# ADVANCED PRAISE FOR "CLICK HERE TO ORDER"

"*Click Here to Order* contains story after story of regular people who saw the opportunity afforded by the Internet and began to think BIG. Joel has done an incredible job of not only capturing and sharing their inspiring tales, but of also inspiring the reader to embrace their passion and become the next Internet success story."

- **Michael Port, Author of *Book Yourself Solid* & *Beyond Booked Solid***

"Joel Comm tells the story of internet marketing as only a living pioneer can. He reveals a pattern of success in the individuals he profiles that you can follow. This is just the book internet marketing has been waiting for."

- **Dave Lakhani, Author of *Subliminal Persuasion: Influence and Marketing Secrets They Don't Want You To Know***

"*Click Here to Order* is the perfect book for anyone that wants to learn about Internet marketing. If you are looking for stories about Billion Dollar DOTCOM buyouts, this is not for you. If you want to learn from the real underground everyday people that have made millions on the Internet and want to share their story with you, buy this book today! - Who knows, you may just find yourself in the Version 2.0"

- **Mike Filsaime, President and CEO: MarketingDo**

"It's about time! There are so many here today, gone tomorrow guys in the Internet Marketing world, but Joel Comm has been there from the start and gives you the inside scoop and the real story on Internet Marketing. He's the real deal - I love this book!"

**- Frank Rumbauskas, NY Times Bestselling Author, MarketingOpus.com**

"When people hear 'Internet Millionaire' they immediately think of IPOs, stock options, and how someone was able to sell their web site (even one that made no money) to a larger company. The majority of the world doesn't realize that there is an 'under the radar' group of online millionaires, like myself, that are building wealth in very a different way... by producing HUGE PROFITS. *Click Here to Order*" is a book that finally tells 'our' story. As more people learn about this untold story, we're going to see a whole new group of successful Internet entrepreneurs!"

**- John Reese, Founder of Income.com**

"If you're not already familiar with the internet's underground economy, the stories disclosed in this book might seem like fairy tales of "pots-o-gold" and buried treasure. But you'd do better to read this book with a notepad and pencil in hand, because what it truly reveals is a map to your own wealth and success online."

**- Mark Widawer, Internet Marketing Author & Speaker,**
**TrafficAndConversion.com**

"Joel Comm is the consummate Internet marketing entrepreneur. He's a creative, innovative thought leader. Read his stuff a couple or three times and apply it."

**- Shawn Collins, Co-founder, Affiliate Summit Conference**

"Joel Comm has been uniquely gifted to empower people to prosper. His insight and his strategies are remarkable. If your goal is to prosper then this book is a one stop online shop."

**- Pat Mesiti, Mr. Motivation, Mesiti.com**

"For me, the best proof of Joel's skill as an entrepreneur was watching him pull off his 'Next Internet Millionaire' reality TV show. An amazing production machine, and a fun event. Not to mention his reputation as an author and Google AdSense expert. I enjoyed contributing to this book and no doubt you'll learn a lot from the many great stories."

**- Perry Marshall, PerryMarshall.com**

"Joel's vast wisdom combined with his sense of humor makes this book sure to be another bestseller. This fun read will keep you entertained all while offering the knowledge that can make you a fortune."

**- Jen Groover, JenGroover.com**

"Discover how thousands of people are quietly making millions of dollars selling information products online. If think working from home, setting your own hours, writing your own paycheck and finally being in control of your life would be fun, read this book now."

**- Shawn Casey, ShawnCasey.com**

FOREWORD BY MARK JOYNER

# CLICK HERE TO ORDER

stories of the world's most successful *internet marketing entrepreneurs*

by

# JOEL COMM

AUTHOR OF "THE ADSENSE CODE"

Morgan James Publishing • New York

# CLICK HERE TO ORDER
stories of the world's most successful *internet marketing entrepreneurs*

Library of Congress Control Number: 2008921795
ISBN: 978-1-60037-173-8  (Paperback)
ISBN: 978-1-60037-174-5  (Hardcover)

PUBLISHED BY:

Morgan James Publishing, LLC
1225 Franklin Ave Ste 325
Garden City, NY 11530-1693
Toll Free 800-485-4943
www.MorganJamesPublishing.com

**MORGAN · JAMES**
THE ENTREPRENEURIAL PUBLISHER ™
www.morganjamespublishing.com

**Habitat**
for Humanity®
Peninsula
Building Partner

GENERAL EDITOR:
Heather Campbell


COVER & INTERIOR DESIGN BY:
3 Dog Design
www.3dogdesign.net
chris@3dogdesign.net

# TABLE OF CONTENTS

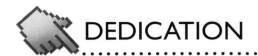 DEDICATION

This book is dedicated to Internet marketers everywhere, whose pioneering spirit and entrepreneurial drive have served to inspire thousands to enjoy the freedom that working at home in your pajamas can bring. Culled from hours and hours of interviews with those in the niche, I have tried to communicate the history of Internet marketing as fairly and clearly as possible. It was nearly impossible to include everyone that I wanted in this book, so please don't feel slighted if you are not mentioned. Rest assured that you hold an important place in Internet history and as my colleague. With so many people telling me their story and mentioning other names in the industry, it became increasingly difficult to know exactly what the facts were. One person may say they invented a certain technique while another would dispute it and embrace it as their claim to fame! I have done my best to tell your stories as accurately as possible and ask your forgiveness if there are any errors in my manuscript. It is my hope that these stories will educate, entertain and serve as inspiration for those who wish to join the ranks of Internet marketers and carve out their piece of the Internet pie. I want to thank Max Gordon for compiling all the recorded content into a cohesive package, Dr. Patricia Ross for her tireless editing, Fletcher Groeneman for an incredible cover design, Robert Secades and Daniel Arzuaga for coming through in a pinch, and David Hancock, Margo Toulouse and all the great people at Morgan James Publishing who have put up with endless changes and revisions. Kudos are also due to my awesome team at InfoMedia, Inc.; Ken, Pam, Sarah Jane, Dan, Joel O, Sarah, Chris, and Gordon for faithfully serving me and putting up with my continually shifting gears.

Remember, it's all fun and games until the flying monkeys attack! Of course, no one on this planet deserves more thanks than Mary, Zach and Jenna who continue to support me in all my endeavors.. Most of all, I want to thank my Savior, who pours out more blessing than I can possibly contain.

# FOREWORD

## BY MARK JOYNER

Twain said, "There are lies, damned lies, and statistics."
Perhaps a notch past statistics is "history."

It's impossible to write history without egregious distortion, omission and an infiltration of the author's bias. Some players will get more credit than they deserve, and some deserving players will get no credit at all.

Joel Comm's history of the Internet Marketing underground (let's be honest, that's what we're talking about here) is no different.

Am I "dissing" the very book for which I'm writing this introduction?

No, I'm just saying: it's history.

But what makes this book important is that it's a first attempt at a story that needs to be told.

You won't hear any mention of the mainstream players on the Internet business landscape ... no mention of Stephen King's famous ebook launching ... no mention of Apple launching iTunes ... instead, what you'll hear are stories from the people who were part of a radical, but largely unknown by the general population, underground clan of "Internet Marketers."

Some of whom actually pioneered many of these innovations long before the mainstream snatched them out of their hands (I, for example, was popularizing the use of ebooks some 4 years before King launched his first ebook), some of whom just rode the wave and cleaned up with wads of cash.

That very term – Internet Marketing - should give you a clue.

If you walk into the boardrooms of Fortune 500 companies, you won't hear anyone using that term. They'll talk about "e-business" "e-commerce" "Internet business" and so on …

But "Internet Marketing" is a phrase used exclusively by the underground.

From the outside it has all of the ear-markings of a cult:
- *A unique language understood only by those in the cult*
- *"Guru" figures of whom many blindly follow*
- *Bizarre rites and rituals*

If you know what a "squeeze page" is, and you know who Corey Rudl was (may he rest in peace), and you spend time obsessing over your "opt-in rate" then you are a member of that cult.

If not you're an outsider.

Either way you'll enjoy this ride.

Here is a small group of people who, at the beginning of a technological revolution, saw opportunity and grabbed it.

I've had the rare opportunity to watch this story unfold, and play my own part in it, both from the inside and the outside.

Not only have I worked with the Internet Marketing underground, but I was also able to take part in several "pre-bubble" Internet IPOs and acquisitions.

The former is populated mainly by home-based small time entrepreneurs. The latter was the domain of the venture capitalists, high level tech entrepreneurs, and occasionally (sometimes embarrassingly) "corporate America").

Two totally different worlds.

The author of this book, my dear friend Joel Comm, is another man with that rare perspective.

Long before he became the Google Adsense "go to guy" who taught the average Joe how to make obscene sums of money by putting a line of code on their web page, he was the developer of a cool little software project that was later acquired by Yahoo. You know it now as "Yahoo Games."

But Joel isn't telling the story here of the big acquisitions, or the famous Internet IPOs, or of the venture-cap melt-downs. The mainstream media has already done that.

Instead, perhaps for the first time ever, Joel is telling the story of some of the prominent players of the underground.

If you are part of "the cult" you're in for a fun ride about the "back story" of Internet Marketing – told by one of its most prominent players.

If you're not, you'll feel like you're peering into a bizarre fantasy world. This fantasy world, though, is one that is populated by very real people. These real people, however, just so happen to have accomplished some fantastic things.

# PREFACE

· · · · · · · · · · · · · · · · · · · · · · · · · · · · · · · · · · · · · · · · · · · · · · · · · · · · · · · · · ·

### Internet Marketing:
*The Unintentional Underground*

# Internet Marketing:
## THE UNINTENTIONAL UNDERGROUND

HISTORY HAS BEEN GIVEN A BAD NAME—UNFORTU-NATELY. Too many teachers have made us learn the boring parts of history, the names and dates of battles fought by people living too long ago for us to really care about. But history doesn't have to be boring, and let's face it, no matter how our teachers made us believe otherwise, history is the story of how we got to where we are now.

This book is a history in that it tells the story of how Internet Marketing came to be and how it has evolved into a world wide movement that includes anyone and everyone who wants to earn some extra cash or even aspires to make a real living selling stuff on the Internet. Now this book isn't about selling your stuff on eBay or Amazon, even though both of those entities are sometimes mentioned in these stories, and even though that's what many people think Internet Marketing is. No, this book tells the stories of real people rolling up their sleeves, burning the midnight oil, taking sometimes giant leaps into the unknown to find out what the Internet could really do for their businesses.

The stories that I tell here are about those who ultimately made the Internet their business. These are the superstars, the men and women who, for one reason or another, figured it out and thereby forged the path for the rest of us. Like the mountain men and cowboys of the early West, these are the folks who weren't necessarily the prettiest or the most popular kids in the class—some of them really were the classic 'geeks' who played video games and were all over learning computer programming languages when everyone else was listening to Duran Duran or Bananarama (some of the hot bands in the 80s,). And make no mistake, most everyone I write about in this book were, and still are, regular joes trying to earn a decent living. But all of them really are the rugged individuals of the Internet who made that once unknown territory safe for the rest of civilization to follow. But unlike the mountain men of old, these Internet men and women didn't ride off into the sunset. Instead, they became the pioneer settlers, reaping sometimes huge profits for their efforts and having a grand time doing it!

It's odd really. I've often heard that the Internet Marketing movement is an underground one. Something is classified "underground" because it is either unknown to the general public—either intentionally or not—or it is somehow trying to defy the powers that be. In that last sense, using the Internet to market a product definitely was "underground" in its early stages, but that was definitely unintentional. It was only defying traditional marketing methods because the general populace didn't all have personal computers until just recently, really, and for Internet marketing to work, an overwhelming majority of people must have access.

We forget how computer technology has made history speed up, in a way. Broad access starting becoming a reality in the late 1980s, but that seems like forever ago, even though it's been less than 30 years!. And the World Wide Web came into its own just a little over thirteen years ago. That's nothing—especially in geologic time. But what still hold true about history is that it has always shown that it takes the establishment (and in this case that would be Madison Avenue) far longer to embrace the "new" than anything or anyone else.

So this book is a history in that it tells the stories of many of the "gurus"—the giants of the Internet marketing world. In that sense, it really is a history of the victors—but that doesn't mean a bad thing, for these stories looks specifically at those who have made selling information about Internet Marketing into both a science and an art form. It 'pulls back the kimono,' as it were, thereby revealing the opportunities the Internet makes available to all. I hope that by reading this you are inspired to go out and forge your own path in the ever changing, ever-growing, but always exciting world of the superhighway of information.

# CHAPTER 1

Working without a 'Net:
*When the Superhighway Was a Cowpath*

# Working without a 'Net:
## WHEN THE SUPERHIGHWAY WAS A COWPATH

COMPUTERS TOUCH SO MUCH IN OUR LIVES that it's easy to forget they haven't been around long. Of course, the 1940s probably *sound* as though they happened a long time ago—ancient history even—to many of the people you'll read about in this book. Most weren't even born. (Hey, *I* wasn't even born!)

But Internet Marketing? That's a different story. Internet Marketing is several generations younger. Even I remember the days before the world wide web brought up Google. You know, we might have seen banner ads and pay-per-click a few centuries ago if Benjamin Franklin and Charles Babbage had ever crossed paths, but Ben died the year before Chuck was born. Neither of them lived to see a vacuum tube, let alone a PC, but they both played a role in the history of Internet Marketing. I'll spare you the technical talk. All you need to know is that Franklin revolutionized (no pun intended) advertising, and Babbage conceived of the first "analytical machine"—that is, the first computer. (Too bad he was so busy perfecting the plans that he never got around to building it. I know people with online businesses like that.)

3

# Dreamers and Geeks

In the introduction to this book, I said that most of the pioneers of Internet Marketing could hardly be considered computer geniuses. That's true. But many of the people who paved the way for Internet Marketing *were* certifiably brilliant in the field—genuine geeks. (Correct me if I'm wrong, but I think that until mathematicians had computers, the word *geek* was used only for those weird carnival dudes who did things like bite the heads off live chickens.)

Don't worry—I have no intention of droning on about punch cards and programming here; tracing the connections that make things happen can be fascinating, but I don't really want this book to weigh more than my laptop, so I'll keep to just a few of the most relevant contributors. I could ignore them all, but I promised a history book, so I have to mention *something* from the old days. Besides, my editor thinks that adding the occasional endnote makes the book look more official—and they're also useful for giving credit where credit it due. And as you'll read later on, that's a key tenet of successful Internet Marketing.

Here's one of those geniuses: Vannevar Bush (no relation to the political family). When things get really dull at your next party, maybe you can liven things up by mentioning that he was the first to predict something that was, for all intents and purposes, hypertext—without which there would be no Internet Marketing as we know it today. He grumbles about how difficult it is to retrieve and make use of all the information piling up (if he felt overloaded *then*, imagine what he'd think if he were alive today) given the primitive resources of his day (filing cabinets, oh my! or card catalogs at the library, good heavens!!):

> Our ineptitude in getting at the record is largely caused by the artificiality of systems of indexing. When data of any sort are placed in storage, they are filed alphabeti-

4

cally or numerically, and information is found (when it is) by tracing it down from subclass to subclass. It can be in only one place, unless duplicates are used; one has to have rules as to which path will locate it, and the rules are cumbersome. Having found one item, moreover, one has to emerge from the system and re-enter on a new path. The human mind does not work that way. It operates by association. With one item in its grasp, it snaps instantly to the next that is suggested by the association of thoughts, in accordance with some intricate web of trails carried by the cells of the brain.... Trails that are not frequently followed are prone to fade...yet the speed of action, the intricacy of trails, the detail of mental pictures, is awe-inspiring beyond all else in nature.

**—Vannevar Bush, 1945**

Enough about him. Fast forward two decades after ENIAC—the first large scale, digital computer capable of being reprogrammed—to the 1960s, and you come to Joseph Carl Robnett Licklider. "Lick," as he preferred to be called, was another visionary. Like many of the people you'll read about later in this book, his contribution came not through dumb luck but through the ability to draw on seemingly unrelated bits of knowledge and experience to synthesize a cogent thought. That is, nothing he did or learned was wasted. As an undergraduate, he studied math, physics and psychology, a seemingly peculiar mix but one that served him (and us, as it turns out) quite well. It played into his incredibly radical belief that engineers ought to know a little something about humans. (He actually introduced a course for Psychology for Engineers.)

Lick was heavily involved in the SAGE project (Semi-Automatic Ground Environment), a computer-operated air defense system. Machines collected data, and humans decided what to do with it. WWII had inspired military researchers to delve into ergonomics, and an

**5**

Army lieutenant named Alphonse Chapanis revealed the startling notion that pilots would have fewer crashes if their instrument panels were actually designed logically rather than randomly. At the time, they were all a confusing jumble of dials and buttons.

In 1960, perhaps inspired by these decades-old concepts, Lick wrote a now-famous paper called "Man-Computer Symbiosis." In it he proposed yet another radical idea: *people should be able to interact with computers.*

Until then, the buzz was all about artificial intelligence—feeding information into a computer and letting it crunch away and spit out answers, translations, and other data. Lick had this crazy idea that people ought to be able to sit down with a computer terminal (and at this point, that's all they were—dumb keyboards that connected to the real brains, the mainframe computer) and *do* things like send and retrieve information and then manipulate it. He would have loved the idea of a "personal computer."

Lick became program manager of IPTO (Information Processing Techniques Office), a newly created offshoot of the Department of Defense's Advanced Projects Research Agency (then called ARPA, renamed DARPA, then re-renamed ARPA and now called DARPA. Gotta love the military...). At IPTO, Lick's role involved choosing to fund those projects that showed promise, and he chose well. Of key importance to us is that he believed in Douglas Englebart's Knowledge Augmentation Laboratory. From this lab came the "mouse," the idea of "cut and paste," and the ability for people to actually interact with what they saw on the computer screen. (The brain was still a mainframe, though).

In 1962, Lick wrote a memo. His ideas there earned him the moniker "father of the Internet." Building on his idea that humans should be able to interact with machines easily and logically, he described his vision—a "galactic network" with computers all around the world

**6**

connected to each other and being used for things like commerce, communication and financial transactions, all operated through a graphical user interface point-and-click operation. In other words, the Internet.

# ARPAnet

Lick didn't stay long at IPTO but went back to his research, and eventually back to M.I.T. where he directed Project MAC (which stands for Multiple Access Computer...or Machine-Aided Cognition...or Man And Computer—no one is quite sure). Project MAC developed the first operating system to use a hierarchical file system (think: folders) called Multics; engineers involved in that project went on to create UNIX. When he left IPTO, Lick made sure that his successor shared his vision and ARPA did develop the first "galactic network": ARPAnet.

ARPAnet started out as just three terminals at ARPA, each connected by telephone line to a different mainframe: the Q-32 at Systems Development Corporation (SDC) in Santa Monica, CA; a computer at UC Berkeley ("Project Genie," another of Lick's creations, a smaller Project MAC); and the Multics/TX-2 in the M.I.T. lab. The terminals sat in the office of Bob Taylor, the director of IPTO (and later a founder of Xerox PARC and Digital Equipment Corporation). The terminals could talk to computers in other states, but they couldn't talk to each other, and Taylor—who had to walk from one terminal to another and log in there to contact the different mainframes—thought things would be a whole lot simpler if the terminals were connected to each other, too. When they were, that was the birth of ARPAnet—the Internet in its infancy. It was 1966.

By 1972, ARPAnet could send email. Woo-hoo!

# Net Wars

The Department of Defense owned ARPAnet. Recognizing its potential, the Department of Energy created its own communication networks, MFENet and HEPNet, for its researchers. Other networks soon cropped up: USENET (Unix-based), BITNET (academic use), SPAN (NASA only), CSNET (academic and industrial use only), DECNet (corporate: Digital Equipment Corp.), XNS (corporate: Xerox), and SNA (corporate: IBM).

Naturally, none of these networks could communicate with the others. They didn't speak the same computer language.

It wasn't until the National Science Foundation and a British network (JANET) announced that they intended to link together academic communities regardless of discipline. That move began to make the networks compatible, and the TCP/IP protocol became the standard. That network became the NSF Backbone known as NSFNET. That was 1986. One by one the independent networks adopted the TCP/IP protocol and connected to NSFNET. Commercial traffic was prohibited.

The commercial sector didn't care that it couldn't use NSFNET; it developed its own networks—among them UUNET, PSI, and ANS CO+RE. By 1988, these commercial networks had finally been allowed to connect to the NSFNET, the backbone of education and research users. In theory, any industrious user could have begun doing Internet Marketing then and there.

Of course, it would be text only.

There were bulletin boards, newsgroups, and email. There was even Internet Relay Chat (a primitive version of today's chat). But there was no graphical user interface, no hypertext and no pictures. There was no World Wide Web.

# From Net to Web

The Internet is not the Web. The Internet is what we call the gazillion publicly accessible computer networks connected together and capable of transferring packets of data from place to place electronically. It's boxes and wires.

According to the man who invented it, Tim Berners-Lee, the World Wide Web is "the universe of network-accessible information, an embodiment of human knowledge." In 1980, Berners-Lee worked as a contractor at the *Organisation européenne pour la recherche nucléaire* (European Organization for Nuclear Research, which, oddly enough is abbreviated as CERN), the largest particle physics laboratory in the world. Berners-Lee developed ENQUIRE, a system that used hypertext (which was developed in rudimentary form in 1965) to let various researchers communicate and share data.

By 1989, CERN had become the largest Internet node in Europe, which gave Berners-Lee an idea: why not join hypertext and the Internet to make it easier to find data? (Ever wonder where "http" comes from? Hypertext Transfer Protocol.) As he put it, "I just had to take the hypertext idea and connect it to the TCP and DNS ideas and—ta-da!—the World Wide Web." (Sure. Like Karl Benz just had to take the wheel idea and connect it to gasoline and—ta-da!—the automobile.) He's quick to point out that Robert Cailliau helped him with the development.

# The Last Component

To be honest, there was some Internet Marketing happening before this latest piece was in place, and I'll touch on this later in the book. But the really cool stuff came after the development of Internet browsers.

Browsers are software that let you interact with text and images on the screen using a user-friendly, point-and-click system based on HTML and hyperlinks (that's hypertext) from one page to another; a hyperlink could take you to the next page in a logical book–style sequence or to a page on another website on another server in another country to a sentence about a topic only peripherally related to the original. There were browsers of sorts before this, but here I'm talking about the ones that took the Internet from the realm of the technophile to people who still viewed computers as fancy calculators and typewriters. I'm talking about the browsers with pictures.

Wait! Why don't I let one of the Internet gurus take up the story for a minute? For the next page or two you'll be reading the words of Ken McCarthy talking about Marc Andreessen. Ken told me a few things I don't think you'll find in print anywhere else. I'm going to wait until a little bit later to give Ken a proper introduction.

# Ken McCarthy on Marc Andreesen
## THE BIRTH OF THE BROWSER

In 1993, Marc was an undergraduate at the University of Illinois, studying at the National Science Foundation's National Center for Supercomputing Applications, in Champagne–Urbana. He was there for computing stuff. He was kind of a geeky guy and hadn't really found his way yet; he spent a lot of time playing basketball. He had a job in the physics lab—a work-study job that paid something like $6.85 an hour—helping out, emptying wastepaper baskets. I don't know exactly what. There he saw the Web, which was, of course, originally built for physicists by Tim Berners-Lee at CERN in Geneva. Those were the original users of the Web; about fifty high-particle physicists. Marc saw that and said, "Wow, this is really cool. Why don't they put a point-and-click graphical interface on it?"

He and his friend Eric Bina got together and did just that. It's a very funny story. It worked just like the Mark Twain story where Tom Sawyer gets his friends to paint the white fence for him: Marc recruited all his hotshot programmer friends to help develop different versions of the browser—a UNIX version and so on. Then they put the browser they created, Mosaic, up where people could download it—and started giving it away. I believe it only took them a year from the start to having a million users....

People just don't appreciate and understand that Marc just put the thing up and *gave* it away. And once you downloaded it, he personally provided a huge amount of customer service. That's how I met him. I wrote him an email with a question, and he answered it. He did that for probably thousands of people in those early years. He ramped the whole thing up from zero to a million users. And then he graduated from college and got a job.

It wasn't much of a job—he was a junior engineer at a nonprofit in Silicon Valley that was working to improve computer networking throughout the Valley. *That* was his job. Nothing grand, nothing high profile. No one rolled out the red carpet for him. Most people just didn't really appreciate the significance of what he had done.

Then came one of those wonderful moments in time, one of those magic things that might just as easily not have happened—just as we could very easily not be having this conversation if certain things didn't happen. What happened was that Jim Clark, co-founder of Silicon Graphics, had just been sort of bounced out of his own company. He was looking for something new to do when Marc arrived. Clark was asking around, looking for a new venture, and some people—the technical people, not the business guys, but the smart technical people—said, "You *really* should talk to Marc Andreessen."

Well, he did, and the first thing Marc said to Jim was, "I'll do anything you want, but I don't want to do another version of Mosaic. I'll do anything, but that."

Part of the reason he said that—and this is another important part of the story—is that, well, they had created this marvel, these kids. I can't tell you how much I admire them. But as soon as it got popular, the college stepped in and said, "Hey, you did this on our time. It belongs to us." They actually took Marc Andreessen and all those guys *off* the Mosaic project—basically booted them out.

So as you imagine, when Marc arrived in Silicon Valley, he was quite discouraged. He created this thing, this force of nature, and it had been taken away from him. It's no surprise he didn't want to touch it again.

I like to tell this story because a lot of people when they are just getting started in business think everything just goes on a nice smooth path. They think if you hit a rock or something, it means there is something wrong with your venture or your idea or your life. Having your amazing project taken away from you—that's a pretty big rock. The fact is we wouldn't have the World Wide Web as we know it if Marc Andreessen hadn't been incredibly flexible and persistent and diligent in not only creating the idea, but also shepherding it through every step of the way. Obviously Clark convinced him to change his mind and in 1994 they founded Mosaic, which they renamed Netscape to avoid trademark problems. Jim Barksdale joined as CEO, and they became a real company.

Interestingly enough, I think this is something that people should also know and appreciate. Bill Gates [Microsoft], Steve Jobs [Apple], Larry Ellison [Oracle], and all these guys who are now pounding their chest about the Internet were, back then, completely unimpressed by the Internet. They made openly derogatory comments about its commercial potential.

In the end it cost the University of Illinois way more money than they may have thought they were going to make. Obviously, Marc and his friends made a ton of money, and the University of Illinois isn't getting one penny of it.

—KM

# The Stage is Set

One of the things Ken forgot to mention was that the new browser Andreessen created, Netscape Navigator, didn't use a single line of code from the original Mosaic program; Marc and his engineers wrote the new browser from scratch. It never occurred to him to cheat or take shortcuts that could have cost him later on, or to try to pass off someone else's ideas as his own. Wannabe Internet Marketers—no, everyone, really—should emulate that kind of integrity.

I wish I could say that after Netscape's extremely successful IPO in 1995, everyone went on to live happily ever after. Yes—and no.

Remember that Andreessen didn't create the original Mosaic for the money. Similarly, Netscape did not charge users for downloading Navigator. Andreessen created the browser because he knew it ought to exist to tap the potential of the World Wide Web. Sure, he wanted Netscape the company to make money, but he also cared about Netscape the Internet too; he had this bizarre idea that every user ought to be able to access and edit files no matter what kind of computer they were using and no matter what kind of operating system that computer used.

Microsoft thought otherwise.

I'll spare you the bloody details. Netscape was David, and Microsoft was Goliath, but this being the 20th Century, the battle ended differently. The short version is that Microsoft introduced Internet Explorer, and Netscape ended up a moribund subsidiary of AOL. (Undaunted, their vision still clear, many of the original Netscape engineers created a new, independent organization that eventually became the Mozilla Foundation, a non-profit R&D company, which then spun off Mozilla Corporation, which developed the cross-platform products Mozilla

Firefox and Mozilla Thunderbird—free browser products that kick butt.)

Today there are five major browsers available. From the most to the least number of users they are Internet Explorer, Mozilla Firefox, Safari, Netscape, and Opera. Why should you care? Because browsers are the keys that opened the doors to true Internet Marketing.

# CHAPTER 2

A Way With Words:
*The Write Stuff*

# A Way With Words:
## THE RIGHT STUFF

AH, THE GOOD OLD DAYS. Life was so much easier then, wasn't it? Not like now when there's so much competition, so many new products launching every week, so many seminars to attend, so many changes in search engine algorithms…and on and on. *Everybody* knows that the so-called Internet Marketing gurus are only where they are today because they got there first, back when everything was simpler. *They* never had to struggle like online marketers today.

If you believe *any* of that, let me tell you about this hot new product at a price only available to a select group of deserving people. That is, the willfully obtuse…

Not long ago there was a discussion on the Warrior Forum, the granddaddy of all forums dedicated to Internet Marketing, where someone broached this very subject. The original poster (I'll call him OP, although I might be doing you a favor if I did name names in case he ever tries to sell you something) suggested that the well-known gurus "got rich and built their reputations when making money in Internet Marketing was easier." What amazed me most was that there were others on the list who also believed this. That's a little like saying it was easier for Columbus to fly across the Atlantic than

19

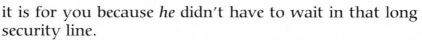

it is for you because *he* didn't have to wait in that long security line.

If you suffered through the somewhat dry but nevertheless relevant chapter on the history of the Internet, you probably already have an inkling of why OP's whiny complaints are just "poor me" poppycock. Because you know what? *These* are the good old days—and they are only getting better. And you have those gurus to thank.

# Here Be Monsters

Newsflash: none of these Internet Marketing gurus got where they are by inheriting the family business. They *built* the business. They are the pioneers who dared to believe that the world wasn't flat, and who had no fear of sailing into the uncharted territories of brand new technology. They created the maps that other Internet Marketers still follow today.

You'll remember that the first users of the Internet were scientists, educators, and the military, along with a few determined technophiles and geeks who finagled access or found a back door. These indigenous peoples, the Internet purists, did not welcome the commercial invaders with their strange customs and foreign tongue. Many were downright hostile.

The very first blatantly commercial "unsolicited bulk email" (that's "SPAM" to you and me) was sent by an eager-beaver marketer at Digital Equipment Corporation named Gary Thuerk. At the time, DEC had a substantial marketing presence on the East Coast, but wasn't nearly as accessible on the West Coast, so Thuerk had what he thought was a brilliant idea. DEC would hold a few open houses for West Coast ARPAnet users to view a demonstration of the company's powerful brand new mainframes, and he would let them know through their own medium. To him, this wasn't commercial use so much as public service; to this day he maintains that his message was a relevant announcement, not a solicitation, since the DEC 2020 Series had the ARPAnet protocol integrated into its operating system.

Unfortunately for Thuerk, his was a minority opinion. Adding to his "crime" was the actual sender's incomplete mastery of the arcane art of using SNDMSG to shove email across the ARPAnet; this unfamiliarity with the protocol caused a very long list of addressees to bleed from the header into the body of the message. Compounding that error, when Thuerk realized that this overflow meant that many of the addressees wouldn't receive the email, he sent it out *again*. Remember, everything was dial-up, and slooooooooow dial-up at that. The recipients watched their systems slow to a crawl as the message loaded and then, when it was finally complete, they discovered that it was essentially a sales pitch. The flaming that followed was immediate and intense.

Here's the offending piece (without the hundreds of addresses):

DIGITAL WILL BE GIVING A PRODUCT PRE-SENTATION OF THE NEWEST MEMBERS OF THE DECSYSTEM-20 FAMILY; THE DECSYS-TEM-2020, 2020T, 2060, AND 2060T. THE DECSYSTEM-20 FAMILY OF COMPUTERS HAS EVOLVED FROM THE TENEX OPERATING SYSTEM AND THE DECSYSTEM-10 <PDP-10> COMPUTER ARCHITECTURE. BOTH THE DECSYSTEM-2060T AND 2020T OFFER FULL ARPANET SUPPORT UNDER THE TOPS-20 OPERATING SYSTEM. THE DECSYSTEM-2060 IS AN UPWARD EXTENSION OF THE CURRENT DECSYSTEM 2040 AND 2050 FAMILY. THE DECSYSTEM-2020 IS A NEW LOW END MEMBER OF THE DECSYSTEM-20 FAMILY AND FULLY SOFTWARE COMPATIBLE WITH ALL OF THE OTHER DECSYSTEM-20 MODELS. WE INVITE YOU TO COME SEE THE 2020 AND HEAR ABOUT THE DECSYSTEM-20 FAMILY AT

```
THE TWO PRODUCT PRESENTATIONS WE WILL
BE GIVING IN CALIFORNIA THIS MONTH.

    THE LOCATIONS WILL BE:
    TUESDAY, MAY 9, 1978 - 2 PM
    HYATT HOUSE (NEAR THE L.A. AIRPORT)
    LOS ANGELES, CA

    THURSDAY, MAY 11, 1978 - 2 PM
    DUNFEY'S ROYAL COACH
    SAN MATEO, CA
    4 MILES SOUTH OF S.F. AIRPORT AT
    BAYSHORE, RT 101 & RT 92)

A 2020 WILL BE THERE FOR YOU TO VIEW.
ALSO TERMINALS ON-LINE TO OTHER DECSYS-
TEM-20 SYSTEMS THROUGH THE ARPANET. IF
YOU ARE UNABLE TO ATTEND, PLEASE FEEL
FREE TO CONTACT THE NEAREST DEC OFFICE
FOR MORE INFORMATION ABOUT THE EXCITING
DECSYSTEM-20 FAMILY.
```

Pretty scandalous stuff, right? From the ensuing ruckus, Thuerk might as well have been hawking kiddie porn. One ARPAnet user, a well-known (within his field, that is) systems programmer who actually wrote a great deal of the ARPAnet protocol for the DEC PDP-10, dashed off this email in May of 1978:

```
The ARPAnet is not...a public resource;
it is available to pretty much a select
group  of  people  (high  school  kids
regardless!).  We  are  all  engaged  in
activities  relating to,  or  in support
of,  official  US  Government  business.
ARPAnet  mail  therefore  is  more  of  an
"interoffice memo"  sort of thing than a
```

> trade journal, not intended for public distribution although not "top secret" either.... I don't see any place for advertising on the ARPAnet, however; certainly not the bulk advertising of that DEC message. From the address list, it seems clear to me that the people it was sent to were the Californians listed in the last ARPAnet directory. This was a clear and flagrant abuse of the directory!

Unfortunately for that "select group of people" (but fortunately for the rest of us), in the following years a growing number of stalwart individuals and brazen companies trekked into this isolated expanse of the networked computers and settled there. The purists managed to repel the interlopers for years, defending the territory they had staked out, but despite their advantages—one of the biggest being federal funding through the National Science Foundation (NSFNet), the backbone of the Internet—they were soon outnumbered. The U.S. military had already declared victory and withdrawn behind the firewalls of MILNET, its own private R&D stronghold, and left the academicians and scientists to their own weakening defenses. There was no ferocious final battle. But soon the sporadic incursions of a few intrepid explorers became a sparse but growing string of Internet Marketing trading posts, and their numbers swelled until finally, despite a valiant effort (and many a strongly worded memo), the labcoats retreated and commerce spread across the Internet.

The Internet gold rush was on.

In an unusually insightful move, the scientists and academics wisely decided to relinquish complete control—and financial responsibility—and let the market take over. Remember: though the Internet was still largely

U.S. government property, it was administered not by bureaucrats but by the prescient band of *brainiacs* who had built the Internet. They recognized that the Internet was in no danger of disappearing regardless of what role they played, and they wisely—and fortuitously—created a peace treaty of sorts.

The story of how it was that the Internet managed to evolve gracefully from a state-owned elitist commodity into an international egalitarian resource is a book unto itself, and not one I'll be writing any time soon. Most of the controversies and negotiations and talk of reparations had no direct bearing on the history of Internet Marketing, with the exception of one crucial element: *universal access*. In the waning days of 1990, a handful of technical gurus and department heads met over pizza in Reston, Virginia, and defined a universal connection point, the Commercial Internet Exchange (CIX, pronounced "kicks"), a "zero-settlement" agreement that enabled commercial gateways to the Internet to exchange traffic with each other. In other words, they opened up the borders, charged no tolls, and imposed no tariffs. A few discreet signs went up welcoming commercial visitors.

There was hardly a mass migration at first. The Internet was still just thousands of miles of wire linking up far-flung computers. But finally enterprising entrepreneurs could send text from point A to point B, and email all their Internet-savvy friends. (All two or three of them.)

## Brave New World

But I digress. Let me get back to the idea of the "good old days" of Internet Marketing. I won't give you the tired bit about how the pioneers had to walk to school in four feet of snow, barefoot, uphill both ways, but they did *not* have it easy. Hear me out on this.

Imagine it's 1987, the year of both Black Monday and the debut of Prozac® (which now that I think of it may not have been coincidental). So much of what would become commonplace is still hot new development in these pre-WWW days: local area networks (Novell, 3Com, Appletalk), "affordable" laser printers (down from $10,000 in 1979 to around half that), and a new ("100 times faster!") 320MHz microchip soon to be available. Most telephone systems finally have modular plugs, but to get onto the Internet on a hard-wired phone, you need hardware, such as a $45 disc-shaped device that screws into the handset (and the handset is, of course, tethered to the phone by an annoying curly cord). The 5.25" floppy drive is *finally* on its way out, and the 3.5" floppy is on its way in, and for $200 you can get software and cables to transfer your data from one to the other via a serial port. Big selling software includes Lotus 1-2-3, WordPerfect, Ventura Publisher, and dBase III.

There are no browsers, no search engines, no pictures, and no WYSIWYG (what you see is what you get) files passing back and forth. (Adobe's Portable Document Format (PDF) is still six years in the future.) There's no hypertext online. Mac users could buy HyperCard stacks—specific hypertext programs and utilities that could be customized with the HyperTalk markup language—that used a WWW-like interactive graphical user interface (GUI) but these came on 3.5" floppy disks and were strictly for offline use. The World Wide Web won't hit the Internet for three more years.

Yet across the country, and the world, a small group of people is starting to "get it." Some of these gurus-to-be were dazzled by the realization that anyone with a computer could, in theory, communicate with anyone else with a computer. In their visionary dreams, they saw a rapidly expanding, nondiscriminating marketplace in the interconnection of hulking high-speed mainframes with PCs from IBM, "PC-compatible" clones, Tandy Radio Shack/TRS-80, Commodore, Amiga, Atari, and Apple. All anyone needed was a modem, a computer, a phone line, and a phone number to call.

By 1987, there are two kinds of numbers you can call. One will link you to one of several Internet Service Providers (ISP). In 1987, this is most likely CompuServe, although it could be GEnie or Prodigy. Commodore users have another choice called QuantumLink, which later will expand to AppleLink and PC Link; later still, Quantum Computer Services will become America Online. Whereas in 2007, you pay an ISP a monthly fee for unlimited access, in 1987 you're most likely paying anywhere from 10¢ a minute at night to four or five times that during the day, plus you have to pay the phone company itself for the call. Since only the major metropolitan areas have access numbers, and darn few of them at that, you're probably paying for a long-distance call that you have to dial repeatedly just to get connected. Paying by the minute is especially painful since you probably use a 300- or 1200-baud modem, although you may be thinking of upgrading to a 2400-baud modem. A few of your wealthier power-user friends might even have plunked down big bucks for the 9600-baud modems just hitting the market.

No matter what modem you are using, when it comes to logging on, you might as well start the process, go fix yourself a cup of coffee, and maybe even walk out and get the mail. You'll probably still come back to a message that says "one moment, please...connecting..."

And far from being dazzled with too many blinking headlines, animated graphics, sounds, and music, once you get online you'll see screen after screen of... text. WYSIWYG programs for personal computers are still brand new. The first desktop publishing software came out two years prior when Aldus PageMaker for the Mac debuted in 1985; that was followed soon after by MacPublisher, ReadySetGo, Ragtime and Quark XPress. Of course, if you have a PC platform, you have to choose between Ventura Publisher and...nothing.) But WYSIWYG online? Not really, no. You will see a lot of colored text, colored boxes, or text in colored boxes, but for now you have to be content with still plain old ASCII text (ASCII is a character encoding based on English).

Could you sell what you sell now online with art that looked like this?

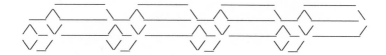

You can send and receive black and white images in RLE format (run–length encoding, and by the end of the year, CompuServe will have brought out the .gif, a new format for graphics, the Graphics Interchange Format, which Unisys actually developed and patented. (It's properly pronounced Jiff, by the way, per the original engineering spec, regardless of what platform you're on.) But transferring images and displaying them in the context of the same page are two entirely different things. You might as well be mailing photos by snail mail.

What, then, is the attraction? Why bother? For the rewards at the end.

If you connect through an ISP, you can read the front page of over 100 different newspapers, updated every two hours. You can check the weather, send and receive email, check a stock price, or talk to customer service. Or you can enter a SIG (special interest group, now generally called a forum or discussion group), and find other early adopters who share your interest in stamp collecting, MUD games, C++ programming, genealogy, dwarf hamsters, whatever—even online marketing.

That brings me to the *other* kind of number you might call in 1987 if you don't have an ISP connection: one that connects you to a "bulletin board service"(BBS). This might emanate from a climate-controlled computer lab with a couple of hulking DEC mainframes, or it might just as likely operate from a basement with a tangle of wires, monitors, keyboards and black boxes cobbled together by some bearded guy in acid-washed jeans and a Mötley Crüe T-shirt. Anybody with a decent computer setup (and some software) can be a SysOp—a system operator, or moderator. How it worked was, you would pay the BBS a monthly subscription fee of a few bucks, and then, for the price of the phone call, you could contact all the other users out there in cyberspace. From 1986 to 1987, the number of hosts had doubled, and the number of newsgroups had shot up from 241 to well over 10,000. Gosh, can you imagine? If there are one or two newsgroups related to your interests, and each one has a few hundred members, you could market to as many as—wow, maybe a thousand users who are potential customers!

Now all you have to do is reach those users.

If you still think those Internet Marketing pioneers had easier than you, try selling your product using nothing but email and bulletin boards.

## Trading Places

In February 1987, Paul Myers was living in Buffalo, NY. If you've ever been to Buffalo in winter and experienced the "lake effect" (a double whammy storm off both lakes Erie and Ontario. In 2006, one of these delivered 2' of snow on a single night—and that was in October), you understand why Myers might have spent a lot of time indoors staring at a computer screen. For $750, he bought a used Amiga 1000 with a whopping 1.5MB RAM (considered a lot at the time). He connected it up to a 300 baud modem, which he quickly junked for a 1200 baud modem. He ultimately got hold of a 2400 baud modem and, with that high-powered system, he thought he was the "cat's meow." He started dialing up the BBSs. Within thirty days of getting online, he was moderating forums for the local Amiga store, and over the next few weeks become a moderator for several of his friends' BBSs.

In 1988 Myers discovered Fido.Net, a networking system that linked bulletin boards around the world. It not only had Netmail (email) but Echomail, a specialized protocol that let users piggyback attachments such as programs onto their emails. Fidonet provided a bucket-brigade for bulletin board posts: Myers would type a message to the Fidonet servers, which would, at several specified times throughout the day, "echo" the message to its member bulletin boards, and the SysOps of those boards would, at some other specified times during the day...or week...or whenever they felt like it...send the message to its subscribers. Myers was delighted with push-the-envelope, state-of-the-art technology.

Of course, the state-of-the-art was dismal.

And what qualified then as "pushing the envelope" was a little like mailing a letter that languished in the mailbox for a while, was sorted when the Post Office got around to it, and eventually got delivered when the mail carrier had gas in the tank and nothing better to do. But Myers was psyched: he could talk to people all over the country—the world. So he did, with something like this:

```
Have 1 first card, first series, 1977
Topps Star Wars card (Luke Skywalker),
M/NM condition for sale or trade. Others
in series, most v. good.
```

His first attempt at "Internet Marketing" did not go rocketing along the information superhighway but jogged along the side of it. What many of his "custom-ers" would see, a few lines in fuzzy white or green dot-matrix-style type on a dark gray background—back then many people made do with monochrome monitors—didn't make for a very spectacular "product launch." Worse, the method violated what would become, in the

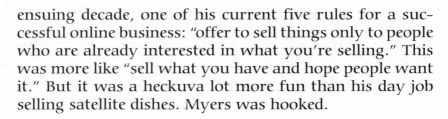

ensuing decade, one of his current five rules for a successful online business: "offer to sell things only to people who are already interested in what you're selling." This was more like "sell what you have and hope people want it." But it was a heckuva lot more fun than his day job selling satellite dishes. Myers was hooked.

## Classified Information

CompuServe was by far the biggest ISP in town in the late 1980s to mid-1990s, but it wasn't pretty. In fact, it was so ugly that it made Quantum Computer Service's user interface look like fine art. (Think Mondrian: squares, lines, colors, meaningless at first glance...). Only Commodore users could access QCS's Internet gateway, QuantumLink. At the time, Apple Computer and Commodore were the bigshots in the creative personal computer market, and those users were thrilled with the new graphical user interface, such as it was.

QuantumLink offered a total of eight choices on its main menu, choices that you selected by moving the up and down arrows until the cute little star cursor landed on your choice, at which point you pressed a function key: Software Showcase (reviews and free downloads), People Connection (slow, public "chat" rooms), Commodore Information Network (company fluff and public relations.), Learning Center (some reference software, a few college courses), News & Information (headlines, stock quotes), Customer Service (help, account info), and Just for Fun (games, sports news).

The final choice was called The Mall.

Like a brick-and-mortar mall, QuantumLink's shopping service offered a woefully finite number of shopping choices. Not many stores were online before the mid-1990s, so the early malls (and most ISPs had some version of this) were more or less fancy yellow pages. There were no "websites" to send people to, no extensive, eye-catching catalogs of goodies to browse through. There was text.

Lots of text. You could buy things, but you had to call the seller anyway since there was no electronic payment method, no shopping cart service or security. The same was true for things like making airline reservations or renting a car. You could find out what you wanted from the computer, but you still had to talk to a human.

But one thing The Mall and other online shopping portals *did* have was a classifieds section—a bulletin board area for buying and selling. In other words, it had eCommerce.

Let me step back about a decade and introduce a tall, rangy Texas/Oklahoma boy by the name of Marlon

## What is Information Marketing?

This may be a good time to point out that while this book covers the history of Internet Marketing, I have focused heavily on an even smaller niche: Information Marketing. While it may seem at times that this is just a small self-sustaining group of entrepreneurs surviving by buying each other's products, you need to understand that the phrase Information Marketing does not mean just marketing information about making money online but marketing any kind of knowledge or strictly online service (plumbing repair, car rentals, dating, astrology) as opposed to selling hard goods (computers, cars, clothing, books).

Information marketing is nothing new, of course. People have always bartered knowledge for goods or services. Knowledge is power, and many a ruthless leader has held on by ensuring that the common people remain uninformed and uneducated. But what has changed is the way this information can now be transmitted.

The Internet allows information to speed around the world in near real-time, but it also represents a highly egalitarian system of information sharing. Anyone with access to the Internet can access billions of terabytes of information, and most of it for free (and currently about 1 billion of the world's 6.5 billion people are Internet users). The entrepreneurs who find interesting ways to package what they know and add unique value can leverage this knowledge into income—and many of those who do this on the Internet are the gurus featured here.

Sanders. Now he's a big-name guru, but back then he was just another journalism graduate asking that age-old question, "Now what?" By day he did telemarketing or sold timeshares just to pay the bills, but by night he sat at the big, boxy computer in his apartment and crafted freelance articles. In 1978 he gambled on a "get rich quick" ad in a magazine and sent in his check. What arrived in his mailbox several weeks later was a book by Benjamin Suarez called *Seven Steps to Freedom: How to Escape the Great American Rat Race.* Suarez, who had worked with the late, great Gary Halbert, got Sanders interested in direct marketing.

Sanders had already tried direct *sales.* In his own words, he wasn't very good at it. Of course, in typical Sanders style, he added in a deep drawl, "Actually, I sold a lot. I sold my house and my car and everything else I had trying to make a living in sales. I learned a lot. You know how Mike Filsaime has the Fire Sales nowadays? (when you get rid of your product at a deep discount price) They had fire sales back then, too. The manager would come in and say 'you'd better sell some of this stuff or you're fired.' "

In addition to trying to sell timeshares, Sanders had started up a retail store that sold motivational books and tapes. As he likes to point out, one thing he has in common with Dan Kennedy (another Internet Marketing guru) is that they both failed at that business. But as a former psychology major with a knack for writing and a keen interest in marketing, Sanders had every reason to believe that direct marketing would be his niche. He started an MBA program to learn more, only to find that nobody at the school, and maybe in all of Oklahoma, had much to say about direct mail and advertising.

Then he saw another ad that changed his life. Jay Abraham had a thirty-two-page ad in *Entrepreneur Magazine* touting his *Protégé Program* which promised to teach someone how to make money using the Internet. At

$5,000 it would be a much bigger gamble than Suarez's book, but if there is one thing that all the gurus have in common, it's the willingness to make serious sacrifices in order to follow their dreams.

He wrote the check.

Armed with his new knowledge, Sanders started prowling the classified section of QuantumLink. Soon he was selling his articles there. He wasn't the first, of course. Others had scouted it out first and were already earning money online, including Michael Enlow, another pioneer who began his Internet Marketing on the bulletin boards—he promoted and sold what were essentially DOS-based eBooks. (No, that's not a typo: DOS.) Another early user, Sheila Danzig, was so successful at working the AOL classifieds that she wrote *Turn Your Computer Into a Money Machine*—and proved its premise by earning millions herself—based on collections of articles posted online. But of that trio, it is Marlon Sanders who remained at the forefront and has earned the honorary title of guru. It may have to do with his rather colorful personality. It could have something to do with the old saying in marketing circles: "when Sanders talks, people listen."—

# The Prospecters
You might wonder how anyone could make decent money, let alone millions, working with ASCII text ads. The answer is that not everybody did. Most people wrote up their ads, put them up on AOL, and then hoped that theirs would get noticed. What set people like Myers, Sanders, Danzig, and Enlow apart from most people in Internet Marketing then—and what sets them and the other gurus apart now—can't be learned from any seminar, eBook, or workshop. Those can teach you tips, tricks, and techniques, but they can't give you what you really need to succeed. Tom Wolfe called it *The Right Stuff*. Athletes often call it drive or the will to win. Survivors call

it heart. By the end of the book, we may have a name of our own for it. Whatever it is, it's what separates the users from the gurus. The people who made money using these primitive features of the Internet shared a passion for blazing trails, not following them—and they pushed themselves hard.

In this case, they all started out at the same trailhead, but soon went off in their own directions. They each had slightly different talents and, more importantly, different products—although all were "information products."

A life-changing event inspired Michael Enlow's specialty, "investigative technology": the first paragraph in one of his old catalogs reads as follows:

> Some of the techniques and devices found in this catalog and/or the books sold in this catalog are illegal. Possession or implementation of certain devices, except by authorized law enforcement personnel, may be illegal as well. The laws regarding electronic surveillance change from time to time and vary from state to state. It is your responsibility to find out what is and is not legal before using any of the techniques or using any of the equipment constructed from our plans, or revealed in our books. In other words, talk to a good lawyer....

Enlow's product was technology related to surveillance. He may have been just naturally nosy, but it seems more likely that his early life had a lot to do with his forming INTEC Investigative Technology later on. Enlow told the story himself in a "sales letter" posted online in 1992 with the headline "Who is Mike Enlow? The story behind one of America's foremost private detectives—who can help you get almost anything on anyone!"

At seventeen, a restless Enlow dropped out of school and lit out in search of fortune. It didn't quite pan out that way. He tossed two pairs of jeans and some T-shirts into knapsack and hitchhiked through the Louisiana bayous to a Labor Camp. There he worked twelve hours a day, seven days a week, wrestling three-ton pipes onto forklifts in exchange for room, board, and a net pay of about $40 a week. Frustrated by his situation, Enlow, by his own admission, went off in search of companionship and "help"—that is, a woman with a car. Before long, they were sharing an apartment, and with his improved prospects, thinking about the future. There was only one problem: the girl's father (and she was, in fact a girl; turns out she was only sixteen) hated Enlow. Before the couple set off one weekend on a trip, the father gave Enlow a really good deal on a .25 caliber pistol he was supposedly selling in a yard sale. Unfortunately, Enlow was carrying the (unloaded) weapon in his pocket later that day when he found himself surrounded by police, guns drawn, demanding that he freeze. The father, it seems, had taken advantage of the couple's absence to torch their apartment, damage a friend's car, and then call the police to report that Enlow had done all this and then run off with a minor.

Enlow spent several months in jail before his case finally went to trial, only to be dismissed when the father failed to appear, having scuttled away with his daughter, never to be heard from again. Enlow had spent those months in his cell writing to the district attorney, who never replied. When the D.A. admitted at the trial that he had never even opened the letters, Enlow made a promise to him: "Mr. District Attorney, I shall return. Someday you will see me again. I will be standing in this exact spot defending people like myself." And he was—not as a lawyer, but as an investigator for the Indigent Defenders' Office. With everything he had learned about tracking down people and information, Enlow showed the D.A. just how important it can be to answer your mail.

You might appreciate the irony in how Enlow's name came to my attention while researching this book. One of my guru friends, speaking of the days when the first Internet Marketers used the classifieds and bulletin boards for commerce, mentioned Enlow's special contribution at the time. It seems that Enlow hired a programmer to write a special utility that stripped out all the email addresses from the online classifieds. Now, that wasn't even close to being considered illegal or even unethical back then: in those pre-Spam days it was considered to be just a clever use of technology to get information. Of course, over the ensuing years, many such "harvesting" utilities have been created by various other Internet Marketers. Some of them were "white hat" (strictly on the up-and-up, and within the bounds of both the law and common decency), though others were "black hat" (unethical, sometimes even illegal, and used without anyone's knowledge or permission), and some were even malicious.

By culling these names from the classifieds, Enlow began creating a database of legitimate Internet contacts who had already—by virtue of their ads—expressed an interest in certain kinds of products. He not only used these addresses for targeting his own online mailings, but he had sold the lists to others. It may well have been the first concerted effort online at list building. And it meant that Enlow's dreams for success panned out. The gold rush boomed.

# On the Shoulders of Giants

It's no coincidence that people like Marlon Sanders and Paul Myers were among the first to stake their claims on the wealth potential of the Internet. In the new online world, words were the coin of the realm, and Sanders and Myers were (and remain today) intelligent, talented, driven writers who could bank on their writing skills. In a world where the ads looked pretty much the same, the marketers who survived were those who knew how to wield words in the most powerful, even seductive ways—or who depended on those who could.

One of the greatest writers in direct response marketing of all time died not long before this book made it to press. Gary Halbert was a legend among Internet Marketers. Cocksure and often controversial, he is best known for having been the man behind "the most widely mailed letter in direct mail history," the infamous "Coat of Arms/Family Crest" mail order promotion, which has allegedly been mailed 600 million times. (That's *eight* zeroes.) Despite all the flak the product caught, no one can deny that the promotion itself was perfectly conceived, written, and executed. Halbert wrote in one of his highly prized newsletters to his clients that he wanted them "to experience what it is like to be flooded with so much mail you will have to hire an extra 40 people just to count it all and help you make your bank deposits! " He always did have a flair for the dramatic.

Of course, he also had a big bank account. Gary Halbert liked to call himself the "Master Shitweasel." He also picked up the moniker (thanks to that successful promotion) as Sir Gary of Halbert. But what most people called him were names along the line of "genius," "giant," "legend" and "inspiration"—and that was when he was still alive. Although Halbert got his start in direct mail copywriting long before the days of Internet Marketing, two things stand out when you read his archived issues of "The Gary Halbert Letter." First, almost every nugget of direct mail gold for the print world that he handed out shines just as bright in the online marketing world, with minor differences. Second, Halbert may have been 68, but he was hardly some dusty old fossil even though in Internet time he had been around since the Jurassic Period. He didn't *have* to keep up with the trends (or start new ones of his own), and he didn't *have* to keep writing, but he did. He just loved to teach, and he did it in his own unique in-your-face, take-it-or-leave-it style. Over the years he raised more than a few hackles with his not-always politically correct comments, but even his detractors grudgingly admit that what he did worked for him—and for millions of others who followed his teachings.

Halbert lived a colorful life (for a glimpse, read "The Dark Side of Success!" at http://www.thegaryhalbertletter.com/Newsletters/zskk_dark_side.htm) that included being scammed by unscrupulous cult therapists, getting robbed by masked thugs in his own home at gunpoint, and even spending some time in Boron Federal Prison Camp ("Club Fed") in the Mojave Desert. But he didn't just get rich and then revel in his good fortunes. He'd earned every penny by doing what he did best—copywriting—and he leveraged that success into something he loved more than any beach villa or houseboat: getting *more* copywriting work. He put it this way in one of his newsletters: "I can't program my VCR. I can't master my microwave. I can't operate the remote on my television. I can't keep my car insurance up-to-date. I can't fill out the forms necessary to join a gym. I can't keep my papers in order. I can't write a check to pay a bill. I can't schedule appointments to see my doctors. These are things I can't do. However, there is one thing I can do… and…do better than anyone else on this earth. That's write an ad or sales letter." Halbert charged $15,000 plus 5 percent of the gross sales. By all accounts, most of his clients considered that a bargain.

Most of the Internet Marketing pioneers mentioned Halbert as someone who had taught them a lot. He's definitely the 'giant among giants,' for his students turned out to be one of the giants themselves. One of those was Halbert's good friend John Carlton—"the most ripped-off veteran freelance copywriter online." (If you've ever written a long-form sales letter, you've "borrowed" from him, too.) John Carlton had great respect for Gary Halbert and recognized in him both his flaws and his genius. Here's what Carlton had to say in one issue of "The Gary Halbert Letter": "I first met Gary Halbert…way back in the go-go 1980s. (At the time, I was trading copy for free run of John's office… a genuine bargain, since I was in my 'suck up every scrap of knowledge from the geniuses' mode.) Gary was easily the most arrogant, dismissive and self-aggrandizing SOB I'd ever met. I liked him immediately."

Carlton would be easy to pick out of a lineup of Internet Marketing gurus. Most of us tend to look like unusually well fed refugees from the chess and science clubs. A handful of the gurus look more like those slick, self-confident classmates voted 'Most Likely to Succeed'. And an even smaller number look like the kids who dressed for success—providing success meant a primo job as a burned-out rock-band roadie or a farmer of alternative crops. John was part of this last crowd, a self-admitted "slacker" who hid his natural smarts and phenomenal talents. His isn't a classic rags-to-riches story, as he proudly points to his "white-trash, blue-collar" upbringing in a happy home in Cucamonga, California (a landlocked burg absorbed, along with Alto Loma and Etiwanda, into Rancho Cucamonga in 1977). He had plenty. He just wanted more.

Carlton wandered out of UC–Davis with a B.A. in psychology ("the biggest joke in college education: there are exactly four jobs waiting in the universe for 4,000 psychology grads from every college") and no particular plan. He worked his way around the country as a dishwasher, a fisherman, and even a cartoonist. Finally he signed on as a commercial artist for a computer supply catalog in Silicon Valley—this was before *personal* computers, mind you—*but* doing paste-up was not particularly satisfying. He never gave a thought to where the catalog's words came from until the day he met his first copywriter, a bitter, uncooperative New Yorker. We have her to thank for inspiring Carlton. When he asked her how someone went about working his way into copywriting, she snarled, "It's way too hard. You'll never figure it out so just forget about it." He took it as a challenge. In fact, she pissed him off so much (his words) that he stole her copy of the 1932 John Caples classic *Tested Advertising*

*Methods*, and he read enough of it to whet his appetite before she stole it back. Caples opened Carlton up to a whole new world, and sent him on a quest for knowledge that drove him to take an Evelyn Wood Speed-reading course and then work his way through shelf after shelf of library books on marketing, sales, copywriting and advertising—in fact, everything labeled 600–900 under the Dewey Decimal System. He was determined to "catch up," to be able to walk into any ad agency and hold his own with the so-called experts, even though he was over thirty without a whit of experience. What he found out was that his Ph.D.-level self-education left him light years ahead when it came to practical knowledge. That was both a shock—and an entry into the business.

Most advertising agencies in those days formed around one or two superstars who had read maybe one or two books on the subject but followed their own muses and intuition. Their goal was to be creative, clever and entertaining—and they succeeded in that much of the time. As marketing tools, however, their work was not so successful. They needed Carlton, and before long he was in demand as a hotshot freelance copywriter who understood direct marketing (the psychology degree came in handy after all). He didn't need seat-of-the-pants marketing because he knew what had worked over and over again in the past—as he puts it, "since the first caveman sold another caveman a cave with a better view in exchange for a haunch of mastodon."

Carlton soon snagged several plum clients, including Agora and Rodale. (It was for Rodale that Carlton created what is probably his best-known ad, the one that became the talk of the country clubs. His classic headline: "Amazing Secret Discovered by One-Legged Golfer Adds 50 Yards to Your Drives, Eliminates Hooks and Slices... and Can Slash Up to 10 Strokes From Your Game Almost Overnight." His second-most famous copywriting is probably what he wrote for what I'll just call the

## Joe Vitale on the John Caples classic *Tested Advertising Methods*

When the American Marketing Association and NTC Books, Inc., hired me to write what was to become The *AMA Complete Guide to Small Business Advertising*, I knew I had a battle to fight. The greatest books ever written on how to write ads were still in print, and they were all by one man: John Caples.

Caples spent most of his long life writing and testing ads. He was a brilliant copywriter. Most agree he was a genius. In 1925, at the age of 25, he wrote what may be the greatest ad in history, an ad that has been duplicated in one form or another for more than six decades. It began with the now famous headline, "They Laughed When I Sat Down At The Piano, But When I started to Play!——"

Caples was elected into the Copywriters Hall of Fame in 1973. He was elected into the Advertising Hall of Fame in 1977. The famous Caples Award, given for the year's best ads, was named after him. He died in 1990, at the age of 90, after spending 58 years in the advertising business. The man remains a legend.

How was I ever going to top the work of John Caples? I spent three years of intense research in order to write my book, and throughout the journey I had one goal: Write something that would be better than what John Caples had already written. I failed. But I had a good time nonetheless. I learned a lot, as well.

So try to imagine my surprise when I heard that Prentice-Hall was revising and reprinting Caples's most popular book, *Tested Advertising Methods*. I was excited. I couldn't wait to get it. When the new book arrived, I held it and smiled, eager to dive in and relish once again the words of one my favorite mentors.

This classic book first came out in 1932. The publisher reprinted it numerous times. Caples himself revised it four times. The last edition, still available in paperback today, was reprinted at least fourteen times. This is a book that has stood the test of time.

Caples wrote it while a young copywriter for the famous BBDO advertising agency (he later became their Vice-President and spent 56 years with the company). He continued to test, refine, revise and add techniques—not theories, techniques—to his book right up to his death. As far as most experts are concerned, his book is THE bible in advertising. It's the one I keep by my side. It's the one I tried to model my own book after.

"sex book." His sales letter shocked the editors at Rodale and got him banned—until he convinced them to mail it. His version quickly beat out the control by one of the company's top writers and went on to mail to millions of names for more than five years. (He says that today it is "the most copied ad online, with literally hundreds of versions working in markets far removed from sex.")

One evening Carlton went to a "Divorce Party" at a house about a mile away from where he lived in Los Angeles. The host was a well-known local copywriter, Jay Abraham, whom Carlton had met not long before. As the night wore on, Carlton found himself talking with yet another copywriter, maybe a dozen years older than he, a big man in both size and personality. When two strong-willed, opinionated, creative types with a great deal of...shall we say self-assurance?...meet up, one of two things usually happens. Within minutes they either start hurling epithets and possibly even small articles of furniture at each other, or they become instant friends and allies. That's how Carlton became friends with the late Gary Halbert. No furniture flew.

So, what? There was a batch of really great writers out there in the olden days. What does that have to do with you and Internet Marketing in the here and now?

Everything. Because what it should tell you—the main thing these guys learned, and what they taught each other—is that (as Carlton sums it up) *copy is everything*. That's wasn't just true then, when online marketing had no banner ads, animated gifs, or video. It's *still* true. In direct marketing, it is always true, and Internet Marketing is direct marketing.

You can have a beautiful site, or one with all sorts of gewgaws and gimcrackery, but if your copy is dull, littered with typos, pointless, or guilty of any of dozen other copy crimes, you might make a sale, but you won't earn a *customer*; no one will be bookmarking, raving about, or linking to your site. They won't come back for more.

A great picture with a bad headline won't keep users clicking through your site; a bad picture with a great headline will. (Of course, for these guys, there was no "site.") That doesn't mean that all successful Internet Marketers can write, but they do have to have the right stuff.

I'll talk more on writing and Internet marketing a little later on in this book. For now, hold this thought: *It's all about the words.*

# CHAPTER **3**

Between the Lines:
*Commercial Zone*

# Between the Lines:
## COMMERCIAL ZONE

THE ROAD TO SUCCESS IS NOT A ONE-WAY STREET. And you have to keep moving; lose your momentum and it can be very hard to pull back into traffic. Having discovered that there were real live people across the world who would—for the right offer—mail actual checks in exchange for information, many of the pioneers realized that it wouldn't be long before what they were doing or selling would have competition from other online marketers like themselves. Without bricks and mortar, they couldn't depend on "location, location, location" to attract customers, so they created new ways to differentiate themselves. Many of these tactics and strategies left them perfectly positioned for the next big technological breakthrough: the World Wide Web.

Even today, though people use the Internet for a lot of different reasons from entertainment to education to business, the common denominator is email. It's a rare person who uses the Internet and doesn't use email. Email existed pre-web, and back then it was still considered by many to be something of a novelty, so people actually *read* what landed in their inboxes—before spam was a big problem, that is. Faster than the post office, more convenient than the phone, and more practical

**47**

than face-to-face communication with far-flung corre-
spondents …what's not to love?

Thus it was that the pioneers embraced email as a
key part of the "products" they delivered. When the first
utility for stripping email addresses from the classifieds
came along, no one thought twice about adding those
names to their mailing lists. First, relatively speaking,
the lists weren't that large. Second, since no one was
receiving much "unsolicited bulk email," the mailings
themselves weren't as bothersome since they were so
easily deleted. And third, the general feeling was that if
people were serious enough about doing business online
to be advertising in the classifieds in the first place, they
could only benefit from receiving new information and
offers, right? Ah, we were so naïve then.

Email became the workhorse. Instead of asking customers to write through the USPO for more information,
the early Internet Marketers listed their own personal
email addresses. To "qualify" for a free report or subscription, people had to enter a valid email address of
their own, and that address got added to the growing
mailing list. When someone bought a report or an article
(which they still had to *pay* for by snail mail, by the
way), more often than not it was delivered via email.
And one of the most popular products at the time was
the email newsletter.

There were probably thousands of newsletters being
mailed around the world in those pre-web days, but very
few of them were targeted specifically toward Internet
Marketing. Talk about your micro-niche market! The
ones that were marketing oriented pulled in an early and
loyal following that carried into the early days of the
web (and in some cases beyond). One of those belonged
to Dr. Ralph Wilson, an avuncular man who built his
whole business around email marketing. He's the author
of *The E-Mail Marketing Handbook*, a whopping 875-page
how-to and reference on everything related to email—

things he learned after launching *Web Marketing Today*. It's still around, with over 110,000 subscribers, so he must know what he's talking about.

Another newsletter pioneer, Dr. Audri Lanford, used her Ph.D. in sociology from Stanford University—with a focus on statistics and research methods—to give her insight into online trends and behavior. After realizing that every one of her secretaries earned more than she did as a professor at Stanford, Lanford and her husband Jim founded an OCR-type document imaging company called Micro Dynamics, Ltd. In 1989, to learn as much as possible about sales and marketing, she signed up for Jay Abraham's "Protégé" seminar, paying an unheard-of $15,000 to attend the week-long course. (You might remember that Marlon Sanders started out with Protégé, too, but he bought the course, nearly seven years before this seminar, which is why he paid only five grand.) Two days into the seminar she called her husband at home to describe a new (offline) marketing strategy she'd learned, and by Friday they had added an extra $60,000 in profit to their business.

Although Jim had ensured that MDL had a presence on the pre-web Internet, Audri Lanford herself didn't get hooked on computer technology until after the Lanfords sold the company. In 1994, always drawn by the entrepreneurial side of business, she started poking around on the online world to see if the Internet and the World Wide Web showed more potential for business owners than she'd been led to believe—most people considered that it was at best a minor distraction from "real" media and wouldn't be much use, to small businesses especially. She saw its promise at once. The couple founded Internet Business Advisory Service, followed by NETrageous, Inc. They began publishing an advisory newsletter called "NETrageous Results" that provided information about online business, marketing and public relations strategies, interviewing successful

Internet Marketers and passing on their success stories in a way that readers could relate to.

Inevitably, since they sent so much time online evaluating and analyzing past successes and burgeoning opportunities, the Lanfords ran across a growing number of Internet Marketing scams, fraudulent offers, and intentionally misguided information. This made Jim especially furious. In response they started a public service newsletter, now the #1 publication of its type, "Internet ScamBusters," which covers the latest twists on Internet scams, identity theft, credit card fraud, phishing, lottery and investment scams, and urban legends.

Despite their frequent encounters with online scammers, the Lanfords never lost faith in the media's potential. Although Audri Lanford did not weigh in on the topic posed on the Internet Marketing Warrior forum ("Did the pioneers become successful because it was so much easier then?"), she has been quoted as saying that she and her husband believe that even today the Internet is still just beginning to reveal its potential. She doesn't believe that everything original has been done and all that's left is a fine tuning here and a tweak there—she loves to tell the (apocryphal but still amusing) story of Henry Ellsworth, Commissioner of Patents in 1843, who is widely misquoted as having said that the government might as well close the patent office down since everything had already been invented. (He was actually just expressing incredulity at the rapidly growing number of creative ideas and inventions, but that's not nearly as good a story.) Her point remains valid though: there may have been a lot of good ideas in the past, but the Internet manages to change and improve at an amazing pace. There are plenty of new ideas just waiting to happen.

When the Lanfords started their online newsletter, they were already online, of course. But the honors for publishing the longest-running newsletter in the industry go to Jonathan Mizel, who started *The Online Mar-*

*keting Newsletter* in 1993. It's still going strong. Building on his encyclopedic knowledge of how to work the pre-Web classifieds, bulletin boards and email system to best advantage, he packed in tips, techniques, real-life examples, and gems of direct marketing wisdom (offline and online). His best-known maxim is "sell people what they want, not what they need." Of course, being too successful at email marketing caused some headaches of its own. Every request for more information, for a newsletter subscription, for a report or an eBook, or even for a confirmation that such a request had been received had to be sent out manually. *Nothing* was easy.

# Do As I Say, Not As I Did

Wait. Before I go on, I want to point out that the most valuable lesson you can take away from this book is this: although they may have made what they do look easy, the Internet Marketing gurus are not superhuman. (All right, so I can't prove this, but I can say I haven't seen any of them in Spandex suits.) They are just like you, or your neighbor, or your cousin Edna. Most of the gurus started out with little or nothing, kept their days jobs for a very long time, and have no advanced degrees in computers or, for the most part, in marketing. They are just average folks with an above-average drive to succeed. One of the best examples of this has to be John Reese.

Reese is the first to tell you that he made some pretty big mistakes working his way up to where he is today. One online reviewer called Reese, "the Albert Einstein of Internet Marketing—just with a better hairstyle." That may be (and I can vouch for the hair; Reese is one of the few among us to still have most of his, too), but it was not always that way.

Reese was one of those kids who are just naturally entrepreneurial—you know, the ones who win the top prizes for selling the most candy in the school fundraiser, and do it without conning their parents into selling the stuff at work. He was also a computer nut from an early age and wrote his first game ("guess my number," with too high and too low prompts), in BASIC when he was just a kid. By the time he entered his teens he'd been reading business, marketing, and entrepreneur magazines for several years, and when he was 14 he answered a mail order ad for a course in, well, mail order—his first exposure to Gary Halbert. He enjoyed reading success stories, but didn't try anything himself until he was seventeen, when he bought a classified ad in *Mother Earth News* (offline), suggesting that readers mail him for more information. Unfortunately, since he'd been skeptical about the whole process, there *was* no more information.

In college Reese changed majors like most of us change our socks, though regardless of whatever his current obsession was, his ADD drove him into the library to study business. When he discovered the classified sections of CompuServe and AOL, he wondered whether anyone really read the ads and responded. Remembering his "success" with the offline ad years before, he placed a little classified ad. This time he had a product: he'd bought resale rights to someone else's product, a business manual that promised to teach people how to get rich. To his surprise, some "goofball" sent him an actual snail mail request for more information, and Reese was hooked. Abandoning his studies in engineering...then law...then marketing...then advertising...then business, he "flunked out and got a crappy job." He continued to get responses for information, but no actual sales, yet he couldn't shake that entrepreneurial bug. He continued writing sales letters, placing ads, experimenting with multi-level marketing programs, chasing after anything that promised to earn him money. He spent a lot of money trying to get rich—money he didn't have.

Here's the part where Reese prefaces his story with a warning *not* to do what he did next. He'd noticed college friends getting credit cards with $2,000 to $3,000 limits, although their requests for additional cards were usually denied. Noting how and when the credit bureaus got their information, he applied for multiple credit cards and sent in all the applications on the same day so that one card wouldn't affect the review for another card. He used the cards to fund his quest for a way to make money, in particular by answering every ad he could find offering more information so he could analyze and reverse engineer what others were mailing out. By the time he was twenty-two, he had over a dozen credit cards—and was almost $100,000 in debt. If placing the classifieds online hadn't been free as well, that number would have been much higher. Just before the World Wide Web hit the Internet, Reese had been selling a small advertising sheet featuring other people's ads, and putting together a newsletter about how to do mail order. As his ventures slowly began to grow, however, it began to take up more and more of his time to fulfill the orders, and with so much debt he could hardly hire someone else to do it for him.

But he *could* get his computer to do it for him. He sat down at his little Mac SE-30 and created what he believes was the first auto-responder available to small online businesses. By keeping the computer connected via dialup, he managed to automate his fulfillment process. Other Internet Marketers began to take notice, asking how he did it and asking him to set up something similar for their operations. Rather than turn his program into a product, so within a year of creating the auto-responder for his personal use he founded a service company, InfoBack, that provided auto-responder service to other direct marketers on a monthly subscription basis. At the height of the company's popularity, Reese had about 300 clients, each paying $20 a month, and it began to look as though he would be able to dig himself out of the hole he'd been trapped in for years. Ironically, although he had no idea who they were or what they were doing with their own online businesses at the time, many of Reese's customers were already on their way to becoming well known Internet Marketing gurus themselves, including Paul Myers, Terry Dean, and Jim Daniels.

For many people, especially those who were running their online businesses as moonlight operations—in other words, *all* of them, when they first started out—the auto-responder was the first major breakthrough in online marketing since the Internet had gone commercial. For the first time, a wildly successful online offer didn't have to bring forward operations and marketing efforts to a halt while marketers caught up with live orders.

I personally didn't need an auto-responder for my premier issue of *The Dallas/Fort Worth Software Review*, my eight-page offline opus. I responded to each request—all eight of them—between classes. Of course, that was before I went digital: after I uploaded the second edition to AOL and at least a dozen bulletin boards, the response rate roughly doubled. That is, I think I hand-sent about two dozen. By that time, I had staff. Several other "volunteer" reviewers worked for me, although we were all paid the same "salary" as I was: we got to keep the software we reviewed. In 1994 one of the more forward-thinking reviewers suggested that rather than coding the newsletter in Visual Basic, I should be using HTML markup. I remember laughing at the idea, mostly to hide that fact that I had absolutely no idea what he was talking about. Back then you could have asked me anything you wanted about MUDs, TinyMUDs, and MOOs, but the Web? I didn't know a URL from a UFO.

# A Banner Year

In 1985, Steve Jobs and the man he'd hired to be CEO, John Sculley, wrestled one last time over the control and direction of Apple Computer. In the end Jobs—the marketing whiz who had founded the company with genius computer designer Steve Wozniak—"resigned" his position and moved on. He didn't move far. His new company was called NeXT, and he designed high-powered (for the time, mind you) computer workstations aimed at the college and business markets from 1988 until 1993. Small, elegant, and loaded with goodies that made software development easier than ever before—Mach kernel, Unix, NeXTStep, Objective-C, drag-and-drop application builders, optical disks, digital signal processors, kitchen sink—NeXT was a commercial failure but a technological success, especially in many elite development environments. (In 1996, ironically, the company was bought out by Apple Computer, a move that plunked Jobs securely into the driver's seat again; he's been steering the company down the road to success ever since.)

At some point during those five years when NeXT was thriving, one of its trademark black computers landed on the loading docks at CERN in Switzerland. It didn't look like much, but by the time Brainy Brit Tim Berners-Lee finished writing the world's first hypertext browser and WYSIWYG HTML markup editor, it was not just a humming, one-foot-to-a-side die-cast magnesium Cube. It was the Web's first server.

Berners-Lee introduced his browser on February 26, 1991. The World Wide Web—a global hypertext-linked space—existed before that, but until then there had been no way for anyone but CERN to access it. The browser used the File Transfer Protocol (FTP) as well as Berners-Lee's Hypertext Transfer Protocol, and in what was obviously a very rare moment of fuzzy thinking, he named his browser "WorldWideWeb," all one word. Very confusing. Fortunately he later recovered and renamed the browser Nexus. The network of information accessible through hypertext links processed by Internet nodes and servers around the world kept its original name, World Wide Web, three separate words. (Yes, technically worldwide should be one word, but you can't change history.)

On August 6, 1991, Berners-Lee sent a post to alt. hypertext, a Usenet newsgroup for people who wanted to discuss hypertext and hypermedia. He included the code, free for anyone to download and use. This was the official public debut of the World Wide Web—the first opportunity for anyone on the Internet to witness a pivotal moment in history.

It was as though CERN threw a party and nobody came.

So it was that the World Wide Web tiptoed into our lives, with none of the fanfare and hype you would expect from something that would eventually revolutionize not just Internet Marketing but so many facets of our daily existence. At the time, however, hardly anyone could explain what the World Wide Web was all about, and only a small number of those people knew how to use it. Many ISPs didn't even offer a way to access it. Overall, people were about as eager to embrace this wonderful new tool as they were to fill out their 1040s.

# The "baby announcement" of the World Wide Web

```
===========================================
=====================
Tim Berners-Lee
Tel:      +41(22)767 3755
WorldWideWeb project
Fax:      +41(22)767 7155
C.E.R.N.
email:  t...@cernvax.cern.ch
1211 Geneva 23 Switzerland
===========================================
=====================
```

In article <6...@cernvax.cern.ch> I promised to post a short summary of the WorldWideWeb project. Mail me with any queries.

WorldWideWeb - Executive Summary The WWW project merges the techniques of information retrieval and hypertext to make an easy but powerful globalfor-matio@ 4 started with the philosophy that much academic information should be freely available to anyone. It aims to allow information sharing within internationally dispersed teams, and the dissemination of information by support groups.

Reader view
The WWW world consists of documents, and links. Indexes are special documents which, rather than being read, may be searched. The result of such a search is another ("virtual") document containing links to the documents found. A simple protocol ("HTTP") is used to allow a browser program to request a keyword search by a remote information server.

The web contains documents in many for-mats. Those documents which are hyper-text, (real or virtual) contain links to other documents, or places within documents. All documents, whether real, virtual or indexes, look similar to the reader and are contained within the same addressing scheme.

To follow a link, a reader clicks with a mouse (or types in a number if he or she has no mouse). To search and index, a reader gives keywords (or other search criteria). These are the only opera-tions necessary to access the entire world of data.

Information provider view

The WWW browsers can access many existing data systems via existing protocols
(FTP, NNTP) or via HTTP and a gateway.
In this way, the critical mass of data
is quickly exceeded, and the increasing
use of the system by readers and information suppliers encourage each other.

Making a web is as simple as writing
a few SGML files which point to your
existing data. Making it public involves
running the FTP or HTTP daemon, and
making at least one link into your web
from another. In fact, any file available by anonymous FTP can be immediately linked into a web. The very small
start-up effort is designed to allow
small contributions. At the other end
of the scale, large information providers may provide an HTTP server with
full text or keyword indexing.

The WWW model gets over the frustrating incompatibilities of data format
between suppliers and reader by allow-
ing negotiation of format between a
smart browser and a smart server. This
should provide a basis for extension
into multimedia, and allow those who
share application standards to make
full use of them across the web.

This summary does not describe the many
exciting possibilities opened up by the
WWW project, such as efficient document caching. The reduction of redun-
dant out-of-date copies, and the use of
knowledge daemons. There is more information in the online project documen-

**58**

tation, including some background on
hypertext and many technical notes.

Try it
A prototype (very alpha test) simple
line mode browser is currently available in source form from node info.
cern.ch [currently 128.141.201.74] as

/pub/WWW/WWWLineMode_0.9.tar.Z.

Also available is a hypertext editor for
the NeXT using the NeXTStep graphical user
interface, and a skeleton server daemon.

Documentation is readable using www
(Plain text of the installation instruc-
tions is included in the tar file!).
Document

http://info.cern.ch/hypertext/WWW/
TheProject.html

is as good a place to start as any. Note
these coordinates may change with later
releases.

```
======================================
======================================
==============
```

Okay, so Tim Berners-Lee is no Hemingway. Still, you
have to admit: it's award-winning material. And it made
sense to some people.

A handful of browsers existed at the time (Erwise,
ViolaWWW, Midas, and Cello), but to say the response
was subdued would be an understatement. Then three
things happened that changed that.

One was subtle: in February of 1993, the University of Minnesota announced plans to collect licensing fees for the use of its Gopher servers, and most people suspected that fees for the program itself could not be far behind. Since Gopher was the main workhorse for most Internet users, the idea of having to pay to send and receive files was not good news.

The second happened two months after that. CERN announced that there would be no fees for access to the World Wide Web. The various nodes and servers could tap into the global network at no charge. ISPs and others weighed the choices: paid access for a simple utility versus free access to the World Wide Web. Not surprisingly, there was a slow shift toward the Web. *Very* slow.

Then came the biggest change of all. On April 22, 1993, the National Center for Supercomputing Applications introduced Mosaic, a new browser developed by Marc Andreessen and Eric Bina. Mosaic unlocked the gates for the average user. For the first time, large numbers of people noticed the Web, for a very simple reason. Mosaic was easy to use, but what made it different from any other browser out there, and what made people's eyes pop out, was that it allowed you to put a picture on the same page as your text. Before, pictures sat all by themselves on a blank screen, and you toggled between them and the copy. Unless you were there at the time, you can't possibly understand what a big deal this enhancement was. It's like the difference between finding something in the library card catalog, and actually reading the magazine. It was like overdubbing a foreign-language film. It was like *real life*.

Gary Wolf wrote this in the October 1994 issue of *Wired* Magazine, "The (Second Phase of the) Revolution Has Begun":

> When it comes to smashing a paradigm, pleasure is not
> the most important thing. It is the only thing. If this sounds

wrong, consider Mosaic. Mosaic is the celebrated graphical "browser" that allows users to travel through the world of electronic information using a point-and-click interface. Mosaic's charming appearance encourages users to load their own documents onto the Net, including color photos, sound bites, video clips, and hypertext "links" to other documents. By following the links—click, and the linked document appears—you can travel through the online world along paths of whim and intuition. Mosaic is not the most direct way to find online information. Nor is it the most powerful. It is merely the most pleasurable way.

Build it, and they will wait. Make it *pleasurable*, and they will come—in droves. Easy to use, nonlinear and graphics-friendly—that is how the Web revolutionized Internet Marketing. Corporate America took notice, of course, and soon many of the largest companies had a web page (and a few had multiple pages—real websites), which were for the most part simply marketing brochures reformatted for a computer screen. Users were usually directed to a phone number and a USPO address for more information or to conduct actual business.

The first issue of *Wired* Magazine, begun in March 1993, made only passing (and rather negative) references to the Internet, but by the end of the year it became one of the first publications to list web and email addresses. *Wired* itself was also on the Internet already, although it was based on the Gopher text storage-and-retrieval program and delivered by email. Being in the thick of new developments, the engineers who handled the Internet version of the publication tried to persuade the publisher, Lou Rossetto, that to maintain credibility, *Wired* had to establish a presence on the Internet.

Now the powerful new browsers had made an Internet presence practical. Of course, magazines get their money, as a rule, from advertising, so the question became a matter of how to make the efforts pay for themselves.

Other publications had been supported by sponsors previously with clickable text ads—notably Global Network Navigator, an O'Reilly and Associates venture—but *Hot-Wired* (the online version of *Wired*) carried the concept much further. Rick Boyce, formerly a media buyer for the Bay Area ad agency Hal Riney & Partners, sold a six-month placement to AT&T, giving the telecom giant a prominent top-of-the-landing-page position for the online component of its extensive "You Will" offline ad campaign. The 468x60-pixel ad—this would become the "standard" size—appeared on October 25, 1994:

This was more than just an ugly intruder on previously sacred territory. This opened the gates for a massive migration onto the Web. Companies scrambled to get their names online, and one way they did that in addition to creating their own pages was to advertise on other sites, and to link those ads back to their pages. Of course, they had no way of knowing how many people arrived at their sites by way of the ads, although today that's the kind of simple, basic stuff we take for granted. But *HotWired* was the very first site to track ad response and, most importantly, made that information available to advertisers. We take it for granted now, and even consider banner ads passé, but the implication was enormous. For the first time websites could compete for advertisers with the support of actual numbers. This was *huge*.

Banner ads changed John Reese's auto-responder business. It started with his customers asking if they could put text ads for their products into his auto-responses. These text ads soon became banner ads, and before he knew it, Reese was in the banner ad brokering business. And paying his bills.

# Gimme Fever

One of the hot catchphrases in the industry these days is "viral marketing," the process where various introductions to something new spread and self-replicate, causing its popularity to grow exponentially. As with a lot of marketing concepts, it's an old standard with a new name (traditional marketing used to call it "word of mouth" or sometimes "whisper campaign"), although occasionally a new twist may get added. Internet Marketing—and even the Web itself—succeeded in large part through viral marketing, although it was not anyone's carefully orchestrated campaign. It was just "Dude, you have got to check this out," repeated over and over until it reached critical mass.

You can trace this spread starting with almost any early adopter, but let's follow just one trade route so you get the bigger view. We'll pick a pioneer: Jonathan Mizel, a former salesman living in the San Francisco Bay area. Mizel explored the bulletin boards, Usenet groups and classifieds from the very beginning, and in mapping out his travels he discovered a way to get his ads posted in the most visible spot in certain online classifieds. Naturally he wrote up a little guidebook, and started selling it online. That was his first-ever Internet Marketing product.

Michael Enlow, as I mentioned earlier, was already a serious power user of the classifieds and bulletin boards in those early, pre-web days. Around the time Mizel was figuring out how to work the system, Enlow started a newsletter that he posted to several bulletin boards. In it he sold both his own products and those of others, and occasionally touted some up-and-comer who'd caught his attention. When Enlow plugged Mizel's guidebook, its sales picked up serious momentum. Mizel was off to a great start, and meanwhile more people felt more confident about getting into the marketplace. More people means more customers.

When he was first starting out, Mizel often hung out after hours at a funky computer store where techies and marketing type people from all the hot computer companies—Apple, Macromedia—got together with their guitars and drums and what have you for a regular jam session. One of the people Mizel met there was a multimedia expert named Declan Dunn. Some years later, when Mizel started a seminar company, he tapped his old friend Declan Dunn to be "the online guy"; the "copy guy" was Marlon Sanders. Mizel, Dunn and Sanders promoted not only other company's seminars but held their own, hitting on average two cities every weekend and spreading the Internet gospel, regaling eager adventurer-wannabes with their tales of online derring-do. Thousands sat mesmerized by their true-life tales. More people joined the online migration.

One of those attendees at a Mizel/Dunn/Sanders seminar who was revved up and ready to explore the new world was an independent auto consultant, a young Canadian from Carleton Place, Ontario, who owned two specialty car companies. Corey Rudl had spent fourteen years doing recon in the auto world, scouting out every chisel and flimflam that some unscrupulous people in the business—the folks we count on to sell, repair, and even insure our cars—could perpetrate on unsuspecting customers. Rudl turned his knowledge into *Car Secrets Revealed*, a book he tried to market offline. It flopped. Nine months after he moved his promotion online, it had driven in over $140,000 in net profit and earned him so much notoriety for exposing the scammers that he was featured on The Maury Povich Show. This inspired Rudl to create another product called *Insider Secrets to Marketing your Business on the Internet*. In it, he compiled his Internet Marketing know-how into a product that many, many Internet Marketers now credit with jump-starting their online careers, including Tom Antion, Randy Charach, and Rosalind Gardner.

John Carlton once remarked that if you look at all the up-and-coming gurus, there's hardly one who didn't follow one of four guides: Carlton himself, Jay Abraham, Gary Halbert or Dan Kennedy (who was geared more to offline, non-information products). As the late Kurt Vonnegut would have said, "So it goes." Students become teachers whose students become teachers. Is it for the money? Sure, in part. But there is also a kind of evangelistic fervor, a technological wanderlust that inspires certain people to keep pushing the boundaries farther and farther out.

There are dozens of product launches each year and nearly as many seminars, and most of them involved can be traced back through the guru "lineage." Whether they will become the gurus of tomorrow will depend on how well they were paying attention, and how well they persevere.

## Business Class

It's easy to picture the earnest New Yorker bustling off the plane in 1981 headed for the Chicago offices of McGraw-Hill lugging his brand new Kaypro "portable," a thirty-pound computer that looked more like a sewing machine than a laptop. David Garfinkel worked as a business journalist for the publisher, but his interest in and knowledge of new technology had somehow made him the in-house expert—no small thing in a technically adept crowd—on telecommunications for reporters and editors outside the main office. This was back in the days of 300 baud modems that required bulky cradles the size of tissue boxes. These had two round rubber wells to hold the phone receiver: you dialed the number, waited for the squeal, then jammed the phone into the suction holders and waited until the next millennium for the two computer systems to finish their elaborate greeting rituals.

A handful of people Garfinkel knew had email addresses, but mainly the connection allowed him to send information and articles from one office to another, an ability that suggested all sorts of possibilities. So Garfinkel was already computer savvy and eager to learn even more when he was invited to a copywriting seminar in Key West featuring none other than the infamous Gary Halbert. Halbert's emphasis was on direct mail and commercial copywriting, which was the same direction Garfinkel had begun to lean. A natural-born writer, Garfinkel had spent years perfecting his craft and his talents for teaching others to write. He watched the emergence of Internet Marketing with great skepticism, appalled by the excessive claims made by fly-by-night, dot-com startups and shady-sounding, get-rich-quick hypesters. But he was as intrigued by the potential as he was repulsed by the reality.

Not long after the turn of the new century, a copywriting friend named Don Hauptman told Garfinkel about a newsletter that needed an editor. At the time Garfinkel had been working freelance for years, and was not too keen on the idea of getting locked into a situation with a single client and project, but when he learned more he changed his mind. He would be editing a $500-a-year subscription newsletter called *What's Working Online*; ironically, it was printed and distributed offline. The readership comprised execs in such big-name corporations as Goldman Sachs, CBS, Playboy, Disney—the hot-shot companies of the day looking to establish an Internet presence.

The current editor had given notice, and with no one internal in place to move up the publisher was looking frantically for a replacement. Still not 100 percent committed to the idea, Garfinkel named an outrageously high fee for what looked like a routine job without much challenge, fully expecting (and half hoping) to be turned down. He was wrong on all counts. Looking back, he says that the newsletter title ought to have been followed by a question mark and had the tagline, "not much," as all around dot.com bubbles burst and companies without solid footing crashed to the ground. But talking with people about what was and wasn't surviving was enlightening. For the most part, the companies that were staying afloat weren't those with snazzy online marketing programs but those that were using the workhorse efficiency of the Internet to automate some key component of their long-distance business, such as manufacturing, shipping, or order taking—for example, Southwest Airlines, which saved millions of dollars a year by issuing tickets online.

Unfortunately, soon one of the things that was *not* working online was the newsletter itself. The atmosphere had changed since the late 1990s, when companies had been told over and over that if they didn't take their businesses online and forget about bricks and mortar they would be left behind—what Garfinkel called the "dot con" scare. First top managers and mid-level executives were frightened that they couldn't stay ahead of their competitors if they didn't fling up a fancy website with lots of the proverbial bells and whistles. Then, as the all-glitz-no-groundwork dot.coms blew up, the same companies got nervous and backed away from the Internet, frightened to get too far ahead. On January 16, 2001, the publishers told Garfinkel that he was doing a great job, absolutely top-notch, and handed him a pink slip. They just couldn't keep the circulation up and had to cancel his contract.

Garfinkel meanwhile had discovered his knack for teaching, and in late 1999 had finished putting together a tape and workbook course that he started selling through traditional sources, clearing around $5,000 in a good month. He showed his materials to his friend, fellow copywriting great, Joe Vitale. Vitale had just been recently asked by his good friend, Mark Joyner, if Vitale knew of anyone else who would be interested in digitalizing their products. Joyner had just successfully put Vitale's videos online with great success and was wanting to do more. It was Garfinkel's lucky day. Putting audio

**67**

online was pretty high-tech in those days, and Joyner not only knew how to do that, but how to market the stuff online too. On April 11, 2000, Aesop.com launched Garfinkel's *Killer Copy Tactics*. His world changed. His life changed. His tax bracket changed. Everything changed. He made more than $60,000 that month.

So even as the media were reporting one failure after another on the Internet, Garfinkel was discovering that there were people out there who wanted his knowledge, and were willing to plunk down their credit cards to get it. Even before *What's Working Online* folded, Garfinkel decided to find out what else he might be able to do with his talents. That's when he discovered one way the online world differed from the offline world: things happen a lot faster.

Joyner worked about as fast and was as smart as anyone Garfinkel had ever met. After the first success, Joyner called Garfinkel and said, "Hey, put together six reports for me today, would you? We're going to offer them to our affiliates." Garfinkel was shocked. Six reports? In one day? He wasn't sure he could do it, but he did, and another surge of sales followed. He started writing articles. About 90 percent of the Google hits on Garfinkel's name today (just over 500,000, if you leave off the quotation marks) have at their root those original six reports, picked up and distributed on scores of affiliate sites.

That first product set off a string of successes. Garfinkel and Joe Vitale did a series of teleseminars that caught the attention of another Internet Marketing copywriter and eBook expert, Jim Edwards, who wanted to create a product with Garfinkel. Edwards had a lot of experience with eBooks, and had built up a great affiliate force; Garfinkel had a lot of experience with traditional publishing and self-publishing offline, and was a fantastic writer. Garfinkel protested that he wasn't technically oriented, but Edwards said, "Don't worry. You create the product. You create the sales letter. I'll take care of all the other stuff." The product, recorded on *idictate.com*, was *eBook Secrets Exposed*—another big seller. Garfinkel had found his niche.

Garfinkel illustrated the appeal of eBooks with this story:

> Okay, imagine that there are two land owners. One of them is a worm farmer. You know, people need worms for bait, for fish, and there might be other things they use worms for. He has an acre, and he needs to keep the whole acre taken care of and keep the toxins out or whatever he needs to do, and he harvests worms. There's this other guy. He only has 1/8 of an acre, but this piece of land has oil underneath, so the guy puts in an oil well. Which one makes more money? The guy with the oil well. Which one covers more ground? The worm farmer. Which one goes narrow and deep? The oil well. An eBook, when done correctly, is like an oil well.: it keeps producing for years and years, and doesn't cover a broad splotch of material the way a typical, traditional published book does. It might go to a niche market that only includes 10,000 people—but if you can sell 500 eBooks for $100 each to just 5 percent of that 10,000 market, you can make a tidy sum.

Garfinkel and Edwards had an oil well. *eBook Secrets Exposed* hit the top of the ClickBank business-to-business lists and stayed in the Top 10 for over a year. Garfinkel was not disappointed, then, when the *What's Working Online* newsletter closed up shop and let him out of his contract. *He* was working online.

# Enclose $1.25 plus 50¢ for shipping and handling

*Just add water! ... Grow and enjoy the most adorable pets ever to bring smiles, laughter and fun into your home.* I was a smart kid, not easily fooled—I thought. But something about those too-good-to-be-true ads in the back of my *Spider Man* comic books just called to me. I was pretty sure that the weird little pink people in the illustration had

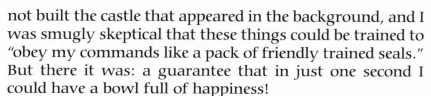

not built the castle that appeared in the background, and I was smugly skeptical that these things could be trained to "obey my commands like a pack of friendly trained seals." But there it was: a guarantee that in just one second I could have a bowl full of happiness!

So I admit it. I used money I'd saved from my allowance and sent away for my very own packet of Sea-Monkeys. What can I say? Maybe I misread the "magnificent, fully illustrated manual," but I was never able to train those tiny brine shrimp *(Artemia salina)* to do much more than hang out in the tank for a month or two before they disappeared, perhaps in search of a bigger castle.

I'm not saying that the ads for spy equipment, X-ray specs and stick-on mustaches inspired my entrepreneurial spirit, but in talking with Jason Potash, a Clark Kentish Canadian Internet Marketer, I recognized a fellow mail-order fan. Potash says he was intrigued by such ads and thought it would be "cool" to sell products that advertise that way and make money, so even as a teen he started reading everything he could find about mail order success. The thought of actually placing an ad—or maybe it was the cost—kept him from trying it back then. "Analysis paralysis" made him just sit and dream, and eventually he got a "real" job in sales.

Still, the desire to start a business, to put something together to sell products through the newspaper or mail order or somehow, persisted. Potash realized that if he were going to get into something more progressive, with long-term growth potential and more opportunity to earn better money, he would likely have to switch industries. He stayed in sales but went to work for a software company, which seemed like the perfect answer. It wasn't. Frustrated, he went to the president of the company, the brains behind the software product—the one who had developed it and hand-coded it. "Mike," Potash said. "I need to get more leads, more prospects. I need more people to sell this software to." Potash knew it was time for a radical change when his boss told him he had all the needs he would ever need right there in the office—and handed him the yellow pages.

Obviously, dialing for dollars or cold calling any kind of company in the yellow pages was not the way to make serious money in any profession. Potash wondered how he might expand his reach. How could he cover more territory since he couldn't duplicate his efforts or clone himself? He started thinking laterally, studying, going back to his early thoughts of direct marketing, and became a serious student of direct response principles, learning how he might apply them to his selling career. The core fundamentals are the same principles used in an online business today.

Potash started by thinking about automated ways to attract prospects and leads, and put together a few campaigns using a new technology called Broadcast Fax that was really big in the late 1990s...before all the anti-spam-telemarketing legislation kicked in. Potash says he could "broadcast freely until the cows came home and people would not complain or take him to court or anything; it was a wonderful time." It doubled his income, and inspired him to even send out regular snail-mail sales letters. The company had a basic website, and in an effort to attract more prospects there, Potash tried to locate resources where he could find his ideal prospects and customers—contractors and construction companies that would use his company's estimation software—and discovered they probably belonged to dozens of industry associations. Soon he had formed alliances with contractors, alarm and security installers—all sorts of people.

His boss may have been impressed, but his competitors really took notice. A company in a related software business approached him and made him an offer: "Look, we saw what you did. We have been watching how you have been growing this business. We see you at trade shows. We see that your booth is always packed. We want you to do exactly what you are doing there, but we are going to pay you a whole bunch of more money to come and work for our company."

He left under happy circumstances—even his boss said, "If your salary doubles overnight and plus you're getting all kinds of bonuses and perks, how can we prevent you from leaving?" His boss gave his blessing¬— and Potash went on to do the same thing all over again, building networks, forming associations. As a member of the local sales association's advisory committee, Potash started writing articles for the monthly internal publication that reached 40,000 members, and was excited to see how it brought in thousands more prospects, built his reputation—his "brand"—and dramatically increased his sales. He wondered if it would have the same effect online, so he created an eZine that he started emailing to prospects online. It did work, sort of. But this was 2000, and there wasn't much happening in terms of ecommerce for companies at that level: there were online brochures, and those gave a phone number or offline address to contact a salesperson to make a purchase.

Potash was still reading traditional direct marketing materials—Dan Kennedy, Ted Nicholas—but he also found a $35 eBook by Ken Evoy called *Make Your Site Sell*. It was the first Internet Marketing product he bought. He spent a lot of time modifying his website and adding new articles, working on his eZine, but he thought of himself as a grain of sand on the beach of the Internet. So he did online what he had more or less done offline: he contacted eZines in related fields and told them about his site and articles, offering to promote their products if they would promote his. He submitted his information to eZine directories one by one.

It paid off, but it was tedious work. At night after his day job, he would sit and punch the keyboard, hand submitting his current eZine. He dreaded having to do it all over again when he launched the other eZines he had planned. As with many an Internet Marketing guru, that tedium was the inspiration for Potash's "Aha!" moment. He was a software guy in an automation field, but he was also a marketer with visions of opportunities. It struck him that if there were others with the same problem, there was probably a money-making opportunity there. He talked to other eZine owners on an almost daily basis anyway, so he casually asked around to see if submitting to directories was a pain to everyone else, too. It was. Potash put together a product, and *eZineAnnouncer* was born. Everything he had learned and studied over the previous years came together: the sales letter, finding potential partners, promotion, direct marketing.

At the last moment before launch, Potash wavered, as many marketers do. He worried that he would sell only a handful of copies. He fretted that he would only net a hundred bucks or so on something he had spent six months of his after-hours time developing. He was ready to shelve the project when his wife convinced him that if he didn't follow through, he would never know, and that he owed it to himself to see it through to the end. He did. None of his partners were the big names we know today. Potash just knew from his offline experience that he needed to develop sales channels, channels of resellers. He launched the product in November 2001, and in the first month he made about $3,500. That may be a small amount by today's million-dollar day standards, but at the time, considering the low-key launch, it was very, very satisfying.

There was only one complication. His business began to do so well and take up so much of his time and energy that he lost focus at work. His boss gave him several warnings until one day, two weeks before the birth of Potash's second son, the call into the office ended with a pink slip.

Just as his confidence had wavered right before his product launch, it wavered now. Not trusting his online business, he found another job. When a friend suggested that the two of them start a software company, he jumped in without planning, and after four months had to pack it in. He found another job, and then once again found himself sitting in his boss's office hearing the familiar warnings. He went home, dejected, and told his wife he just couldn't handle doing both anymore, and he didn't know what to do. It was November of 2002, and the holiday season was coming up. He had a family and was drawing the larger paycheck of the two, but he hated his job, his boss, his commute. The money he was making from *eZineAnnouncer* was good, but not enough to pay a mortgage, make car payments, buy clothes and diapers and food.

But once again his wife weighed in, and the next day Potash gave his notice.

Potash likens the next few months to those situations where the seemingly impossible happens, like when a mother sees her child pinned under an SUV and draws on some superhuman strength to lift the vehicle. He threw all his energy into growing *eZineAnnouncer* exponentially, started a new site called *picktheirbrains.com*, and started doing webinars (online seminars) to pull money in. He started making connections with other Internet Marketers—not yet the big names like Terry Dean or Ken Evoy, but others in the same generational wave as he was, like Joel Christopher, with whom he shared a passion for list building. He met John Reese at a Christopher seminar and they became friends and helped each other hone their products. Potash found that unlike the popular notion that Internet Marketers can just sit around working all day in their underwear all alone, getting out and meeting others in the same business helped build his confidence, his contacts, and his sales. Potash's eZineAnnouncer established him, but he made himself a success by devoting himself to giving more than he took.

> I was just trying to assist people, helping them or spreading my knowledge, doing free teleseminars—to really give and give without asking of people. I found this generosity and good karma came back to me ten times over through the years…. One of the things I prided myself on even in the offline world was really offering great customer service, going that extra mile and being very attentive, listening, being responsive, always having a squeaky clean slate—doing nothing shady, sleazy or underhanded…. When you run your business that way, you end up developing a loyal base of customers who are, as John Carlton puts it, evangelists for your business. They literally spread the word and talk about you and really do a lot of your marketing and word of mouth promotions for you.

Since then Potash has had a number of big successes, most notably *ArticleAnnouncer*, released in June 2005. It comes in two parts: the training component teaches people the inner workings and mechanics of creating good content. The software component helps people automate the submission process to article directories in much he same way that *eZineAnnouncer* automated that process. The years and years of behind-the-scenes training, studying, and hard work paid off, with a half a million in sales in the first few weeks. To outsiders it may have seemed that Potash was an overnight success, but it's clear that he invested a lot of that old blood, sweat, and tears to get where he is today. But you don't have to take my word for it; just ask his wife.

# The Unknown Copywriter

Michel Fortin was a big baby. Literally. His mother, on the other hand, was tiny—just four-foot-two in her stocking feet. Fortin filled out to eleven-and-a-half-pounds in that nurturing space, and came out happy and healthy but with one minor problem: folded into that petite space his legs had grown in crooked—crooked enough that doctors would eventually decide to break them and then fit Fortin with braces for the first three years of his life. Children, we all like to say, are resilient. But adults can be less forbearing, and Fortin's father was one such man. Feeling like a failure for having a "disabled" son, he began drinking heavily, which only confirmed his sense of failure. As many alcoholics do, he lashed out, physically and verbally, and young Michel Fortin grew up afraid of his own father yet desperate for his approval. He did not get it: his father pronounced him a failure, too.

In his typical glass–half–full style, Fortin managed to see this rejection as one of the best things that ever happened to him. To avoid confrontations, Fortin spent all his time either at school or locked in his bedroom. When he was ten or eleven, he found a way to stay in touch with the outside world from behind the safety of his door: he bought a Radio Shack computer and a 300 baud modem and used his text browser to get onto the bulletin board services, where he discovered online role playing games. The local favorite in Fortin's native Ottawa was *Sceptre of God*, a variation on *Dungeons & Dragons*. It was completely text-based, of course—this was 1980, after all—but it allowed him to be whomever he wanted. He didn't have to be Michel Fortin, the guy who was born with a disability, the guy with the abusive father, the guy who feared rejection tremendously. He could be anyone, without being judged at every turn.

Then when Fortin was sixteen, the years of alcohol abuse caught up with his father. Dad had to be institutionalized for Korsakov's Syndrome, a degenerative brain disorder caused by a lack of thiamine (vitamin B1) in the brain that causes irreversible memory loss and confabulation. With his father out of the house, Fortin resolved to fight his fears of rejection. He steeled himself with a quotation from Henry David Thoreau: "Do what you fear and the death of that fear is certain." He reasoned that there could be no better way to fight his fear of rejection than by inviting it over and over again. He dove into sales.

Fortin was determined to prove his father wrong. To avoid being a failure, he put himself into a situation where he had no choice but to succeed—selling on commission—or literally go without groceries. Unfortunately, it didn't work out as planned, and by age twenty-one Fortin had declared personal bankruptcy. But like so many times when plans go awry, leaving direct sales in the end had a positive effect. Fortin found that while he couldn't sell life insurance policies by knocking on doors unannounced, he could sell them if he were invited—that is, if he sent a sales letter first by way of introduction, offering a presentation. Because the only people who responded were those who were genuinely interested, he wasn't rejected. His sales shot up, and after about a year he became the top-producing salesman at the Fortune 500 company where he worked. He won awards. He made the million-dollar round table—a coup in the life insurance biz. He succeeded.

That was the beginning. At first, although he was selling on paper, Fortin didn't think of himself as a copywriter. He thought of himself as a salesperson who happened to enjoy incredible success with his sales letters. But as he gained confidence, he wanted to extend himself and do something else with his newfound skill. He left the insurance business to become a copywriting consultant—not a copywriter yet, but more of an instructor. He'd been positioning himself to sell to professionals and decided to stay in that niche, focusing mainly on the medical profession. Somehow (and he does not say how, although I have my suspicions) Fortin stumbled onto a hair-replacement firm that needed his services, and, with his copywriting prowess, the company grew from a single office to a twelve-franchise empire spread across Canada and the U.S. Once again, though, Fortin reached a plateau and was eager to move on.

He knew he didn't want to work for another company. He'd done that between 1989 and 1993. He preferred being self-employed, and was beginning to chafe under the knowledge that he was earning pennies while those he wrote for were raking in millions. So he formed a company he called The Success Doctor. After all, he specialized in working with physicians, particularly cosmetic surgeons, and he was helping them become successful. It was 1996, still the wild and woolly days of the World Wide Web, and he was eager to get online himself. He'd helped his previous employer set up a website; he was already well acquainted with bulletin boards, and he thought of the Web as just a fancy electronic Yellow Pages (which it sort of was, back then). His first attempt at a site was little more than a resume, a static display-ad-style page with no real attempt at marketing—despite the fact that Fortin was a big fan and follower of Dan Kennedy, had gone to numerous seminars, and had studied a lot of direct marketers and sales trainers out there. He didn't even own his own website but parked his site at geocities. com/eureka/concourse/7770/successdoctor—not something all that easy to remember or type.

Fortin did something offline that would soon serve him well online: he formed a joint venture to move closer to his goal of giving copywriting and marketing seminars. He'd found conference rooms in the back of a struggling office supply company. This company was having trouble getting traffic into the store; Fortin was having trouble finding clients. The two cut a deal: he would give free marketing seminars in one of the conference rooms, talking about positioning, marketing, naming a business, niche marketing, joint ventures, and other marketing techniques. To get to his seminars, people had to walk through the company's store, and more often than not, they would stop to buy something—paper, pens, whatever. The seminars drew only modest traffic until Fortin decided to package his ten best tips into a booklet, which he would offer as a gift to people who attended a seminar. With that simple change, he started packing the room.

The book wasn't even written yet, and already it had become a best seller. Attendees readily gave over their names and addresses so Fortin could mail them the booklet as soon as it was available. It took two days to write and edit it. Fortin included a coupon for the furniture store in exchange for having them print it up, and soon *The Ten Commandments of Power Positioning* drew many people into the seminars. Curious to see if it would do the same for a website, Fortin registered *SuccessDoctor.com* and started offering the booklet in exchange for people joining his mailing list. It did well, and Fortin occasionally scored a contract for his copywriting services, though the bulk of his clientele remained offline. Most of his clients were cosmetic surgeons, chiropractors—those sorts of medical professionals.

Then one day a well-known Internet Marketer hired Fortin to write a sales letter. When Fortin's copy quadrupled his sales, Simon Grabowski *(GetResponse, GetSubscribers)* started recommending him to his friends.

Fortin became Grabowski's regular copywriter, and eventually one of his letters crossed the screen of another Internet Marketer, Kurt Kristensen. Kristensen started calling Fortin the Unknown Copywriter since his work was well known, but hardly anyone had ever met him. People occasionally sent Fortin emails asking if he was this hot-shot Unknown Copywriter they kept hearing about, but he was still largely...well, *unknown*. Then in 2002, Fortin went to his first Internet Marketing seminar, one of Ken McCarthy's System seminars, where Kristensen was speaking. During his spiel about how to make money online, Kristensen said, "Oh, if you want to hire a copywriter who is proven to have the highest conversion ratio, I highly recommend Michel Fortin. He is the Unknown Copywriter." Not for long. Kristensen asked Fortin to stand up, which he did, and the room broke into applause. Right after Kristensen finished speaking, people lined up in the hallway to get Fortin's business card, find out his web address, and talk with him. After that, Fortin's client list exploded as one big-name marketer after another hired him to help out: Stephen Pierce, Jay Abraham, Rich Schefren, Shawn Casey, Armand Morin. It was about as far from "rejection" as you could get.

# Do you copy?

*It's all about the words*, I said earlier. Although some would disagree, the top piece of advice you'll get from the Internet Marketers—after the obvious one, which is "have something to sell that people will buy"—is "create good content." (In deference to Marlon Sanders and the late, great Corey Rudl, I will say that the next-most touted piece of advice is "set up a good affiliate program.") But what makes copy "good" content? Is it the quality of the writing? The relevance of the subject matter? The depth, breadth, and accuracy of the information? Does it inspire the reader to think, feel or—better yet—do something (such as buy your product)? Does it get picked up by the big search engines?

Well, yes. To all of the above.

While hypertext and the Web definitely opened the borders to a whole new continent in the world of Internet Marketing, they didn't change the reality that what people flock to the Internet for is, by and large, information. That doesn't have to be just words, but words must be involved. And although you can now search the Internet for images, video, music—all sorts of things—the big search engine algorithms deal mainly with words. There's an entire industry, search engine optimization (SEO), devoted to improving a site's page rank, which is essentially a page's distance from the top in a list of search results.

"Black Hat" SEO techniques, namely, those that flout the rules and guidelines of the search engines, but that sometimes yield spectacular results in the brief period before their deceptive tricks are discovered and the sites are banned from all future searches (and the techniques are foiled by adaptations to the search algorithms)— flourish as the unscrupulous and the lazy look for shortcuts to success. "White Hat" SEO techniques, however, reign supreme.   Search engines are finicky. They like things the way they are in the real world, meaning they like content that is targeted towards people, not search engines.  A "Black Hat" website is built with its creator trying to game the system.  A system like Google is set up on algorithms, which change frequently, and there are those who write for the algorithm.  A "Black Hat" embeds key words or inserts title tags.  They'll do anything to get their site links through tricks so that they can get their website a higher ranking.  The "White Hat" webpage creator builds a site that will be indexed properly.  That is, they create content to attract users first—and only then do they consider whether the search engine "spiders" that tippy-toe through their pages can easily browse and categorize the copy. Writing for algorithms is relatively easy, although the methods have to change frequently. Writing for people is by comparison extremely difficult, as we humans are a fickle bunch. We want information, but we don't want dissertations; we want creative writing, but we don't like to read; we need facts but we respond to flattery. Above all, we're jaded. We've seen it all, read it all, 'been there done that. '

There's a site online called GuruDAQ (like NASDAQ) that shows the "rankings" of the top Internet Marketers currently active, with a "share price" based on their Alexa Rankings (traffic statistics), the number of back-links to their sites, their sites' longevity, and their popularity. At the top of the list currently, by a long shot, is yet another Canadian Internet Marketing guru, Dr. Ken Evoy. (Rosalind Gardner may have had a point when she commented that the cold weather keeps people inside hunched over their computers becoming Internet savvy....)

While Canadian, Michel Fortin is the Success Doctor, Ken Evoy is truly a successful doctor. He graduated from Montreal's McGill University in 1979 as an M.D., and for years practiced and taught emergency medicine there. He loved the work but hated the system. Soon he turned his attentions elsewhere, starting a toy company in 1983 and eventually designing, patenting and marketing 23 toys and games, many of which still earn him millions in royalties.

In 1990 Evoy began developing a strategy for investing in Canadian penny stocks, and successfully turned his $5,000 "experimental stake" into a $150,000 bonanza. The problem was, although the strategy worked, it was time consuming. It was tedious. It was boring.

In 1996, he discovered the Internet, and at once realized that it could be the answer to his problem. Working with his voluminous notes and existing database, he created a software program that would help him sort through the market and identify potentially lucrative investment opportunities. He likened the Internet to a digital Wild West, which would make him the eager cowboy. Quickly becoming enamored of the technology and its potential, Evoy decided to sell his program on the Internet. The Internet is a high-density marketplace, a concept he has explained this way: "Manhattan can sustain high-niche retail stores because millions of people are on one tiny island. Well, with the Internet, you have hundreds of millions of people sitting right inside your computer!"

Evoy did not get into Internet Marketing to become an Internet Marketer; he got into it because he wanted to market and sell an information product, and thought the Internet would be an ideal venue. He wasn't out to teach people how to make money on the Internet *per se* but how to make money investing in Canadian penny stocks without having to devote prodigious amounts of time and energy to what amounted to busywork. His product's target market, a very tiny niche indeed, dealt with a segment of the investing world that had a very negative reputation. What's more, when it came to convincing prospects that the system he had developed had been proven to work, people resisted at first—he was, after all, a "nobody," a medical doctor, not a well known financial whiz. As a toy designer and entrepreneur, he had proven business and marketing acumen, but selling in this high-tech, still largely untapped medium was something new for him. What wasn't new, at least, was his ability to communicate, and by dint of stubborn determination and the same diligence and industry that had served him well in med school, Evoy managed to turn *PennyGold* into real gold. Along the way he learned what worked with a website and what did not, and ended up with two products: *PennyGold* and *Make Your Site Sell!*

Some of the techniques he used early on he would now consider Black Hat. At the time, nobody thought too much about the implications of what they were doing. It really was the Wild West in that way. Evoy started out relying heavily on SEO—first doing invisible keyword stuffing (words typed in the same color as the background), and when that no longer worked, he started using doorway pages (pages designed exclusively to spam a search engine, yet often invisible to the user through redirection or a quick refresh). Then it happened. Those and other similar methods were eventually deemed unacceptable by the search engines, and Evoy found his site dropped. Evoy worked his way up the telephone food chain until he found out why: he was "stuffing the database"—basically, labeling his site with every possible variation of his keywords —and that was simply no longer allowed.

Now Evoy speaks about good copy and rich content with all the evangelistic fervor of the newly converted.

He learned the importance of "White Hat," copy, and, ironically, his later sites have thrived because they are designed not to work around search engines like Google but with them—as does his banner product, *Site Build It!* In fact, he says that had he gone to Google "hat in hand with a complete spec sheet" asking them to create a product that would be ideal with his clients' sites, he couldn't have gotten a better result than AdSense. (And as an AdSense expert, I'll be happy to tell you all about AdSense in my other books....)

Evoy proudly talks about how the lessons he learned about the importance of "good copy"—"White Hat" SEO copy that has engaging, informative content—got incredibly personal.

He has taught hundreds if not thousands of people how to 'do it right,' but perhaps he is most proud of how his lessons in "White Hat" copy stayed personal, well at least familial, as he taught his daughter how to do it right as well:

> "Favorite Anguilla beaches?" That's a question we were asked a lot. You see, we had visited all 33 Anguilla beaches during the 30 days we were first here (since then, we've been frequent visitors). It's amazing that such a teeny speck of a Caribbean island in the BWI (British West Indies), a mere 35 square miles, could have so much sand! And I don't just mean that we saw the 33 Anguilla beaches. We walked them. We swam, snorkeled, and snoozed on them. Of course, we photographed every one of those spectacular Anguilla beaches....

That's the beginning. Literally, and figuratively.

Montreal in March gets very, very cold. So one winter, when the family flew south for a vacation in the Caribbean, fourteen-year-old Nori hit the sand running—love at first sight. The whole family felt the magic, and no one resisted when Nori's dad suggested they return in the summer to spend the entire month of August in their new-found paradise. Nori's family doesn't spend much time hanging out at hotels chatting with other travelers. They rent the local vehicle of choice, in this case a Jeep 4x4 , and trace every drivable road they can find (and a few not-so-drivable ones, but don't tell the rental company…). They explore. They play. They go native. Several weeks into the trip, Nori realized that she didn't like Anguilla—she loved it. She asked her dad, who had some insight into these things, if he thought people would be interested in a website about their trip. He did, and when they finally flew home, reluctantly, to their office laptops and high school study halls, Nori made a web page. No, make that a web site. Not content to just create a hobby page filled with gorgeous vistas and candids of her dad enjoying yet another rum punch, Nori wanted a real website.

The big question was, how could the site pay for itself? Nori was a student, and had no "product" to sell, just a fascination for and infatuation with a low stretch of sand half the size of Montréal lazing in the waters of the Carib-bean. What she could do, though, was contact local busi-nesses that had no websites and offer to promote them in return for a finder's fee. She could also become an affiliate and earn commissions from Amazon.com and Barnes & Noble (and later, Google AdSense). Now all she had to do was get people to visit her site.

This is where her dad's life lessons paid off for Nori. Ken Evoy told his daughter what he knew about the Internet: "…the World Wide Web is really nothing more than hun-dreds of millions of people looking for information, and millions of sites that provide that information…. Anguilla would…be a wonderful theme for a site if there was enough demand for information about Anguilla and not too much competition. If there was, then Nori could indeed attract visitors by providing good information—and she was becoming an expert on Anguilla." Evoy's most impor-tant advice, according to Nori, was that she should write to

**85**

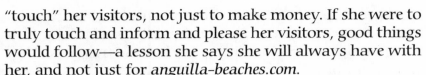

"touch" her visitors, not just to make money. If she were to truly touch and inform and please her visitors, good things would follow—a lesson she says she will always have with her, and not just for *anguilla-beaches.com.*

I've been to Anguilla. But even if I hadn't, her site would give me the sense that I had, at least for a moment, because she took Evoy's advice. Her writing pulls you out of your computer chair and onto the beach, hands you a cold drink, and shows you the sites. She tells you things you really want to know. Not just where the restaurants are (or whom she has a deal with), but which are her favorites and why: "Ask for their conch roti— it's not on the menu, but it is out of this world. Now that I'm back in Montréal, I really feel like flying back to Anguilla, just to gulp down a fresh conch-filled roti!" She doesn't just list car rental agencies, hotels, and attractions; she takes you there. Because she writes as though you are her best friend and about to visit Anguilla for the very first time (and not as though she is trying to say "Anguilla Beaches" a minimum number of times per page), her site gets a phenomenal amount of traffic. And why shouldn't it? Over a two- to three-month time period, her site has a "Long Tail" of over 10,000 distinct keywords. Alexa shows the site with a five-star rating, and as having almost identical stats with a well-known, ten-resort vacation chain in the Caribbean (think multi-million-dollar company versus now college freshman).
Nori has also made her site fit the "Web 2.0" model, which essentially means Websites where the users are important participants (e.g., MySpace, youtube). Anguilla-beaches.com now solicits stories from Anguilla vacationers, which she approves (or not) and posts on the site, keeping her content fresh, unique, entertaining—and profitable. Nori's had her site for five years now, and earned enough to pay her own way through the college she's attending. Unlike some kids, though, she will probably look forward to heading home for the holidays: her dad,

her mom Janice, and her younger sister Yuki just bought property…in Anguilla.

# CHAPTER 4

Naming Names:
*Lists, Leads and the Curse of Spam*

# Naming Names:
## LISTS, LEADS AND THE CURSE OF SPAM

THE I.Q. TESTS PLACED HIM AT ONLY SLIGHTLY ABOVE AVERAGE, yet he somehow managed to become Valedictorian of his class, a fact that puzzled even him at the time. He knew he wasn't the smartest kid in the class. But he may have been the kid with the best system for learning, something he developed for himself without even knowing it at the time. All he thought he was doing was tutoring a couple of friends. Of course, to do that, he had to figure out how to teach the material. Maybe that analysis-synthesis process that gave him an edge.

Or maybe Joel Christopher Remadan was just homesick and trying to avoid thinking about the family that he had to leave behind so he could go to a good school and get the type of education that would take him beyond the dirt roads of his little town. That town was Tabango in the northern part of Leyte Province in the Philippines. When he was just nine, his parents sent him to a school on another island five hours away. In August 1988, with the ink on his degree barely dry, he moved to the United States to set up his own private practice, and for thirteen years he worked as a licensed physical therapist. He dropped the Remadan from his last name in all but legal matters, but his heart remained in the Philippines. His dream was to retire by age 45, buy his own private island there, and concentrate on his philan-thropic endeavors, which focused largely on scholarships and "netrepreur" education, employment and empower-ment for the people back in his hometown. You probably already know this, but Joel Christopher is a really great guy. (Not surprisingly, one of his heroes is Dr. Muham-mad Yunus of the Grameen foundation, who won the Nobel Peace Prize in 2006 for his pioneering program in micro-lending.)

Physical therapy was not going to help Christopher achieve his dream.

In April of 1999, he married, and he and his wife Sheila bought a two-story, three-bedroom house. In one of the extra bedrooms sat the computer Christopher suppos-edly used for work, but since his business manager han-dled most everything—including reading and answering emails, and since Christopher didn't even have his own email address—the PC mostly sat there gathering dust. One day, as he walked by the library for the Nth time, he stopped and on impulse fired up the computer. He'd been hearing that people could make money on the Internet and was curious to see how it could be done. The fact that he knew nothing about computers seemed a minor detail. He'd been Valedictorian, right? Surely he could learn.

Soon he had an email address and an Internet connec-tion. He started surfing around, checking out websites, looking for leads for a personal network development company he was part of called PDN. He was certain the Internet could help him find leads, but he didn't have a clue how, so he began searching. In July 1999, he found a book by Jim Daniels called *Insider Internet Marketing*, and bought it. In the fall of 1999, Christopher made his very first online download purchase, a $97 product from Terry Dean. His computer skills hadn't advanced much: after he downloaded the file, he had to call Dean and ask where on his hard drive the file would have landed since he couldn't seem to find it. Once he finally located the file, he read it, and everything else he could find, including what he found on Allen Gardyne's website *AssociatePrograms.com* where he learned about affiliate programs. Gardyne was promoting Ken Evoy's *Make Your Site Sell*— and Christopher knew he needed the kind of step-by-step instructions he'd find in that thousand-page monster, so he bought it. He also bought his very first domain, *successaccess.com*, to set up a how-to site for rank Internet Marketing beginners like himself.

He started out with a newsletter filled with anecdotal tidbits about his own Internet Marketing experiences so far. There was no sales pitch (after all, there was no product). The tiny newsletter took him two weeks to compose—he's a very slow typist, even now— and just after the Y2K New Year's Eve festivities, he walked up to the computer and hit SEND to everyone on his mailing list. That was a total of nineteen people, including his wife, his brothers and sisters, and a few former clients. It was an inauspicious start for the man who would become known as "The Master List Builder" seemingly overnight (actually, it took a little less than two years—and a lot of hard work).

How did he do it? Several ways, based on bits of information he'd gleaned from the mailings from Evoy, Gardyne, Dean, and Daniels, and other things he'd read. Christopher bought a lot of eZine ads, inviting people to his site where he could capture their information. He also used two popular methods at the time: ad swaps (you place your ad on my site and I'll place my ad on yours, and we'll send each other traffic—and leads); and Free-For-All advertising (FFA), which turned out to be worth exactly what you paid for it—nothing. What worked very well for him, however, was offline lead generation. He printed up free offers on the back of postcards and mailed them to everyone he knew from old coworkers to high school classmates. It worked, but very slowly. It took him almost six months to have a database of just 300 names.

About the same time, he got pulled into network marketing, a fancy new name for the old mirage of multilevel marketing success, and ended up losing around $10,000. He was making a little money off affiliate programs—his first $10 check most likely came from selling Evoy's *Make Your Site Sell*—but that wouldn't pay the mortgage.  It did prove, however, that the market was out there; he sold others' products for nearly two years. But his list was still growing agonizingly slowly. In June 2000, Christopher went to a seminar and hired a mentor for a few hours of coaching. He came away with a plan that helped him grow his list from the measly 300 names that had taken him six months to accumulate to 2,000 names—in just six weeks. The crux of the plan was a joint venture program based on banner ads. Eight months and eleven days (but who's counting?) after his stellar Y2K debut, Christopher finally quit his day job.

Christopher developed a real appreciation for the value of seminars, and soon realized that the big money was in promoting big-ticket items, such as mentorships, coaching programs, and seminars like the one Terry Dean told him about called the Internet Money Machine Boot Camp seminar (hosted by Ron LeGrand's daughter, Vicki Sessions, Global Publishing). He began promoting the Boot Camp and in four days made $2,400 just by mailing the offer to his list—more than he had been earning in a whole month. He signed himself up for the September 2001 seminar. He also signed up someone named Armand Morin. It hadn't taken Christopher more than a few months of selling the Boot Camp to realize that when someone pays $1,600 for a seminar, they call with some kind of question, although perhaps just to verify that the sale is legit. Morin didn't call, and Christopher began to worry that there had been a mistake. Although he was traveling in the Philippines at the time, he called Morin to confirm the seminar reservations. When Christopher happened to mention where he was calling from, Morin offered the fact that he was half

Filipino, and the two spent a considerable amount of time swapping stories. When they met at the seminar, they hit it off immediately.

Christopher wasn't making as much online as he had as a physical therapist, but the two or three thousand a month he was making was enough to get by, and he could at least do it from home. At the "Boot Camp" seminar (moved from the weekend of 9/11/2001 to September 28), he met not only Morin but also David Ledoux and Marlon Sanders. They had lunch, and Marlon said something that stuck in Christopher's head: "If you want a best selling product, talk to your list." By that time, Christopher had built a list of about ten thousand people. The very next week he sent out an email asking subscribers to describe their biggest problem in business at the moment…their biggest challenge in Internet Marketing. About six hundred people replied out of the ten thousand. Two thirds of them, in one way or another, said that their biggest problem was figuring out how to build an optimum list from scratch. Christopher went back to his notes, the eBooks he'd read, the audios he had played, and realized that while there were only scattered bits and pieces of help with list building—do ad swaps, buy ads, do SEO—there was no step-by-step system.

He decided to create one.

As it turned out, he not only created a list building system, he also created a list-building niche within Internet Marketing. The industry went from nobody teaching list building to *everybody* teaching it. But only Christopher was the *master*. He didn't just learn everyone else's tricks and techniques and collect them into a single source, he made up his own. He also made up a few new words along the way, like "co-opetition"—literally, cooperating with your competitors—finding others who want to sell to exactly the same people but who don't have a product that competes directly with yours and then finding ways to enhances each other's lists and then share. In his best selling book *Mining Online Gold with an Offline Shovel* he talks about bricks (offline) and clicks (online), and the importance of using both. His most important tool, though, one he developed over the years, remained relationship building—remembering that the names on the list are real people.

Christopher may be the only Internet Marketer I know who loves the telephone. When someone on his "hot list" (those who have previously spent X number of dollars, or bought X number of products) buys something new, he picks up the phone. He calls and says thank you. (Did I mention yet what an approachable, amiable, warm-hearted guy he is?)

When Christopher was still promoting the Internet Money Machine Boot Camp, he made an offer to his list: the next five people who sign up for the seminar in February 2002 could have him coach them for the next ninety days, about an hour or two hours a week for twelve weeks, and he would share with them how he was doubling his list. One of the people who signed up was George Callens (who five years later became vice-president of operations for Armand Morin). During that private coaching period, Christopher managed to double his list from 10,000 to 20,000 in 74 days, but kept pushing. He'd challenged himself to do it in 90 days, and he had sixteen left. In the end, he managed to more than triple his list to 30,903 opt-in members (not yet buyers) in 99 days. Around a month later, Callens interviewed him during a teleseminar, introducing him during the live call as "Joel Christopher, the master list builder who even Internet veterans go to for help building a list." And all Christopher could think of was, "Man, that's a great name." He immediately registered the *masterlistbuilder.com* domain.

What's so hard about building a list? Can't you just buy a mailing list? Of course you can. But there are names, and then there are names. The difference between a subscriber and a customer is what pays the mortgage.

As Christopher himself pointed out in one of his books, during the 2002 Internet Lifestyle Summit in Hawaii, someone once asked three Internet Marketing pioneers if their offices caught fire and they could save any one thing what would it be? All three—Stephen Mahaney, Corey Rudl and Jonathan Mizel—gave exactly the same answer: their subscriber lists. The reason is that these lists represent not just lists of random names but genuine prospects who have already shown an interest in a product. And better yet, there is a subdivision within the larger list of buyers—those who have already bought something in the past. Christopher would trade a list of a million subscribers for a list of a thousand buyers. With a list, you can rebuild a business in a fraction of the time it would take to work from scratch.

A strange thing happens when you start getting tagged as "master of this" and "Dr. that"—people start expecting you to stand up at seminars and share some of the great wisdom. So it happened that Joel Christopher, Master List Builder, found himself a last-minute addition to the speaking roster at Mike Filsaime's April 2002 event when the scheduled speaker's wife went into labor. Christopher had been talking with Ron LeGrand and David Ledoux, and both mentors had been telling him that his coaching fee was too low, and when an unmanageable 41 signed up for his $700 services, Christopher was beginning to agree. They both told him to double his fee and reduce the number of classes. Reluctantly he tried it, charging $1,200, and 22 people signed up—still too many to be workable. He was toying with the idea of upping his price even further to $1,500, and he decided to test out the idea at Filsaime's event.

Maybe it was the fact that people bought his list building coaching services at the higher price. Maybe it was the pressure of his first public speaking at an Internet Marketing seminar. Maybe he was just tired. For whatever reason, many of the attendees—including Armand Morin, who thought it was so funny he wrote it down—remember Christopher's first stage appearance not for that test offer or for anything he taught them but for something he said that didn't come out quite as he intended. Christopher still thinks in his native Filipino, then translates his thoughts into English to speak them aloud. All weekend he'd been growing excited at the idea that with the probable increase in income from price restructuring, he and Sheila could finally feel comfortable enough to start the family they wanted. That's what he meant to say, anyway. But what came out of his mouth when he answered a question about how very important it was to attend live events was this: "You've got to go to events because so many great things happen there—you can even get your wife pregnant!" The audience howled; they always love Christopher's easygoing, warm, downright neighborly way of speaking to them as though they had all just stopped by for a barbecue. Christopher is still puzzled about what on earth was so funny.

# Spam, Spam, Spam, Spam, Lovely Spam! Wonderful Spam!

Lovely, that is, only in Monty Python's Green Midget Café in Bromley. Years ago, when email was still new enough that most people had to ask what the word meant, the first "unsolicited or undesired bulk commercial electronic messages" started popping up. People shrugged. *How bad can it be?* They wondered. How many "unsolicited or undesired bulk commercial electronic messages" can I get in one day? How many "unsolicited or undesired bulk commercial electronic message" *senders* can there be out there? It didn't take long for early Internet users to realize that there were two big problems. One, if they didn't do something about it, soon email could be overrun with "unsolicited or undesired bulk commercial electronic messages," filling up inboxes and dragging servers to their digital knees. And two, the name was too long.

Happily, some wit recalled the 1970s comedy skit in which Mr. and Mrs. Bun attempt to order breakfast in a café where every item except two contains Spam—a food despised by Mrs. Bun (Graham Chapman, looking especially matronly and proper in his, I mean *her*, sturdy Mackintosh) and adored by Mr. Bun (Eric Idle). The menu, in fact, aptly foretells the growth of the "unsolicited or undesired bulk commercial electronic messages" problem that would follow two decades later. In the skit, the hapless waitress (Terry Jones, in full frumpy-drag regalia) recites the items on the menu, and each contains even larger servings of Spam. At the sound of the word Spam, the horn-helmeted Vikings burst into "song," an *a capella* ditty with the attention-numbing bass line ("spam spam spam spam") and the trilling yet equally annoying melody ("spam, lovely spam! Spam, wonderful spam!) In the beginning, it's not so bad, much as those early "unsolicited or undesired bulk commercial electronic messages" weren't too bothersome with their still somewhat personal pleas for you to buy this piece of real estate or this self-help product ("egg, bacon, and spam"). There have even been the very occasional "unsolicited or undesired bulk commercial electronic messages" that were actually useful or entertaining such as those sent by the early Internet Marketing pioneers before they knew better ("Lobster thermidor aux crevettes with a Mornay sauce garnished with truffle paté, brandy and with a fried egg on top and spam"). Today though, most "unsolicited or undesired bulk commercial electronic messages" are virtually worthless to readers, and used largely for the benefit of the senders, as in the case of the email-spoofing "warnings" from fake PayPals and eBays hoping you'll give up your passwords and credit card numbers ("spam, spam, spam, spam, spam, spam, baked beans, spam, spam, spam and spam").

Small wonder that users decided to call email's evil twin "spam." (Hormel, the makers of the canned meat, reputedly liked the skit enough to add it to the Spam museum, but were less happy, naturally, about being associated with the scourge of the Internet.)

It would be comforting to think that responsible Internet Marketers never, ever sent spam. But it would also be false. In the beginning, most of the pioneers didn't think twice about the precedent of mass-mailing the electronic equivalents of the sweepstakes entries that once flooded everyone's real-world mailboxes. The first mass spamming sent out in 1994 went to just 6,000 addresses. A decade later it was nearing 30 billion per day. Various anti-spam groups estimate that in 2007 that number has risen to a staggering 12 billion plus per day, or roughly six spam messages for each of us online (someone out there is not getting his or her fair share: I personally get scores of spam messages every day). The Messaging Anti-Abuse Working Group (MAWWG), working from a sample group of 100 million mailboxes in 2005, estimates that as much as 85 percent of what's landing in our inboxes today is spam. (Others say it's closer to half, which suggests that one person's spam is another person's long-ago-forgotten opt-in.) Poor Bill Gates gets 4 billion emails each year, or about 10 million each day—that is, between 5 and 8.5 million spam messages every day, most of which promise to help him get rich.

So? Let's separate out the spam estimated to be scam-related (about 10 percent) such as all those sad Nigerian princes needing you to hold onto their millions of dollars, the spoof emails, the chain-mail letters used by phishers to capture addresses. Now take out the spam vaguely categorized as adult (another 20 percent—2.5 billion per day), which includes not just nudie photos and ads for, well, enlarging devices, but serious hardcore pornography. You're still left with a gazillion emails that may well have some sort of legitimate product or service to sell, or some information to deliver. That is, some kind of *marketing*—on the Internet. That means that some Internet Marketers are doing this spamming. But not the gurus or the responsible newcomers, who all recognize now that spam is more than a nuisance, it's a crime: theft of our valuable time. How much time does it take you to delete an email? How much is your time worth? One estimate says that U.S. corporations alone lost a total of $8.9 billion to employees and IT departments having to deal with spam—and those are the figures from 2002.

It's a difficult thing to police. The U.S. passed the CAN-SPAM Act of 2003 (who says the government has no sense of humor?), which made it illegal to send out messages without a means to "opt out" of receiving any further communications from that source. The problem is that scofflaws don't care and so don't include the opt-out link, and the people are hesitant to use the link in the messages that do. The pervasive fear is that doing so just alerts the sender that your address really exists, inviting even more spam. That would be illegal, of course, but when is the last time anyone asked you if you had spotted any unsavory spamsters hanging around your neighborhood? It is only the major offenders who even get noticed, let alone charged with a crime. The latest American to wear the mantle of "spam king" (no queens yet) is Robert Alan Soloway, indicted by a grand jury for identity theft, money laundering, and mail fraud—including email fraud—among other things. Yet another reason we Americans should be thankful: Soloway could have had it much, much worse. Moscow resident Vardan Kushnir was believed to have spammed every Russian-language Internet user trying to sell his American Language Center courses. In 2005 he was found dead of "numerous blunt-force blows to the head." Makes several decades in a white-collar crime prison sound like a vacation.

The role spam will play in the future of Internet Marketing is unclear at best. As quickly as ISPs find ways to filter out the latest spamming techniques, determined spammers devise new ways to slip through. The message you should take from this if you are an Internet Marketer is clearly "don't spam!" but be aware that your idea of what constitutes spam and what doesn't might vary significantly from the legal definition—and that of your prospects. An important lesson is that Internet Marketing mailings should always, always, always (did I say always?) include an opt-in/opt-out provision. It's best to use a "confirmed opt-in," where recipients must click a special link or reply email to confirm that they really wanted to join whatever they think they just joined, and to give people an opt-out provision every time you send a mailing just in case someone decides to leave the list. Better still than the confirmed opt-in is authentication, wherein you send a "nonce," a special code or verification sequence that confirms a subscription.

On a lighter note, earnest spammers have come up with some maddening but clever ways to slip past the guardians at the gate, such as applying random character and word swap algorithms to real text passages. Annoying though they can be when it comes to your own inbox, you have to give credit to whomever came up with some great names for these spamming techniques: "dissociated press" and "travesty generators" are among my personal favorites.

# Winging It

Mathematicians and physicists like to study chaos theory. No, that's not the explanation of how it is that holiday lights, no matter how carefully you store them, manage to weave themselves into birds' nests from one year to the next. It actually has to do with finding order in seemingly random systems. (Don't worry; you won't be tested on this later.) It has three properties, but I want to mention the one first described and named by a meteorologist in the early 1960s. It seems Edward Lorenz was working with his twelve-variable computer model for weather prediction when he decided he needed to re-run a previous sequence. To do that, he had to enter data from a printout, and he did, but to save time he started in the middle, not the beginning. He let the computer chew on the numbers for a while (we aren't talking super-speed microprocessors here), and when he returned he was baffled. The exact same numbers in had produced a different pattern out. How could that be? As it turns out, the numbers weren't exactly the same. In entering them, to save time and paper he had used only the first three decimal places, where the original data had used six decimal places. Logic suggested to Lorenz that the patterns should still have been roughly the same, if not identical, but in reality he discovered that minor changes can cause chain reactions that lead to major effects. In 1972 he presented a paper to the American Association for the Advancement of Science in Washington, D.C., called "Predictability: Does the Flap of a Butterfly's Wings in Brazil set off a Tornado in Texas?" This component of chaos theory—and everyday life, it seems—came to be called "The Butterfly Effect."

A few years ago at the *Focus 4 The Future* event in Charlotte, NC, I met the Long Islander who tied "The Butterfly Effect" to Internet Marketing. Mike Filsaime is another "kid" (all right, so he'll turn forty this year) who seemed to come out of nowhere. In reality, of course, he'd been building slowly but steadily for years. After graduating Filsaime picked up an Associate's Degree in Computer Science and Business Administration from the New York Institute of Technology only to discover that he could make $13 an hour at Pathmark, a local grocery chain, working his way up from pushing grocery carts to maintenance, register, and grocery to frozen foods manager. He earned $38,000 a year, a decent amount for a young, single guy in his twenties, but by 1990 he knew that he had not found his life's work. His brother was in the car business. His dad was in the car business. After trying some different home-based businesses bought from magazines, Filsaime followed suit and took a job at a dealership.

At NYIT, he'd learned to do a little coding in BASIC, Pascal, and Fortran, and in 1989, just before jumping from carts to cars, Filsaime had been doing some programming at home. Filsaime's father loved to play the lottery and stayed up late checking the winning numbers. Sometimes he'd get busy and not check his numbers for a while, and then have to check several weeks' worth (at 120 games a week) of numbers at a time. Filsaime said, "Why don't you let me put these numbers into a program? I'll just enter the winning numbers, and it will give you a report of what you won." Filsaime wrote a short program to do just that, and ended up selling the program to *Lottery Players Magazine* for $5,000.

At the dealership, Filsaime started out as a salesman, and by 1993 was leasing manager, then sales manager. He did well for himself over then next decade, and in 2002 he was at Millennium Toyota in Long Island, a rapidly expanding dealership (from seven to thirteen dealerships), with a sales force growing so fast that every week he faced a crop of fifty new trainees. Not only did Filsaime end up spending hours on end training neophytes to sell cars, he also needed a manual of sorts, and for that he turned to the Internet. He discovered that he could find hundreds of free articles and pointers that could be combined into a manual to hand out, and he was constantly online looking for new material to upgrade it.

Anyone who spends much time online has to deal with the constant influx of spam, most of it promising amazing sexual, medical and financial results. Filsaime must have seen "The Secrets to Online Profits" email at least a hundred times before he decided one day not to delete it. When he did, he saw an image of a man with his fist up saying "Yeah!" and copy saying something along the lines of "make a thousand dollars a day." The offer turned out to be Frank Kern's *Instant Internet Empire*, although Kern himself wasn't the spammer; he'd sold resale rights to someone with no compunction about flooding people's inboxes with unsolicited advertising. Filsaime printed the salesletter—all 27 pages, it being a "long-form" sales letter—and read it on his break.

This was Filsaime's first exposure to resale rights. The letter pitched actual websites that he could get and resell: moneymaking website number one, moneymaking website number two, and three and four and so on. He bought it. Of course, all he had done on the Web before was surf, so it helped that Kern, who is known for being an early adopter on many fronts, had produced a sort of starter course that showed Filsaime how register, find a web host, get FTP software, include a PayPal button, send a thank you page, use an auto-responder—many things that he didn't know how to do and some he didn't even know he needed to do. He started up *LetsAllWork-AtHome.com* (WorkAtHome.com was taken).

Like many newbies, Filsaime had no list. So he went to Google and typed "email addresses for sale" and found a million addresses for $297. The spam-ee became a spam-er, but only for a day. Filsaime had a desktop email program called *GroupMail Plus*, and he loaded about 10,000 addresses into it and sent out an email: his wife's pumpkin pie recipe, in honor of the season. The next morning his wife called him at work and said she couldn't get onto the Internet. He suggested she try some things like resetting the modem, but nothing worked. When he got home, he called his service provider, Optimum Online, to complain about paying for a service he couldn't receive, and so on, when the customer service rep cut in: "Mr. Filsaime, we have received thirty-three spam complaints about your account." Filsaime cringed. Spam? The CSR read back his email and IP address, and the subject line, "The World's Greatest Pumpkin Pie." Oops. Busted.

Filsaime couldn't apologize fast enough. "I'm sorry. I took a course on how to do this but I didn't know there was anything wrong with it." She pointed out that it wasn't illegal (back then, though in less than a year it would be a violation of the CAN-SPAM Act of 2003), but it was against their terms of service. She promised to reconnect his service but warned him that if the company received another complaint it would terminate his high-speed access forever. He would have had to return to dial-up, there being no other high-speed services available at the time.

Then Filsaime checked the website's host and found that the same thing had happened. He'd lost his account due to complaints about spam. Finally, he could see that he had made a $19 sale, but he couldn't retrieve it because someone had reported him to PayPal for spamming. He never spammed again.

That left him with no list at all. Again, he turned to the search engines, and looked for "spam-free email," which is how he happened upon safe lists. This is a community of people who want to advertise their product or service, but in return they have to agree to see other people's ads. In the early days, 2002 and 2003, safe lists were a relatively effective way to drive traffic to your website. You had two emails with a safe list, one called admin that the list managers used if they needed to make contact, and a second one where all the emails landed. Filsaime had barely logged in to confirm his address and account when the mail started pouring in. He saw several thousand offers a day for everything from herbal tea to get-rich-quick schemes. It worked...sort of: he got a handful of $19 orders every week. He wasn't concerned about the low return since he was earning good money at the dealership. The online thing was just a hobby.

What he soon realized, though, was that if he made five sales a week, he could make over five thousand dollars just by coming home and hitting the button at midnight every night. The Internet was filled with safe list junkies, and the best safe lists had seven, ten, twelve, even fifteen thousand members. Since safe lists were free, the only way you could start a new one with any success would be to offer the first four thousand people special privileges. Only then would the list be big enough that someone would consider it worth joining. It was March 2003 when he first read that he ought to get an auto-responder. That sounded like one of those bounce-backs that tells people you are away on vacation and will return on such-and-such a date. Filsaime didn't realize that auto-responder meant a full database software where he could capture a name and email address on his site and then email to those people over and over, or send sequential messages, and do other things. Finally, it sunk in. He started with AutoResponse Plus (later he switched to *prosender.com* and *aweber.com*), and he was sold by a single bullet item in the promotion that said, "The average person comes to your site four to seven times before buying anything. What you want to do is focus on gathering the name and the email address rather than trying to make the sale." That is still Filsaime's philosophy—it's all about list building. Around that time, he also saw a video of Mark Joyner's outlining a concept Joyner called Target, Tie-in and Collect—target an audience, tie-in a bonus that someone would like, and collect the name and email address by giving something away for free. In other words, if you're trying to reach other Internet Marketers, don't offer a free toothbrush, offer something that would improve the business, like an eBook about driving traffic to a site.

Filsaime created a directory of the most powerful free safe lists and called it PowerLists. He advertised it on each of the safe lists—"PowerLists. Email millions of people spam-free and get four bonus gifts"—and was getting at least twenty opt-ins a day. Two things came onto the scene that exploded his business. The first was something called a submitter. This was a program that let you store your email ad, and then send that ad to all the lists whose URLs you supplied; it would paste the ad into emails to that list. If Filsaime entered the URLs of ten safe lists, each with 10,000 names, he could reach 100,000 inboxes with a single click.

The second thing that changed things was Filsaime's realization that since he was joining so many safe lists, he was getting about fifty validation emails a week, and he would have to pick through thousands of emails every day to find those validators. Realizing that he could sort emails, and then use a one-click delete that emptied his inbox every day at midnight and leave behind only the ones that included the word validation, he began typing into his subject line "Validation for PowerLists Starts Here." His opt-ins went from twenty a day to seventy-five, or more than two thousand per month. He still wasn't selling anything, but after three months he had a list of over 5,000 opt-in members. When he discovered that he could email offers from Clickbank, he suddenly found that selling forty copies of *The Whole Truth* (Stephen Pierce) or Rosalind Gardner's book was making him significant money. With two thousand members he made two thousand dollars—about a dollar per member name—and that was true when he made $3,500 with a list of 3,500 contacts, and $5,000 with a list of 5,000 contacts. That correlation has remained relatively constant over the years.

Filsaime decided to go on a quest to find different ways to drive traffic for free, give things away, and monetize everything with offers—and to teach others how to do the same thing. He likened his product, *Carbon-Copy-Marketing*, to "Frank Kern's *Instant Internet Empires* on steroids." It included a blueprint people could follow to do exactly what he had done in the past three months: get a website, get FTP software, get Microsoft's FrontPage, get free resale rights products, use a squeeze page, and so on. (A squeeze page, by the way, is any page—especially a landing page—whose primary purpose is to capture names and email addresses that can be added to a list. Credit for thinking of it must be spread among Stephen Pierce, Marlon Sanders, and Scott Covert, but everyone agrees that it was Jonathan Mizel who gave it the colorful name.) *Carbon-Copy-Marketing* still sells extremely well today, although some of the particulars have become a tad outdated as others' products and websites come and go.

Around the same time Filsaime was getting into Internet marketing with his first information product, Mark Joyner was retiring. Filsaime had read a quote from Mike Litman calling Joyner "the Tiger Woods of Internet Marketing," which of course sent him scrambling to read all he could about the man and his products. Joyner was selling every product he owned, including the source code sites and the viral sites, for $1,497—with the price going up to $1,997 after the first one thousand copies sold. Filsaime was making good money at the dealership but was still having trouble making ends meet. He really wanted to buy Joyner's *Farewell Package*, but his credit cards were maxed out and his wife was worried about using the mortgage payment to buy the product.

Another Internet Marketer, Mike Chen, had bought the product three weeks earlier and had done some tweaking, and had created a site called *fly-in-ads.com* that talked about how he had 100,000 hits in a few days—so many he crashed the server—and had 25,000 join the site in just five days. Chen had two products: *WebLock Pro* for $97 and *Biz Automator* for $37. Filsaime wanted both but couldn't afford both at the same time. He joined the site, and that introduced him to a special thank-you offer: "Thanks for joining. If you would like, here is an opportunity to get *WebLock Pro* and *Biz Automator* for $19, but you can only buy it right now. If you pass on this, you will have to buy it at the retail price." Filsaime could afford that one. Working his calculator, he figured that if Chen had 2,400 names on the list, and maybe 10 percent of them went for the $19 deal (for products that probably cost $10 to put together), Chen had made $54,000—in four days. Convinced he'd made a math error, he tried again. Same thing. Now, John Reese had had his million-dollar day, but Filsaime was taking home $150,000 a year—and spending $200,000 trying to keep up with the sales managers.

Immediately he created a product called *The-Best-Deal-Ever*, combining every resale rights product he could, including his own *Carbon-Copy Marketing*. He included everything he had rights to and created a massive one-time offer. In December, 2003, he also created *MyViral-Ads*. He called it, *Dont-Touch-My-Ads.com*, and its "unique selling proposition" (USP) was that a constantly changing series of ads showed up on people's computer screens whenever they stopped typing or using the mouse for more than a certain period of user-defined time. They're called "fly-in" ads, and they were just little three-by-five-inch rectangular ads advertising a text ad; if you wanted to investigate it, you clicked on it and ended up at the advertised site, and if not, you just closed the box. No ads appeared while you were working. They only came up when you went off to the restroom or stopped typing to talk to someone. When you came back, you'd see an ad. And for every ad that came up on your screen, you earned a credit for your ad to be broadcast, too. You also got credits every time an ad appeared on the screen of someone you referred to the site. It was sort of multi-level marketing meets viral marketing, but this in itself was really nothing new as it used the exact same model that Mark Joyner pioneered in the 90's with sites such as StartBlaze. Between *The-Best-Deal-Ever.com* and *Don't-Touch-My-Ads.com*, Filsaime made $19,000 in four days. It was his earliest experience first-hand with the power of viral marketing. And it was the cocoon that turned into Butterfly Marketing.

Filsaime started a site called *ListDotCom*, and he contacted Mike Chen, who had a hot product at the time called *MakeYourOwnSoftware* that sold for $197. Filsaime wanted to know if Chen was interested in doing a joint venture where he did a one-time offer on Chen's product for $97. Chen said he didn't think they would have to discount the price if they added another benefit and said he wanted to think on it and call him back. When he called, Chen said, "Hey, Mike. I got somebody on the phone, a friend of mine named Mark who wants to say hi to you."

Not knowing who was at the end of the line, Filsaime played it safe. "Hey, Mark. How are you doing?"

It wasn't just Mark, it was *the* Mark—Mark Joyner. "Hey, Mike. I like what you are doing." It floored him to hear that from one of his Internet marketing heroes; Joyner called because he was Chen's silent partner, directing the marketing for Chen's project at the time. Joyner started describing something he called the "boutique" concept, which involved positioning yourself as different from everyone else. Joyner also told him, "You should do the one time offer for $197."

Filsaime was skeptical that it would work.

"What you need to do is you need to create something where people can email the people in *ListDotCom*— five thousand members—every two days. That would be huge. What you need to do is charge $79 a month for that," Joyner said. "By creating this service for $79 a month, you could give it to people for free when they buy *MakeYourOwnSoftware* but only on the one-time offer." Joyner was well versed in one-time offers. He had been doing upsells and cross-sells on the back end of his eBooks for years and knew how well they worked, in fact many credit him with being the first to give one-time offers on the web.

That completely changed Filsaime's thinking. Extending a one-time offer and adding a bonus to get people to join sent his conversion rate up to 7.8 percent when it launched in October 2004. In twenty-four hours it brought in $78,000 in sales of which $35,000 belonged to Filsaime.

Chen also benefited. Joyner had told him, "take my StartBlaze model and just change the medium." Joyner then took Chen's idea of putting ads on a browser tool-bar—the product that launched *Instant Buzz*—and devised a whole marketing system for Chen. Chen called it the "Elite Membership" for his site *Instant Buzz*, which he launched with Joyner's help. It did even better than Fil-saime's deal. Three months later, Chen sold his site to Fil-saime—he was just eighteen years old, and he wanted to go back to school. (He could afford it, and then some.)

When John Reese had launched *Traffic Secrets* (August 2004), he released a report that said "One man. One product. One day. One million dollars." Reese likened his million-dollar day to Roger Bannister breaking the four-minute mile for the first time, saying that although it had never been done before, it would happen again and again after that because he'd shown people they should set their goals higher: "What I encourage you to do right now is to envision your million-dollar day." It had to do with viral marketing—a lightening fast "word of mouth" marketing where a product is picked up all over the 'Net. Filsaime had read the report and immedi-ately registered the domain *Butterfly Marketing*, already planning his own million-dollar day. (Of course, there was a lot of planning involved: the site didn't go live until January 31, 2006—a year and a half later.) Sev-eral months after registering it, January 2005, he went to Stephen Pierce's *Unleash Your Marketing Genius* event. That year Filsaime cranked out an astounding number of new sites, although it wasn't until Rich Schefren came along that he stopped creating them haphazardly and created a "marketing funnel." Finally, it was a seminar by Mark Joyner that cinched the deal. Joyner's seminar was all about viral marketing where he basically taught the crowd his old "StartBlaze" model. Filsaime was no stranger to the model as he had modeled most of his earlier work on what he had learned from Joyners' *Farewell Package* and calls that surrounded it. But at this seminar Joyner revealed an even deeper understanding on how the model works. Filsaime took that model and said to his software engineer in Romania: "If we can make a script so people can make their own sites like we do and then just install it, people will be begging us, pounding on the doors to get access to it—once they see what it's done for us. We'll call it the *Butterfly Marketing* script."

On the first of October, they dropped everything and started designing *Butterfly Marketing*. He borrowed liberally from Joyner's work—even acknowledging that "most of these ideas are not mine—most of them I got from Mark Joyner," and it was a huge success. It went live three months later, a little buggy at first, but eventually running smoothly as they made changes and enhancements based on feedback. Internet Marketers could use it to create their own viral sites. The customer testimonials he received (not the usual "Gee, Mike. Why didn't I think of this? You've done it again" variety) suggested that he struck a nerve out there. They made such claims as "I've made $48,000 in twenty-one days and have a 21,000 member opt-in list."

Up-and-coming Internet Marketer Keith Wellman is the product of the Butterfly Effect. Wellman was deeply in debt, struggling to keep his marriage together under the stress of feeding his family with another child on the way, and trapped in a dead-end job in Oregon. He signed up for one of Filsaime's free teleseminars and when he got frustrated at not being able to afford the product, he wrote a flaming post in Filsaime's blog: "I'm sick and tired of you Internet Marketers telling us how to make money, but really the only way that you make money is by selling us products on how to make money. It's a vicious cycle..." The teleseminar call had, in fact, been about someone making hundreds of thousands of dollars in niche markets that had nothing to do with Internet Marketing. After Filsaime wrote about it in his newsletter, he received an email from Wellman: "You know, Mike, that was a slap in the face and a total reality check for me. I've got to tell you that I just wanted that course so bad, and I am struggling so much that I took it out on you and your members on the blog. That's not like me. That's not who I am. Something clicked in me, and I did something that I regret and I wish I could take it back. Please forgive me. I know you probably hate me, and you won't reply."

Filsaime emailed him back, giving Wellman his phone number, and moments later the telephone rang. The caller I.D. said K. Wellman. They talked, and Filsaime was shocked to find out that Wellman had been online longer than he and yet didn't even own the domain *KeithWellman.com*, and he had no opt-in list. Filsaime offered him a deal. "Here's what you need to do. You need to get out to this event. I'll pay for your hotel, and I'll pay your airfare, but you're going to pay me back. Without a doubt, you will pay me back. We're going to get you there."

Once they were there, Filsaime had Wellman create a product by interviewing another speaker. Wellman called it *ViralFX.com*, and it was just the first of many sites he went on to create. If he hadn't gotten so frustrated that he chewed out Filsaime on the blog that day, who knows where he might have turned up? But thanks to the Butterfly Effect, he started making twenty grand a month minimum, and when he bought a house in Atlanta and wanted to put in a new kitchen he didn't have to put it on a credit card, he just offered another promotion to his list. He's also paid Filsaime back, in full.

# Big Brother Meets Madison Avenue

One reason the Internet appeals to so many people is its promise of anonymity. Sometimes we find we can say things in blogs, personal ads, chat rooms, comments, surveys and such that we would have trouble admitting to or stuttering out in person or even on the phone. Sitting at a keyboard staring at a screen, we feel that if we aren't exactly invisible, we are at least largely hidden behind a backlit curtain, and at that most people might see our silhouette but none of the details.

Nothing could be further from the truth.

Big Brother is watching. And while that goes doubly when we're talking about the government, I'm speaking here of everyday civilians in the business world. Think for a moment about how ads evolved online. We started with mass mailings to email addresses that may or may not have been part of targeted lists. From there we added banner ads, tiny electronic billboards that we planted on the cyber real estate of our choice, hoping that interested parties might chance upon them and click through.

That led to the concept of ad targeting, a component of ad serving. Ad servers are the hardware and software that together determine which advertisement will be placed where, and when. As the technology became more sophisticated, ad servers evolved from being able to select from a specific queue of ads to dictating many of the different page components that appear on a page, from content to graphics to appearance; these components change according to information fed back to the server—information about you and your computer. The advantage to users and advertisers both is that ad servers can tabulate impressions, clicks, post–click activities, and interaction metrics; bar or at least isolate competitors' advertising; keep track of ads so that a given user sees them only a specified number of times; or dedicate whole pages to a single advertiser running multiples ad formats. The disadvantage to users and advertisers both is that this happens every time every user goes online now. The ads can be targeted more effectively than ever... because "they" know more about you.

Of course, it's not part of some evil conspiracy, it's just business as usual, doing what can be done to keep out of the red. The refinements are intended to make the marketing work so well that we welcome the ads as helpful hints and don't see them as intrusive or impolitely personal. But consider some of the targeting methods that let ad servers automatically (or nearly so) customize ad placement and even bid pricing. Contextual Targeting places ads according to relevance as determined by a page's content, and the more the server can infer, the more closely the ads should reflect your interests. Thus, if you're looking for vacation information, you might see ads for anything from plane fares to motion sickness to rental cars to beach resorts; if you're looking for ski vacations with children, you might still see plane fares, but you won't get beaches. Behavioral Targeting creates a profile of your prior behavior. If you're reading an eZine article on home buying, when you click to another section on vacations, you may get ads for vacation homes.

The next logical step is likely to be some sort of predictive targeting—a way of determining what you are most likely to do and want. Of course, the best predictor of future behavior is past behavior. It's the classic good news, bad news scenario. The good news? The chances of you seeing an ad you really want to click on at just the right time are much increased, and the chances of an ad you don't want to see much decreased. The bad news? Complete strangers record and analyze your every move—the subject and sequence of your clicks, the duration of your visits, the colors and shapes and sounds that attract or repel you, the kinds of content that inspire you to action. It's powerful stuff, and even though it's done with perfectly innocuous and even helpful intentions, it's vaguely creepy. It's not a backlit curtain of anonymity; it's a spotlighted recording.

The serious and successful Internet Marketing gurus understand this. They know that people do not want to feel as though someone is watching their every keystroke from over their shoulder. They also know that hucksters, scammers, get-rich-quick schemers, and other criminal elements have made many people leery and distrustful of others' intentions. Some of the gurus have addressed this directly—both Terry Dean and Declan Dunn have gone on record discussing the need for integrity in the Internet Marketing world, for example—but every one of us knows that it's crucial that we treat visitors and customers as people, not numbers or eyeballs or seats. We understand that markets are conversations, and that in those conversations anything less than honesty is not only just plain wrong, but it will hurt us in the end. The Internet is not a small town with limited resources. Just as people offline "vote with their feet," people online vote with their hands, clicking away at the slightest sign of disrespect.

# CHAPTER 5

## Share the Wealth:
### *You Click My Site, I'll Click Yours*

# Share The Wealth:
## YOU CLICK MY SITE, I'LL CLICK YOURS

ANYONE WHO HAS EVER HUNTED FOR AN APART-
MENT, a used car, or a limited-edition doohickey can
relate to this: words don't always tell the *whole* story.
One person's "great view" is another person's eyesore.

Pictures made the web much more appealing not only
to Internet Marketers but to the average computer user.
But that doesn't mean that suddenly the Web was awash
with color. It wasn't. It was all still brand new, exciting
and—to most people—something akin to magic. Anyone
who could do something special with pictures immediately attracted attention.

Several years after his success with the auto-responder creation, John Reese got interested in an upstart
auction site called Auctionweb. Unless you have been in
a coma for the past decade, you've heard of this company: its loyal users always thought of it even back then
as eBay, which later became its official name. Reese had
an old PC kicking around that he wanted to get rid of,
so he decided to try out the auction site everyone was
talking about. His ad joined a long list of other people's
old PCs, with nothing special to draw attention. Being a
self-professed nerd, he used FTP to post pictures of his
PC, and added a clickable link so that people interested
in buying it could be taken to a page where they could

actually see the computer first.  The response was incredible. Nobody really cared about the PC, though. What everyone wanted to know was how they could add pictures to *their* auction listings. We don't give that concept a thought now, but at the time people were dazzled. To most people it seemed exotic and out of reach although, as it turns out, it was quite simple. Reese's company was, among other things, a web hosting service. He had simply uploaded the images to a page on his own server. After answering the same questions for the Nth time, Reese had one of those four-in-the-morning brainstorms we get sometimes, and hired a programmer to design a simple web-based utility that people could use to upload their photos. The photos would reside on a page separate from the eBay site—on Reese's servers, in fact—but that fact would be transparent to both the potential bidders and the seller. Bidders would click on an icon on the item's page—"Click here to view this item"—and a page would load that displayed the photographs, just as if it were right there on the eBay site.

He gave the service away for free.

Though Reese is a nice enough guy, this was not pure altruism but a shrewd business move. Now that people were enamored of these new things called banner ads, Reese started placing his customers' ads on the photo pages. But what changed everything was when he added a banner for his own services that said "Do you want free image hosting for your auctions?" A viral marketing storm followed, and thousands of people began hitting on *MyItem.com*, Reese's eBay-related site. Within a few months it had gone from obscurity to being one of the top 500 sites worldwide in terms of traffic. And John Reese was finally debt free. For now, anyway.

# Traffic Jam

Traffic? Even the terminology of the Internet changed with the advent of a friendly Web browser, which became even friendlier when Marc Andreesen was booted off the Mosaic project and started his own company with Jim Clark; the lofty goal of the new browser, Netscape Navigator, was to allow users on any operating system to access and view Web pages in exactly the same way, to "level the playing field." From an Internet Marketer's standpoint this meant a broader, happier prospect base—pages would look identical regardless of platform, so designers could concentrate on content rather than coding. (Microsoft had a different perspective, but that's for another book.)

When online marketing was all about classifieds, having anyone see your ad was a coup; discussions of how to drive thousands, even millions to your little offer just didn't take place. The hyperlinks in the Web, however, allowed users to leap from place to place without cumbersome addresses and a lot of technical "handshaking": as long as a link was valid and the server where it resided was operational, users could follow it without requiring any action from the destination site. As the number of commercial sites ballooned, drawing customers in became less a matter of luck and timing and more of a science.

Reese's success had its roots in something the late Corey Rudl had possibly introduced and definitely perfected online: affiliate marketing. This technique existed in offline marketing in many forms, but it was a new concept to the Internet Marketing niche when Rudl started using it. Most of the gurus agree that while Amazon.com had started an affiliate marketing program before he did, and that several others in the field may have had basic affiliate programs in the works before he did, Rudl was the one who tweaked the standard concept of the joint venture and affiliate marketing for the industry. Many in the business who would otherwise have been struggling to keep their businesses out of the red have him to thank.

Rudl was a true pioneer in the sense that not only was he one of the first Internet Marketers on the scene but he also carved out a path for so many of those who followed. He couldn't take a course—there were none yet—so he taught himself HTML and managed to get a website up to sell his *Car Secrets Revealed* book (actually, in its original edition it was *Kit Car Secrets Revealed*; he was an avid kit-car builder, which is how his career got started in the first place). He sat at his computer and dreamed up all sorts of "wild and crazy marketing ideas," and although he maintained that 95 out of 100 of those ideas failed, the other 5 percent were obviously incredibly effective: within eighteen months his was the #1 best selling car book online. He credited his success to several things. First, he tested and retested every change he made; second, he became a master of opt-in email marketing; and third, he developed affiliate programs.

The key to affiliate programs is finding sites that have the same basic target audience as your site. A survey in May 2007 found more than 118 million websites out there today, with 12.8 million of those added just since the beginning of the year. If you look at those staggering numbers from the point of view of someone looking for sites that have something in common with your own, that's a bonanza. A quick Google search on "kit cars" or "custom cars" turns up roughly 600,000 sites. There ought to be thousands of potential affiliates in there somewhere, right? By the end of 1994, the year Rudl went online, there were 10,000 websites. Not car websites, total websites. And there was no Google. (That came along in 1998.) The big search engine at the time, which used a powerful set of Boolean modifiers but was still only a fraction as sophisticated as today's software, was Infoseek, founded in 1994. (Infoseek, like many of the other search engines of the day, has changed hands, names, styles and markets multiple times since then.) In other words, even searching through those 10,000 websites for potential affiliates wasn't an elegant process.

Rudl found them anyway. The quick rundown on affiliates, for the uninitiated, is this: you find websites that share the same potential customers and have those sites post a link on their site that will send anyone who clicks on the link to your site; a counter keeps track of how many people land at your site through each affiliate link; for every one of those referrals that leads to a sale, the other site (your "affiliate") gets a commission. Referrals that go nowhere earn them nothing. Obviously that means that other sites—maybe thousands of them—send customers to your site, and you don't pay a dime for it unless they buy something.

Rudl managed to get over a million visitors, and when people started to get a peek at the site counter he was deluged by requests for the secret to his success. How, everyone wondered, could a site with just one simple product be pulling in so much traffic? The answers became his first course, *The Insider Secrets to Marketing Your Business on the Internet*. To say that the course succeeded, too, would be an understatement. Rudl's company, The Internet Marketing Center—this is not a huge operation, by the way, but just a handful of talented folks—pulls in well over $6.5 million a year. Not bad for a kid who started out working from his parents' garage.

It's amazing when you start listening to stories like Rudl's, one after another—ordinary people with extraordinary energy carving out a trail for others to follow. The Internet has made all sorts of connections possible that would have been much less likely in the days before we had such easy, instant global communication. For instance, it's unlikely that a woman who had a comfortable twenty-year career as an air traffic controller would

**125**

have crossed paths with a young kit car buff—and had it change her life. But it happened.

Rosalind Gardner spent her days glued to a bank of radar scopes, fixing "the picture" in her head that helped her keep track of the dozens of props and jets that blinked at her during the busy shift, packing the airspace but keeping the craft safely separated. She made a good living—the base pay for air traffic controllers beats that of most other jobs with the same minimal education requirements—and handled the legendary stress with aplomb. One way she relaxed was through the Internet, where she exchanged banter—and seeds— with other avid gardeners around the world. She'd put up a three-page website, and spent her leisure time either actively gardening or, since she lived in the cold northern section of British Columbia, talking about and planning gardens. (As she describes it: "That is what you did. You sat inside and played online. That actually explains why there are so many successful Canadian Internet market- ers. We just spend more time inside getting pasty white and making money.")

In 1996, things changed at work. Her supervisor had to change the schedules radically, and Gardner ended up with crazy hours, sometimes working from six in the morning to one in the afternoon and then having to come back again at midnight. It played havoc with her health, and she knew she couldn't keep it up. Then one day while she was relaxing online, Gardner spotted a banner ad that said, "Webmasters make money," and she clicked through it. She landed on the one and only real dating network, which was looking for help to promote its site. Her first thought was, "This has got to work so much better than chat rooms—you have people's information right there." Her second thought was, "I can probably sell this." And she did. Within twenty-four hours Gardner had her own site online, *sage-hearts.com*, and made her very first sale, earning her a 50 percent commission. Once she listed her site with Yahoo! things took off. Gardner had become an affiliate marketer. Of course, she didn't quit her day job—yet.

She spent the month finding new ways to market her site, including trading links with others and getting herself listed in free directories. Before the end of 1998, *sage-hearts.com* brought in $5,000 a month. Still she kept her day job, religiously lugging her laptop to work and going online during her break periods. While she wrote reviews of new dating sites and kept up communications, her friends at work would come by and laugh, kidding her for working so hard on something they apparently thought of as a silly diversion or hobby. After all, Gardner was still living in a rented house and driving a ten-year-old pickup—and she was still working. By the time 2000 rolled around, though, she was earning $10,000 every month, so she quit her job. Some of the same people who'd laughed asked her how she'd done it and traded the control tower for the PC tower themselves.

It was at that time that Rosalind Gardner and Corey Rudl's paths crossed, though they were separated by an entire continent and several decades of experience. By then Rudl had another site, *secretstotheirsuccess.com*, spotlighting people who were earning up to a few hundred thousand dollars a year with online businesses by following Rudl's business model and affiliate marketing strategies. Gardner sent him a blurb about her own affiliate marketing success (she later bought his Internet Marketing package, her first business course ever), and wound up being interviewed for his monthly online magazine. That started an avalanche of emails in Gardner's inbox.

Affiliate marketers are often portrayed as a bunch of people who do nothing but lie around in beach chairs all day sipping Mai-Tais. As it happens, Gardner does enjoy vacations—so much that she jokes that lying in beach chairs could be her career, and making money on the Internet just a sideline. Since the last thing she wanted to do was answer hundreds of repetitive emails, she started a newsletter. After about six months she had enough material that she turned her knowledge into an eBook called *The Super Affiliate Handbook: How I Made $436,797 in One Year Selling Other People's Stuff Online*, which is what she had done in 2002. She sent a note to affiliate maven Allan Gardyne of *AssociatePrograms.com*, letting him know about this book that his readers—everybody on his list was interested in affiliate marketing—might find useful. The next thing she knew, the book shot to the top of the ClickBank marketplace and stayed there at Number One for the next two and half years. She never looked back.

## How Many Clicks from Here to Success?

The Army made Mark Joyner a millionaire. At least, that's where he learned more than just how to break down an M–16 blindfolded. He also learned the secret to Internet Marketing success: concentration. Not mental concentration—he'd always known how to do that. That explains how a high-school dropout graduated at the top of his class at the Defense Language Institute, learned to speak fluent Korean, and then earned a B.S. in psychology while simultaneously working as a military intelligence operative. (Joyner had a security clearance at the highest level possible in the U.S., Top Secret SCI, for several years.) No, it was in the Army that he encountered a book that he credits with teaching him about strategic concentration, which he sums up this way: "[not just] concentrating your strength on the enemy's weakness, but first tricking the enemy into thinking you're doing something else and then creating a weakness.... That concept of concentration is really, really powerful in marketing. If you can get a concentrated force of marketers to push something of yours on a particular day or a short period of time, you get a Gestalt effect or a buzz."

(Think: Jeff Walker, *Product Launch Formula*. If you don't know who he is yet, hold that thought.)

The book has nothing to do with marketing or the Internet. It's called *Strategy*, and was written by English biographer, military historian, and WWI veteran Sir Basil Henry Liddell Hart. Seeking to determine the reasons behind the high casualty rate during the war, Hart studied its battles as well as victorious battles fought long ago by Sun Tzu, Napoleon, and Belisarius. In the end he proposed that good strategy could be summed up in two words—indirect approach—with two fundamental principles: direct attacks against a strongly entrenched enemy almost always fail, and defeating the enemy requires misleading or confusing the enemy before the main attack. He further ventured the opinion that the indirect approach was generally a successful approach in other fields—including matters of the heart and, as Joyner believes, in business.

Joyner bought his first personal computer while he was in the Army. It was 1990, and he hadn't really touched one since the decade before when he had used his uncle's teletype connection to the ARPANET to play a text-only adventure game called Cave (originally "Colossal Cave Adventure," although it passed through many evolutionary phases). Running an early version of Microsoft Windows, Joyner learned his way around the computer and the Internet, checking out the bulletin boards and classifieds, and the pre-Web Internet. Once browsers hit the scene and he could access the Web, Joyner leaped in with characteristic determination; he started selling various products online on domains he didn't own. Joyner then registered his first domain, botree.com which later became HotrodYourHead.com, a self-improvement site that started getting all kinds of attention, including attention about the attention; the site kept winning traffic contests and was the most popular personal development site on the Web at the time.

How did he do it? Not by reading someone else's how-to book on driving traffic to your website. No, he did it mostly through tactics he figured out on his own: analyzing the algorithms used to rank pages by the main search engines of the day (Alta Vista, SearchHound, Excite, and Lycos), learning about Meta Tags. He wrote everything down and packed it up into what is sometimes considered the first eBook ever but is always credited as the one that made eBooks the hottest thing since removable storage—*Search Engine Tactics*. By 1998, his eBook had been downloaded over a million times. It was certainly not lost among thousands of other titles as it would be today since it was the only eBook on ZD-Net's download website for a long time, and may have been the only eBook to win a ZD-Net five-star rating for software (there was no eBook category).

He gave it away for free. Now one of the most tired approaches to sales letters these days is the "I can't believing I'm making this offer!" or the "So-and-so has lost his mind!" ploy. Make no mistake. You don't become a millionaire and retire before you've got a single gray hair without knowing *exactly* what you're doing. The only reason a good businessperson would give away a valuable product would be that doing so makes good business sense. In this case, it did: there was information within the eBook that was practically an advertisement for Joyner's paid products and services, and the more people who saw that information, the better off he would be. You can shrug and say, "Big deal? Who doesn't do that?" but at that time, *no one* was doing it.

Joyner was also "monetizing" his site (that's marketing-speak for figuring out how it can earn some money) with affiliate links. In this he was helped by his good friend and business partner Dr. Arapaut Sivaprasad—friends call him Siva—who started a company in 1995 called WebGenie. Although Siva's degrees are not in IT (he has several, including a B.S. in Agriculture, an M.S.

in Genetics, and a Ph.D. in Molecular biology), he started WebGenie to develop, among other things, the first off-the-shelf affiliate marketing software. WebGenie and Aesop (Joyner's company) formed a joint venture to develop SearchHound, the first-ever child-safe Internet search engine. Siva moved from his native town of Cochin (Kerala, India) to Adelaide, Australia, while working on his Master's; there he encountered Joyner, and they began their successful and lucrative partnership.

Over the years Aesop managed to introduce a number of what seem to be Internet Marketing firsts. For instance, Joyner developed a product called ROIbot. As the name suggests (ROI stands for "return on investment"—aka profit), the product tracked an ad's effectiveness. ROIbot was the first remotely hosted ad tracking service on the Internet. Although counting clicks was by then commonplace, complex tracking and analysis were not, nor did any other company handle the tracking from its third-party site. Aesop was apparently the first, too, to add tracking codes to affiliate URLs so they could track not just traffic but conversions. For Internet Marketers, that's what it's all about: not just having people walk into your "store" but getting them to buy something before they leave. Nowadays these kinds of tracking techniques are commonplace, too. And it's big business, since Internet Marketers today depend on knowing exactly which affiliate relationships, joint ventures, and other connections are the most cost-effective.

Joyner used the remotely hosted application model for several other innovations that may have existed in other online industries but were new to the Internet Marketing world, such as remote locking for software. Customers who purchased a product needed a code to launch the software; the host system verified whether or not the license was valid. That way, if a customer had gotten a refund, for example, the product software would no longer work. That system also worked with bundled services: Aesop started bundling third-party services with its own. The monthly fee for ROIbot, for example, gave customers access to other software as well—but only as long as they were active members. If they cancelled, the access to the client-side software went away, along with the ROIbot service. In other words, Internet Marketers now had ways to track not only the effectiveness of their ads, with ROIbot, but the remote locking service allowed them to cut down on pirating, the online version of shoplifting.

# All in the Family

While I'm talking about this "I'll scratch your back and you scratch mine" sort of marketing, I have a few points I'd like to make before we move on. They're not about tips or techniques but about the Internet Marketing *family*. It may sound corny and trite, but there is a real sense of family among many Internet Marketers. There are several generations—the pioneers, the settlers, the immigrants—and as with any family there are internal rivalries and petty squabbles. But in all, there is no other industry I can think of where the main participants share so much.

When I talk later about live events, you'll get a feel for what I mean. We aren't one big homogeneous group of best buds who hang together during everything we do. We're more like far-flung relatives from a close-knit family. Some of us know certain people really well; others know a different set of people really well, and some of us might know a lot of people not well at all. Some of us are friends and confidantes; others, just peers and acquaintances. But when we get together in one place you can't even begin to imagine the energy level of the room. It's like being at a combination family reunion and tent revival (and it almost could be, since more than a few of us are or have been pastors), and everyone comes away with a fervent mission.

Sometimes we Internet Marketers seem to spend a lot of our time talking about how great everyone else is. Certainly in other industries, you don't find many top executives sharing the secrets of their success with other execs in the business. Sure, they'll get a four-some together and play a few holes, then brag about their latest deal. But to really talk about how they did it and what exactly they did to improve their product? In this industry, it happens all the time; you find that the big guys are eager to share. We help each other; we learn from each other. We give away big secrets for free (especially when we're on to something new, but that's beside the point). Sometimes we sell to each other, or cross-promote somebody else's product, but only when it's something we believe in. We aren't afraid of the other gurus stealing our best work. That's for amateurs.

That's another point I'd like to bring up. Many people say that the Internet Marketing industry is completely self-invented, self-generated, and self-sustaining. That is, some cynics like to say that the only reason we make money is that we buy each other's products. Leaving aside the fact that doing that would have eventually put us all in the poorhouse, not the clubhouse, the logic doesn't hold up. It's true that the big buzz always seems to be about the marketers selling and teaching amongst themselves—but that's because the people we coach and speak to and share with get our help because they want to run their businesses better and are out there doing just that. These people are Internet Marketers and some are even Information Marketers as I outlined earlier in the book. As I said in that side-bar, this book is primar-ily about Information Marketing, and while Information Marketing is huge, the niche devoted to improving the marketing part of the industry, the part that we're talk-ing about in this book, is just a small part. We aren't talking about the millions of people who have worked through our courses, listened to our teleseminars, or hired us as consultants and then gone on to turn their specific passion into successful online businesses—the grandpas and single moms and college kids selling everything from antiques to zipper pulls. If you surf the 'net, you'll find them, but they're not in this book because they are out there living out their dreams. They're busy practicing what we preach.

## Thank You, Mary Alice

When you're six years old with two little brothers being raised on a tobacco farm mostly by your 65-year-old grandma, you learn early on the meaning of collaboration—or else you have a real tough time. Willie Crawford learned it well. His parents had separated around 1962. Crawford's two older brothers went to stay with his father, a career Army man posted mostly overseas. His mother moved North to find a job that paid better than what she could find in Fairmont, North Carolina. Crawford's grandma, Mary Alice Jones, stayed behind to look after the three youngest boys, teaching them not just how to work together but also how to be independent, patiently instructing them in how to sew, do laundry, iron clothes, and cook. *Especially* cook.

At first, Crawford says, it was mostly simple things like grits, eggs, and toast, but he soon moved up to scratch cakes, hush puppies, and his personal favorite, chitterlings. He had a lot to work with from their own garden, a veritable rainbow of fresh fruits and vegetables from tomatoes, strawberries, squash, butter beans and cabbage to potatoes, collards, turnips, okra, peas, and string beans. They had hogs, rabbits, and a few chickens, and a basic pantry of government surplus staples like dried beans, powdered eggs, powdered milk, huge blocks of cheese, milk, cereal, and other goodies. He says he still likes the taste of powdered eggs.

Crawford graduated high school in 1977 and went off to college. When he finished his degree in economics and business, he dreamed of owning his own business someday. The trouble was, he had no idea what kind of business, and he decided that rather than getting lost in some dead-end corporate job while he figured it out, he'd join the Air Force. There he flew C-130 cargo planes, touching down in 47 different countries in both combat and peacetime deployments. Though he'd never intended to make a career of it, in 1996 he looked around and realized that he was still there—and decided it was time to move on. But first he needed to find a business he could start while he still had the safety net of being an Air Force officer.

At that time Crawford was posted to Hawaii, where he spent a lot of time on the computer surrounded by a network of Macintoshes connected to the Internet. Surfing around, he found many of the same affiliate programs that exist today, although in their embryonic forms, and decided that what he needed was a website of his own. Everywhere it seemed were sites with flashy banner ads exhorting him to get rich selling dating services, telephone services, just about everything possible. What caught his interest were the Internet Marketers with newsletters that talked about how he might earn money online— some of the ones he recalls were those from Jim Daniels (whose writing style Crawford admired and tried to emulate), Marty Foley, and Paul Myers. He subscribed, and read everything he could. Like most Internet Marketers, he started out dabbling here and there, selling to and for other Internet Marketers and selling how-to-make-money information. Then he then put up a site on Free Yellow that talked about the money making opportunities he had found and tested for himself. He steered people there with the search engines of the day: Alta Vista, Lycos, Excite, InfoSeek. It was easy to get listed back then, although the flip side was that there were far fewer people online interested in what you had to sell or say.

He managed to sell some products. Though he had a staff job, he was also on flight status and could choose the flights he wanted to fly. Often he'd print out the Internet Marketing newsletters and read every word as he flew across the Pacific, encountering variations on the same information that holds true today: register a domain, find a niche, build a list, work with affiliates.

Crawford developed a keen eye for telling the good guys from the frauds. He calls them the "naked men," after something he read in Harvey MacKay's *Beware the Naked Man Who Offers You His Shirt*. It was obvious to Crawford that a lot of the marketers online who promised him success and wealth hadn't become successful or wealthy themselves, mainly because they were either passing on bad advice or failing to follow any good advice they might be promoting. Sure, a lot of people were doing okay online, but many more were crashing and burning—buying shirts from naked men.

In 1997 Crawford joined a discussion group, Links Exchange Digest, and quickly learned his first valuable Internet Marketing lesson: if you run your business from a free host account you will have zero credibility since people assume you don't have enough confidence in yourself and your product to buy your own domain name. He registered *WillieCrawford.com*. Then he asked himself how a beginner with no major online marketing success could possibly establish himself as an expert, and realized that there were two fairly simple answers: one, partner up with or learn from someone who does have the knowledge and skills, or two, create a product in an area in which he was already an expert—something he knew inside and out.

Willie Crawford knew cooking.

Oddly, the General that he worked for spent a lot of time on the Internet searching for recipes, so Crawford knew there must be a market for what he knew. He decided to put up a website with some of the rustic recipes he grew up with in the country, figuring that he could lure people to the site that way and, while they were recipe-hunting, hit them with a banner ad or two trying to sell them some of his "how to make money online" knowledge. *Chitterlings.com* was an instant success...sort of. Many people did visit the site, and they even joined his mailing list starting from the very first day it was offered. But nobody cared about the money-making offers; they just wanted the recipes. Soon they were sending in recipes of their own, and Crawford had a steady stream of new material, enough to send out a regular newsletter. It was as easy as breathing for him.

Then his subscribers started pestering him for a cookbook. He promised to write one if enough people said they would order one. And sure enough he soon found himself typing away. He started out selling it as an eBook, but found that readers really wanted a physical book and were taking the file to a copy shop to have the book printed out and bound, so he started offering both options. These days *Soul Food Recipes—Learned on a North Carolina Tobacco Farm* is doing six figures, and Crawford figures it would do even more if he'd had a title that suggested it was the authoritative text. (You know, like *Soul Food Secrets Revealed!*)

What he learned while selling his cookbook online did finally make him an expert in Internet Marketing. While he was busy selling recipes, he was also building his *www. WillieCrawford.com* site which sold not recipes but "how to make money" products. He brought in traffic to those sites with an early version of Adwords and other pay per click programs. This is where advertisers can enter keywords of interest, and Adwords or the other pay-per-click program offers to place ads on what they claim are relevant sites within their content network.

Because Crawford became so successful at the pay per click game, he started doing speaking gigs at various seminars. He even hosted a few of his own and met a lot of

the other big names and up-and-comers: Ramon Williamson, Paul Myers, Marlon Sanders, Terry Dean, Jeff Walker,
Armand Morin, Marty Foley. It was his connection with
Foley that led Crawford to the place where he picked up
his current title. He's not "guru" he's "King."

Foley and Crawford did a teleseminar on using pay-
per-click search engines, and right after that Crawford
went to Joel Christopher's Master List Builder Workshop
in San Antonio. There, Marlon Sanders took the stage.
Though Sanders is a fellow Southerner, the two had never
met. Yet when Sanders started talking about ways to generate traffic and make sales and the subject turned to pay-
per-click, Sanders moseyed to the edge of the stage. He
pointed directly at Crawford then asked him how much
he earned for each dollar he spent on pay-per-click. Crawford answered with his then-current numbers: "Oh, about
seven." Sanders responded as only Sanders could. "Wow.
Didja hyear how eeeeasy that is? This hyear is Willie
Crawford, folks, the King of Pay-Per-Click."

It was a shiny crown to wear, but "King" Crawford
knew about a lot more than just pay-per-click. He was
an excellent teacher, a natural speaker, and an invaluable mentor (maybe invaluable isn't quite the right
word, as lately he's mentioned that his price for mentor-
ship is going up...). Crawford has cited another defining moment that came as he was talking shop with
John Reese and Ramon Williamson. Reese said, "When
you're having trouble just making the rent payment, it's
really hard to imagine making an extra $50,000 or extra
$100,000 a year. But once you make that hundred, it's
easy to imagine another 200 or 500. And if you can do
that, then you can do a million."

Crawford's thinking shifted. He recalibrated his goals
to include seven figures, possibly even eight long-term.
He didn't grow up around people who made that kind
of money; the people he knew worked on the farm until
they were old enough to drop out of high school, then

they went and got factory jobs. Mostly the boys bought cars, and the girls got pregnant and started families. Nobody made six figures, let alone seven or eight. Most made five. Crawford had endured counselors at college telling him, in essence, "We don't think you'll make it through, because you don't have the right background." He wanted to prove them wrong, and while he'd known that there were many people who were much better trained and better prepared than he, and probably some who were more intelligent too, he also knew that they hadn't survived a lot of things he'd survived. He's joked that it's possible he was just too stupid to give up, but I know better. I think it was the "bumblebee syndrome." You know, aerodynamics ought to make the bumblebee physically incapable of flying; it's just too heavy. But the bumblebee doesn't know that, so it flies just the same— and carries its own weight.

# AdWord-tising

In 2000, Google launched the much-anticipated AdWords (still its main source of revenue), a pay-per-click advertising product that showcases text and banner ads on its search pages according to their relevance to the sponsors' ads. Advertisers decide which keywords they want to use to call up their ads, and bid for them, setting the maximum amount they are willing to pay Google every time a user clicks on the ad. These are the "sponsored links" you see running down the right margin of the screen when you do a Google search. Where your ad appears in the stack is not simply a function of the bid amounts but also a quality score relative to other sponsors. This score comes from an evaluation of the historical click-through rates, the keywords themselves, the relevance of the ad, the landing page for the ad, and some top-secret algorithms, parameters, and mystical incantations that Google must update on a regular basis to keep Black Hat SEO hackers from cheating others out of their rightful rank.

In 2003, Google added site-specific advertising in AdWords. Now sponsors could place cost-per-impression bids to have their ads pop up on particular sites (or groups of sites). These bids are priced as "cost per mille" (CPM), which is the cost of one thousand "impressions"; the number of impressions is the number of times an ad is placed on a search page, a web page, or on a product page in the Google Network. Confused? Here: 1 CPM = 1000 impressions, so if the CPM is $5, the CPI (cost per impression) is a thousand times less, or $0.005.

If you are new to Internet Marketing in general, or know nothing about cost-per-click, all that might have made your head spin. Fortunately for guru Perry Marshall, that's a common response. See, while some people call me Dr. AdSense , Marshall is Professor AdWords.
But let me back up a bit. For Perry Marshall, the first step toward becoming a rich and famous Internet Marketer was getting laid off.

The year was 1995, and Marshall had switched from engineering to sales not long before his employer decided to downsize. Anyone who's been out of a job without much warning knows that there follows a period of anywhere from days or weeks to months (years?) of searching for The Next Big Move. So Marshall was hitting the streets, so to speak, heading off to interviews and such. That's when the connection between "marketing" and "Internet" first hit him in the form of a towering billboard for Southwest Airlines. There, in foot-high letters, was a Web address, the first one he'd ever seen on an ad, let alone on a billboard.

It wasn't a life-changing event, just the first line between two dots, something he filed away without much thought beyond, "Hmm, the Internet's going mainstream. Interesting. Now, where the heck is 423 Hatchootucknee Boulevard?" Then within a week of that, Marshall had lunch with a buddy who lived down the street, and the guy signed him up for a bulletin board service—$15 for six months, what the heck—and he got his first email account. Of course, Marshall only knew about five other people with email addresses, but he figured that might change. A few more points got connected, but it was far from being a complete picture.

In 1997, Marshall moved from the job he had finally found in '95 into a sales job with a company selling similar technology to a similar market, but nationally rather than locally. At the first company, the routine had been to go get the manufacturer's directory and page through it, or sift through boxes of old leads from trade shows, and then hit the phones trying to score an appointment with someone who wanted to see inside the magic suitcase full of samples. Being a manufacturer's representative turned out to be a very painful job. After two years of chasing down leads, Marshall had had enough. It seemed every deal he set up slipped away or fell apart. He was not making a lot of money, and he was not very happy.

When the national company offered him a position, there was a lot to like. Okay, they had no money for travel and airplanes. No money for endless phone calls. No money for pounding pavement. What they did have was a website, and it was getting some modest traffic. A few more lines connected a few more dots, and Marshall started to see that the old picture of business had begun to change. In the old picture, the sales force went out looking for customers who would buy their product. In the new picture, the customers went looking for companies with products they wanted to buy. The customers came to *you*. Actually, Marshall was helped in this realization by reading books by the man who *coined* the term "direct marketing." Now one of the oldest living pioneers in that field, Lester Wunderman conceived American Express, the Doubleday Book Club, and Columbia Records, to name a few. He's in the Advertising Hall of Fame, was named one of "Top Twenty Advertising Legends and Leaders" by *Adweek* magazine, and in 1999 was one of the "Top 100

People in Advertising" according to *Advertising Age*. Marshall calls him brilliant.

According to Marshall (and Wunderman), if you have to climb over barbed wire fences and break through the back window to get into a company just to talk to somebody, they *might* still talk to you, but they aren't really going to consider you to be some kind of genius expert who probably holds the solution to the big problem they've got. More likely, they'll think of you as a pest. Online, Marshall didn't have to scale other people's fences, he only had to open up his own gates. Engineers looking for specialized information found the company's website and filled out a little form and the information then went to Marshall. So when he called, he knew the people he spoke with wanted to talk to him because they had invited him.

For the first six months it felt like therapy, not having to wear down someone's resistance, just being able to be a helpful resource to people and having customers buy from him because he gave them all the information they could need. Marshall got the biggest sales commission check that he'd ever gotten (although at the time, he admits, that wasn't saying much), and it sold him on Internet Marketing.

Along with Wunderman, Marshall was reading the work of other direct marketing gurus, such as Dan Kennedy's newsletter, since he saw from the start that the Internet was a direct marketing medium. It may have been a new medium, but nevertheless it had a lot in common with direct mail despite being made up of ones and zeroes and electrons instead of ink on paper. The same principles and metrics applied even though the specifics were a little different: cost per lead, cost per conversion, response rate, average order size, ROI, and lifetime value.

Marshall started actively applying an information marketing model to his sales process, creating white papers, troubleshooting guides, reports, newsletters and magazine articles, and offering the information free in exchange for people's contact information. He became a lead generation machine, and the reps and distributors were beside themselves. The company was usually one of the smallest companies represented, yet it kept out-generating sales leads compared with the big product lines. Reps would call Marshall, puzzled but nevertheless delighted: "I get more sales leads from you guys than from anybody else, and they're all good. When I get a lead from you, I know that company has a project, that they plan to spend some money, and even what that project is sometimes. I love your leads. Keep 'em coming."

Marshall finally connected all the dots: the ones who control the leads and traffic run the show.

Marshall's group starting experimenting with "positioning," beginning by creating a class called "Device Net Boot Camp" (after the name of their product) where they explained the technology while customers downed free coffee and bagels—a "lunch and learn" session. The customers sat there with their arms folded, listening but with no real interest in or intention of buying. At the end, they'd thank Marshall and his crew for the free food and information and leave. Marshall had an inspiration. He and the group created a three-day class with real equipment right there, and charged customers $1,500 to attend. They made up a direct-mail piece, sent out emails, and the classes sold out. The industry hadn't respected "free," but the minute people had to pay to learn something they assumed it was first rate. The company had successfully positioned itself as the expert: the company that offered training that explained the whole industry. *Information* marketing.

A large trade organization added its private label to the class which opened it up on a grander scale, 300 customers per class, and Marshall's company got a huge P.R. boost from the deal. Their competitors were furious since they felt *they* were the experts, not Marshall's company and the industry had apparently forgotten that. Marshall's company was making the big waves and had all the credibility and the others had to settle for being swept along in its wake. The timing was perfect. A company working on a similar technology bought Marshall's employer out for $18 million, and Marshall escaped with a check five weeks after 9/11.

That check became his stake for a consulting business. Since his positioning had made him well known in the field, Marshall got job offers from all around, but he turned them into consulting contracts, unwilling to be fettered once more by a corporate tether. He wanted to sell information products, so he developed a course on lead generation, called it *Guerilla Marketing for High-Tech Sales People*, and put it up on *PerryMarshall.com*. It was free, but it promoted a full-length $1,000 course, and helped Marshall build his list.

In April 2002, Marshall talked to Ken McCarthy, mentioning a new thing called pay-per-click and an advertising system called Overture. McCarthy had invited Overture guru, John Kiel, to speak at his upcoming "System Seminar" and recommended that Marshall come and see what it was all about. Kiel expounded on Overture and pay-per-click, and also mentioned that Google had just come out with a product that seemed similar but that he didn't fully understand yet. Kiel's impression was that it seemed expensive and complicated.

Marshall considered his options. He was a consultant with a few clients; he needed to keep them coming to him, and he needed to sell product. He said to himself, "I don't use Yahoo! I don't use MSN. I use Google." He decided to learn their new system, AdWords. By the end of the week, he was hooked. With AdWords, he could change ads and the next day see the click-through rate change or see how people had responded. He could test keywords, rearrange them, add new ones—evaluate all sorts of things. Marshall learned Adwords inside and out. He quintupled the number of leads he was getting daily, and started offering the service to his clients, but he was hesitant to tell anyone too much about it. Most of his competitors were using Overture, doing SEO, and found AdWords mysterious.

Months later, McCarthy mentioned that he needed someone to speak about Google AdWords. Marshall suggested Andrew Goodman, the better known AdWords expert, but Goodman had already declined. McCarthy convinced Marshall to speak. Certain that his "15 minutes of fame" would be just that—intense but brief—he planned to make sure he had as much product as he could to sell at the seminar, so he got all his tapes and books ready for orders. He was thinking he could create interest for three, maybe four months, then everything would go back to normal. But he underestimated the need. People were stumbling into the AdWords program and starting out before they understood how it really worked. When tossing $5 here and $10 there didn't work, they fed in more money, like a slot machine, and people were maxing out their credit cards and going broke trying to figure out something that had taken him no time at all.

Marshall, however, was still convinced that his guru status would be short lived. He had better "make hay while the sun shines." Shortly after the seminar, he had listened to *Unlimited Traffic Technique*, in which Jonathan Mizel said that anyone who can convert visitors to dollars better than everyone else in the market would dominate that market. Marshall knew that while AdWords would get him a lot of clicks, it ultimately wasn't enough to be good at getting clicks, he had to convert those clicks to sales.

Then, about six months after Marshall read Mizel's book, Mizel called him up. They'd run into each other at several seminars—Marshall was being asked to speak about AdWords more and more—and Mizel wanted to hire Marshall to consult on a project. When Mizel then suggested that they do an AdWords teleseminar together, Marshall agreed, even though he was a little concerned that it might affect his eBook sales—again, still thinking he should have a plan for when he dropped back into obscurity at any moment. They did the seminar, a live call for $60, sold the reprint rights to affiliates, and moved on to the next project. Or they meant to move on. What they found was that the teleseminar was hot. People were buying it up and MP3s were crisscrossing the country, going overseas, and finally the dots were all connected. Marshall was an Internet Marketing guru. His fifteen minutes of fame has lasted years.

# AdSense and Sensibility

I didn't write this book to toot my own horn. Compared with the rest of the Internet Marketing "band," I'm just one piece in the ensemble. I do, however, want to toot the horn of Google AdSense, an ad serving program you can join to have text, images and, video advertisements placed on your site. It basically lets you sell advertising space for other people's ads on your website. It's also really user friendly because you don't have to pick the ads, Adsense does it for you, based on what Google sees on that page.  And Google is very good at choosing ads that are relevant to your site's content pages.  It also is nice for everyone involved because its contextual and geographically relevant ads are less intrusive than most other types of ads.

I discovered AdSense in June 2003. At first I made so little money off it that I barely paid attention to its capabilities. But as I started to hear from others what it was doing for them I began playing around with it in earnest, trying different combinations of code placements, ad colors, and ad blocks. Now, I've had a bit of success online already, so I am not easily impressed, but what I learned astounded me. By adding AdSense to more of my pages, I went from making $30 a day to over $500 a day in just three months. When I shared a few hints with some of my Internet Marketing friends, their successes convinced me that I should learn even more, then compile what I knew into a product. I started with an eBook that soon evolved into *The AdSense Code: What Google Never Told You About Making Money with AdSense*, a print book that actually hit the *New York Times Paperback* Business Best Sellers list. I still get email every day from people who have followed my suggestions and watched their income skyrocket.

AdSense uses a Javascript program to format ads of a given style, color, size, shape and placement from banners and skyscrapers to rectangles and leaderboards. When visitors to your site click on one of those ads to buy something, you get paid: it's that simple. Of course, what's not so simple is encouraging the maximum number of people to click on those ads (otherwise, why would you need a book like mine?) without violating Google's rules for how you can do this. (You can't, for example, have a blinking arrow that exhorts visitors to Click Here! and most of the restrictions are far more subtle than that.) What draws visitors to the site is your content, and what dictates which ads appear is an ad's relevance to that content.

What Google doesn't allow, though, are sites that put advertising before content, either by using design or search-engine optimization techniques created specifically with AdSense (and not the visitors' best interests) in mind, or by buying cheap traffic (low price clicks, literally, a penny or two a click) from one place and then selling it to AdWords advertisers through their AdSense units. It is called "arbitrage," and it is when you buy traffic to your site with low-price clicks—cheap—and then put articles on your site that lead to high paying clicks. These kinds of sites have been warned that their "unsuitable business models" will get them banned from any future AdSense business—and rightly so. Those sites are those frustrating, time wasting pages filled with nothing but links (often broken or otherwise useless) and no useful content. AdSense is not a get-rich-quick scheme but a serious tool— an opportunity to monetize something you feel passionate enough about that you would probably do it anyway. If you don't have the time or talent to produce engaging, useful content, find someone you can pay to do it for you, or risk losing your account. And if that seems like too much work for you, you are in the wrong business in the first place and need to move on.

# CHAPTER 6

Stagecoach:
*"Showing Off," from Seminars to Workshops*

# Stage Coach:
## "SHOWING OFF," FROM SEMINARS TO WORKSHOPS

IT SOUNDS LIKE A MOVIE SCRIPT: "Handsome young half-Filipino vacuum cleaner salesman so shy that he walks six miles in the September heat to buy a bookstore's last copy of Napoleon Hill's *Think and Grow Rich*, becomes a millionaire and runs a wildly successful series of seminars, then fulfills his lifelong dream of becoming a Country-Western singer."

*Yeah, right. Sorry. Sounds pretty far-fetched.*

As they say, sometimes the truth is stranger than fiction. Armand Morin's first sales had nothing to do with the Internet. In fact, they started out like this: "Hi, my name is Armand. I'm in the area. I'm showing a few things, and I have a gift for you, just for taking a look. Which one would you like?" No chance for a No. He'd hold up a can of cleanser in one hand, a roll of paper towels in the other—his first "opt-in" offer. Once they accepted their gift, Morin would wrestle a huge box up to the front door and step inside. For five and a half years he sold vacuum cleaners door to door even though talking to strangers was so painful he'd often cross a street just to avoid bumping into someone coming toward him on the sidewalk. He'd dropped out of college after a single year, thinking he'd make a little money and then go back, but when he was already making $40,000 in a

**153**

single summer, he couldn't get excited about the idea of three more years of school.

Besides, his sales job was teaching him quite a bit. In addition to getting used to speaking with strangers, Morin learned valuable lessons that he would later apply to his online career, such as target marketing: when he and his crew would choose a neighborhood, Morin preferred trailer parks since their density let him essentially cherry-pick the houses he wanted to call on. His reasoning was that people who owned a trailer would have financing, and if they had a nice car in the driveway they probably had decent credit. Those things were important when you were selling a $1,395 vacuum cleaner. Most of the time his reasoning proved correct.

He also learned that you get the best response when you treat whoever answers the door not as a prospect or customer but as a person—another human being with the same basic needs, dreams, issues and fears. He learned that from his boss, Lenny. Morin has called Lenny the greatest salesman he's ever met, bar none. It took Lenny about three minutes to sell the pathologically shy Morin on the idea of selling vacuum cleaners door to door. Lenny had style. Lenny could inspire people to do, and to want to do, things they had previously had no desire to do—and to walk away thinking it had been their idea in the first place. Lenny believed that selling was a system, and he instilled that belief in Morin, a belief that works well in Internet Marketing.

Morin sold many, many vacuum cleaners. But in 1995, after years of traveling all over New York State, knocking on doors from nine in the morning until midnight, he wanted more. He was twenty-five years old and just didn't want to do it anymore. He started to pour over the classifieds but quickly decided that if he wanted a better job, he needed to look in better places. He set aside the local paper and picked up a copy of the *Wall Street Journal*. The ad he had answered for the vacuum cleaner job several years prior had gone something like this: "Wanted—Ambitious people looking to make an unlimited amount of money. No experience necessary." At the time, he thought, "perfect." This time around Morin spotted something similar but with slightly more stringent requirements: "Wanted—Telecommunications sales reps. Must have door-to-door sales experience." Again, perfect.

Morin called the company. The entire conversation lasted about three minutes. They said, "This is what we do. We sell long distance service door-to-door." Morin asked what, like AT&T? MCI?" Exactly like that. They asked what kind of experience he had, and Morin answered, "Well, I've sold vacuum cleaners door-to-door for five and a half years, but..." and that's all it took. He was hired. The company FAXed a Letter of Authorization (LOA) to him at the local print shop, where Morin was inspired to do two things. One, he had 200 copies of the LOA printed up. And two, he bought a clipboard. Already he'd learned the marketing value of presentation. The clipboard changed people's perceptions of him, subconsciously "promoting" Morin to someone professional, someone with authority. He'd learned that concept from Robert Cialdini's *Influence: The Psychology of Persuasion*, which he'd read on his own years before.

There was no training, no script, no experienced advice. Morin needed something to work with, so in a burst of inspiration he opened up his phone book. Inside he found a page that "saved his butt." It contained a table of all the carriers' rates, which they were required by law to disclose. This he inserted into his clipboard.

At the first house he tried one approach, and got a No. At the next house, he tried something different, and got another No. At each house he tried a subtle variation on his pitch, and every time he heard No. Finally he had an inspiration. At the next house he started out something like this: "Hi, my name is Armand. I'm in the area. I'm asking a few questions about your phone bill. Do you use AT&T, MCI or Sprint?" When the woman answered AT&T, he said, "Great," and showed her the yellow paper in his clipboard. "This is what you are paying right now. This is what you could be paying. You'd be saving X number of dollars in a year. That's 3X in three years— several hundred dollars, and all you have to do is sign up." As he said this, he would flip to the order form under the yellow sheet and, pen poised, ask, "Now, how do you spell your last name?"

She said yes. The next five people said yes, too, so he quit for the day. It was a small town; he didn't want to burn through it too fast.

It didn't take Morin long to have another inspiration. "If I can do this, I wonder if I could get other people to do this, too?" He called up the company and asked if he was allowed to hire other people to help. When he explained that he would pay them half of whatever he made, they said sure. He had started his own first affiliate program without even knowing it.

He hired ten people *and* wrote out a script for them to follow. When a few tried to deviate from the script, he'd go out on a call with him or her and follow the script word for word; inevitably his way was more effective. Soon he had twenty reps, then forty, then fifty. He was earning even more money than he had selling vacuums. Then he had a wild thought. Since he'd learned that long distance services paid a monthly residual for every phone bill he signed up, he decided that the real money would lie in owning the long distance company. He may have had no technical ability, but he was a master at selling long distance service door-to-door.

Despite his successes, though, he was broke. He had a two-year-old son, and he and the boy's mother were struggling to get by. Morin had spent the past 5 months working out a plan for a new business, but his wife was fed up. One night she said, "You know, you're putting all this time and effort into this, and you're just playing businessman. You'll never make anything out of yourself. You'll never succeed. You're going to be stuck in the exact same lifestyle you've always had. What makes you think that you could succeed at any of this?" When she finished her tirade, she packed up and walked out the door.

Morin was at the lowest point in his life. The woman he loved had just taken his son and left him. He had spent a lot of time working out a plan for his new company but didn't have a thing to show for it. He felt he had no choice. He didn't want to keep selling phone services for someone else, and he had no other fallback plan. Determined to make it work, he found two partners.

Two weeks after his family walked out, Morin started Global Telecom. He had just $1.73 in his pocket and a vision in his head. *Literally*. He'd read that successful people often used visualization, so he'd been passionately visualizing everything right down to the smell and feel of the stacks of phone bills with his company logo.

It worked. Seven days after he launched the company, he had over $100,000 in the bank and a smile on his face.

He still wasn't on the Internet. He was, however, on the computer. His high school exposure to programming hardly made him an expert, but of the three partners he was the most technically savvy so he had been elected to turn the blinking, humming eMachine in their new Biloxi office into the heart of their business. After all, their "phone company" wasn't built of wires and switchboxes but of contracts and shared networks. Keeping track of the "paperwork" was crucial, so Morin slogged through the manuals and learned the basics. He also started plotting his exit strategy, as it was clear that the long-distance battle would be a fight waged with technology, and Global Telecom had nothing along those lines. It did have clients, though, and in its ten months of operation the company brought in $1.8 million, so in exchange for a hefty lump of stock (all but worthless) and a small amount of cash, the partners sold out to American Nortel and closed the doors.

Morin's actual share for all his work left him with only about $40,000, but he had almost no expenses. He was single, living in a company-owned condo, and spent all his time working. His biggest outlay was a trip for his mother to return to the Philippines to arrange, pay for, and attend her mother's funeral services. Once the company was sold, Morin lost his swanky digs on the Gulf of Mexico, but he did get to keep one perk: the computer. He was 26. Once again he was without much in the way of financial resources, but he did have a connection to the Internet. He poked around, trying out the search engines—Is Elvis alive? Do UFOs exist?—and stumbled across a website that changed the course of his life. It said, essentially, "For $25 you can put your link on our website. Since we advertise a lot, many people will click there and go to your website."

Morin didn't pay the $25. He used a web page creator in AOL to build his own site, and at the very top of the site he typed these words: "For $25 you can put your link on my website. Since I plan to advertise a lot, many people will click there and go to your website." One of the specialized software packages he'd inherited from Global Telecom was a package that let him accept checks over the phone and print them out; they were legal tender he could take to the bank and they allowed him to get paid right away. Morin put up ads everywhere he could, including the classifieds on AOL, CompuServe, and other ISP sites, as well as on newsgroups and bulletin boards. By the end of the first week (that is, one month after he first figured out how to get onto the Internet—his first exposure) he'd made $8,000, without once having to go door to door.

Amazed at all the free stuff he found online—not physical goods but online services such as free email accounts, online diaries, website hosting—Morin started a list of bookmarks to the free offers. When it grew to five or six hundred entries, it struck him that people might be willing to pay him for having collected them all into a single resource. He found software that let him password-protect the file and he created just that, a list of freebie stuff amassed into one file. The software happened to also include an affiliate program setup, so he started selling his list of freebies. After just a few weeks his web hosting service begged him to drop them and go to their massive hosting service because his little business was getting so much traffic that their servers kept crashing. He had the right product at the right time, and the help of 25–30,000 affiliates. After three months he had $4 million and an addiction to the Internet so strong that the only way he would ever be able to feed it would be to make it his life's work. He did. Armand Morin is the man behind the "Big-Seminar," one of the best and definitely the classiest Internet Marketing seminar around. Through it and related products, he has taught thousands of people how to tap into the huge marketing potential of the Internet. The only time he knocks on anyone's door these days is if he's paying a social call.

## First, Foremost and Famousest

We all know that it's not about whether you win or lose but how you play the game—at least, most of us know that—but it's still fun to be first. You'll notice that throughout this book, I have faithfully passed on certain assertions that so-and-so was the first to do x, y, and z, even though in other sources, someone else might be laying claim to the very same thing. Now, we could all wrestle over who's right, but the fact is that we probably all are—we're all just using different criteria and definitions. Ultimately, as far as I'm concerned, it doesn't really matter who did what when; it just matters that it got done. That may be the coward's way out (I do not want to get between two of my pals while they duke it out over dates and data), but that's my story and I'm sticking to it.

Most of the Internet Marketing pioneers started out by taking their offline passions online—the stock market, real estate, magic, cars—but eventually most them found a second outlet: teaching others what they'd learned. The bulk of their product offerings were how-to courses on the various specialties within the fledgling industry, such as ad tracking, list building or search engine tactics. But another popular way to both disseminate information and earn a living while doing it was through the time-honored business tradition of holding seminars. But not everyone who ends up on the stage had plans to be there.

Take Michael Enlow, who I mentioned earlier. He started his online business in 1989. He'd been married for twelve years, working hard to earn a living, not spending nearly the amount of time he knew he ought to with his family. Then his wife was killed in an auto accident. Suddenly being away from home all the time didn't seem like such a great idea. Enlow had already found success marketing on the bulletin boards on the Internet, and around that time he had written a how-to book and had an online readership of over 150,000 people for the test-run chapters. With his experience of the costs and time involved with traditional direct marketing, he was delighted with this new, essentially free marketplace, and said as much to his good friend, direct mail maven Gary Halbert. Enlow showed Halbert how quickly he could convert the online release of a report or a newsletter into a ringing phone with a live customer at the end. Halbert had made upwards of $40 million a year in direct marketing, and now he was watching Enlow reach thousands and thousands of people without paying a penny for printing or postage. Halbert didn't understand computers at all, but he did know exactly what he was seeing: the future.

A few weeks later, in August 1993, in front of several hundred people in traditional marketing, Enlow stood on the stage at Gary Halbert's "Atom Bomb Seminar" and talked about what he'd been up to back in his quiet little enclave in Mississippi. Later, appalled by the hype, the scams, and get-rich-quick schemes that seemed to take over the industry, Enlow regretted saying "yes" to his friend's request that he speak about this "marketing breakthrough of the century." But at the time, it was just so…exciting. The folks who had spent years elbow deep in wax pasting up type and then sending boards off into the void to be printed, fell into two camps. One camp backed away from Internet technology, muttering about fads and hucksters, and returned to their rulers and stat machines. The other camp sat wide-eyed and open-mouthed at the possibilities, and many of them abandoned (or at least semi-retired) their X-acto knives and leaped into learning about the pre-Web Internet. Among those who made the successful transition, there followed a free-for-all of would-be wizards and millionaire wannabes scrabbling to position themselves as Internet Marketing experts. Not all of them really were experts, but most of them knew at least one thing: they could make more money teaching others about direct marketing than by actually doing direct marketing themselves—at least, in the "old" ways.

Halbert charged people $3,000 to attend his "Atom Bomb Seminar." He could because he was the undisputed "king." In the coming years, the industry shook out many of the pretenders to the throne, leaving the real royalty of Internet Marketing to sponsor live seminars, conferences, workshops, courses and press events aiming to teach the uninitiated about what Enlow called "Electronic Marketing." Not long after that "Atom BombSeminar," at another seminar being held across the country from Halbert's, one of the pioneers who *did* know what he was talking about, Ken McCarthy, was chatting it up with Marc Andreessen of Mosaic/Netscape fame. McCarthy and Andreessen had been discussing at length, with a handful of other marketing visionaries, how the Internet would manage to support itself.

McCarthy's pre-Internet career path had perfectly positioned him to become the guru—and seminar host—he is today. He did a bit of everything over the years, although he mostly focused on promotion and media, as these snippets from his C.V. suggest: events and concert producer and promoter; radio show producer and station manger; manager of a record label; partner in a film post-production studio; technical developer of Wall Street trading stations; and conference coordinator for people in the mortgage industry. Along the way he had become pretty comfortable with technology, but even more important, he developed an interest in and gained knowledge about direct marketing and direct mail copywriting.

This was all offline, of course. McCarthy had seen the Internet in the late 70s, although he didn't actually use it: his college roommate did. A bright guy, the roomie used the connection to timeshare, sending his files up to the programs, compilers and processing mainframes in the Columbia University computer labs. (Incidentally, the roommate was Stanley Jordan. Yes, *that* Stanley Jordan, the famous jazz guitarist.) The memory stuck with McCarthy.

By 1993 McCarthy was spending enough time on the online bulletin boards that he was moved to attend BBSCON, an event put on by Jack Rickard, founder and editor of *Boardwatch*, a print monthly originally dedicated to the online BBS community. (It later became ISPWatch.) At that Colorado Springs conference, he met (and later befriended) Mark Graham, co-founder of Pandora Systems and the Institute for Global Communications which includes PeaceNet and EcoNet; Graham is one of the strongest forces and contributors involved in the commercialization of the Internet. There McCarthy got an enticing taste for the online world. That same

**162**

year, the first version of Mosaic hit the Internet, and it was then that McCarthy found himself emailing the developer off and on—at first with support questions, and later just as friends.

McCarthy mentioned that he knew a great many people in San Francisco who were involved in multimedia and doing other kinds of high-tech promotion. It seemed logical that they would be a perfect audience for a conference to discuss the potential of the World Wide Web not as a technical marvel (though it was certainly that) but as an exciting new commercial marketing medium.

He knew that ad agencies, direct marketers, and multimedia experts would be interested. On June 11, 1994, McCarthy convened a small seminar called "Making Money on the Internet—Yes, You Can Do It!" There McCarthy, Mark Graham, and a third Internet expert, Mark Fleischmann, sat down with one ad agency connection—not someone technically inclined but a bright guy named Rick Boyce. McCarthy explained the basics: *there's a page; you put a square on the page; if someone clicks on that square (the ad) it leads to another page (the client's home page); you can count how many times you displayed the page and how many times someone clicked on that box.* In other words, you could track conversions—visits that turn into sales. That got Boyce's attention. Six months later, Boyce was head of business development at HotWired, and the banner ad made its splashy debut.

But McCarthy's real coup came on November 5, 1994, when about 150 people crowded into a conference space in San Francisco. Many were drenched to the skin from an uncharacteristically heavy rain, while others stood shaking out their dripping umbrellas and shuddering the rain off like dogs. The carpet grew soggy from the amazing array of shoes soaked through and squishing with every step: wingtips, Birkenstocks, rubber flip-flops, high heels, sneakers, expensive loafers, biker boots. This eclectic mix showed up for what has been called the first Internet Marketing Conference ever: "Multimedia Publishing on the Internet." McCarthy was the keynote speaker; Graham, the guest speaker; and Andreessen, the featured speaker. A panel of people already engaged in online business and marketing rounded out the day; they included Maurice Welsh of Pacific Bell; Anna Couey of The Well; Bruce Moore of CareerMosaic; John Barnhill of Silicon Reef; and Mark Fleischmann, of Internet Distribution Services.

Just to give you a feel for the state of things at the time of the conference, let me just point out Fleischmann's most recent accomplishment at the time: he helped launch the *Palo Alto Weekly* online in January 1994. It was the first-ever commercial newspaper to make its content available, free of charge, to anyone with access to the Internet. The press release issued a month after the paper first began "testing its Internet presence" proudly reported that more than 2,000 different computer systems had accessed the paper despite there having been no public announcement of the publishing project. The press release had to include two paragraphs explaining what the Internet was: "The Internet is a world-wide computer network linking more than 20 million people in commercial, educational and government organizations. With Internet access to individuals now available for as little as $20 or less per month, the current growth rate is more than a million people a month." Computer users were advised to check with their ISPs about how to gain access to the World Wide Web— *that's* how new it was.

McCarthy's conference wasn't a "how-to" so much as a "what-to" introduction to the possibilities. He was plugged into the multimedia world at the time, and although his main income until around 1996 came from the mortgage conference business, he was already doing trainings and seminars aimed at helping people who wanted to make the transition from offline multimedia promotion to Web multimedia. In his talk at the conference, McCarthy offered a number of visions about the future, and at least 80 percent of them have already come to fruition. At a time when most people were skeptical that the Internet would ever be a successful, self-supporting commercial enterprise, he was so convinced that things were about to change dramatically that he published an article not long before the conference called "Why You Should Stop @#!%&*-ing Around and Get on the Internet NOW!" Since then, he has codified Internet Marketing into a comprehensive blueprint that he presents in both his products and his highly regarded, annual "The System" seminars. And he's still advising others to "Stop @#!%&*-ing Around."

# When the Student is Ready...

...the Master will appear. This bit of ancient Chinese wisdom can apply to nearly every part and parcel of our lives. In the Internet Marketing industry, however, it needs a small caveat: the student must *really* be ready. There are now dozens of major seminars and conferences, and literally hundreds of specifically targeted ones each year. Many of these can run up to five figures a head. Yet if there is one thing that all the gurus have agreed upon, it is that anyone who is truly serious about succeeding in Internet Marketing needs to go to at least one major live event. In the early days, the easy choice would have been Jonathan Mizel's seminar. From 1995 to 2001, Mizel and his company, Cyberwave Media, held *the* Internet Marketing seminar. As Paul Myers put it, that was where the cool kids hung out. (Of course, that would be just the first wave of "cool kids"; not every Internet Marketer who fits that description had hit it big at the time, or even gotten started.) If they weren't attending, they were speaking: Paul Myers, Corey Rudl, Jim Edwards, Marlon Sanders, Declan Dunn, Ken McCarthy, Tom Antion, Stephen Mahaney, and a little later Yanik Silver and Terry Dean.

Other Internet Marketers have hosted seminars throughout the years, notably Carl Galletti and Ron LeGrand, but when Jonathan Mizel gave up his twice-yearly "Online Marketing Power Summits" (and all the speaking engagements in between—an exhausting schedule), there were two consistently held, reliably top-notch seminars to fill the void: the "System Seminar" (Ken McCarthy) and the "BigSeminar" (Armand Morin). The students of the early seminars frequently became the speakers at the later seminars, although the pioneers in the first wave still speak at these and other conferences around the globe.

It's been said that the only thing most people fear more than death is public speaking. Most of the gurus I know hadn't planned on careers that involved standing on a stage in front of strangers; they became speakers almost by necessity, by virtue of their successes as Internet Marketers. But at least one well-known guru did exactly the opposite: already accustomed to the stage, he became so successful he took his "act" online in 1994.

Tom Antion hasn't had a job in thirty years. He's worked—and worked hard—but he's worked for himself all his life. By the time he graduated from college, he already owned five apartment buildings and a hotel. Built like the football jock, Antion went to a big-name college on a football scholarship and was a starting guard for two years (he even received an award from the National Football Foundation and Hall of Fame in 1973). His helmet protected the keen mind (he was Valedictorian of his high school class) of a determined entrepreneur who has owned and operated the second-largest night-club in West Virginia, a print shop, a video production company, and an internationally known entertainment company. He's survived two gun fights, one knife fight, and one car fight–he had a car drive through his living room. But he made his millions online by talking about what he does best: public speaking.

Antion was online back in the days when posting anything even vaguely commercial online would enrage the technical people who would send out flaming curses: "You're going straight to hell for this because we own this place. This is not for marketing."

But marketing was what he knew. Antion spoke about sales and customer service and always did fairly well for himself although he was never a worldwide known figure like Tony Robbins or Zig Ziglar. He did well enough, though, that he often got requests from people asking if he could teach them how to speak in public. He was happy to oblige because public speaking was something he enjoyed, but it didn't take him long to realize that individual and even group coaching would take up all his time. That moved him to create the *Wake 'em Up Video Professional Speaking System*, still the best selling professional speaking system available. In keeping with his goal of never working for someone else, he decided to market it online. It was not as simple as it sounded.

In his characteristic smooth style, Antion tells a story that is the modern-day equivalent of the grandparents' tale of walking ten miles barefoot in the snow to get to school:

> Speaking of online sales, I wonder if [a company that shall remain nameless, because they are] is still in business? They had a shopping cart, the Cadillac of the industry, that required a $2,000 licensing fee as I recall—totally outrageous. You could only put it on one website. You could not find anyone to work on it to customize anything…there were no auto-responders…there was nothing. It was like a dumb cashier at a convenience store: it would barely take the money, and all the time it had this glazed look on its face….That's what we had to work with. And if you wanted an affiliate program? You had to buy that separately and have it connected to your shopping cart. Big surprise: it took six months before they got it to work. You know how it was——and still is today—you get a bunch of things and try to get them to work together, each company blames

**167**

each other when it doesn't work. If you're not technical, you can't do anything about it, just wait until they finally get it to work. That was the atmosphere in those days. There were no people with multiple websites—you'd need a separate $2,000 licensing fee and some really serious hosting to get another website. Then you'd need a separate merchant account and a separate bank account. I think you could dump it into the same bank account, but you'd need to have another merchant account—which again in those days was no easy feat. To have a home-based business merchant account by itself was trouble. Then to try to tell them it's going to be on your website, you could hear them fall off laughing and telling all of their buddies they have some alien on the phone.

Antion persisted. It wasn't so much that he had such a prescient vision that the internet would become the major force in our lives that it did. But he could see that it had enormous potential for guys like him who wanted to stay at home. He was anxious to cut back on his traveling, particularly after an extremely taxing speaking engagement: an eleven-hour flight each way for a twenty-minute speech. The flight was so long Antion's feet swelled and he couldn't get his shoes back on, so when he stepped off the stairs onto the hot tarmac in Hawaii wearing only his socks, he was hopping so fast to keep his feet from burning that the girl with the lei couldn't get it over his head.

He finally got his website up, although he says it took his webmaster a year to set things up in such a way that someone could actually see and buy the *Wake 'em Up* book on the website. Although Antion had plenty of money from his speaking career, he was determined to master Internet Marketing, and he spent quite a bit of his cash checking out the get-rich-quick offers (one of Antion's early lessons: never take financial advice from someone driving a beat-up old Pinto), with no success. Then he discovered Corey Rudl's course, and everything changed. Money started to trickle in, then flow in, and before long the site averaged $30,000 a week. Although the foundation for Antion's success was the information he learned about database development—list building— Antion relied heavily on (and gives lofty praise for) Rudl's concept of the online advertorial.

An advertorial, in case you aren't familiar with the term, is a sales letter that looks like straightforward information such as a report or an article. Nowadays ads that look like editorial copy are tagged, in teeny tiny type, with the disclaimer "advertising." But it was Rudl's contention, and Antion swore by this too, that a well written advertorial will work even when customers *know* they are reading a pitch. People want free information, and if you give it to them (even as you're teasing them about the other 99 percent you could be telling them if they buy your product), they are more likely to regard you as an expert than as just a slick salesperson. Oddly, part of the appeal seems to be the lack of appeal, as people seem more trusting of gray expanses of text than of blinking banners, bold graphics, and flashy product photos. Embracing Rudl's psychological approach to sales made Antion the multimillionaire he's become.

It's ironic that Rudl, the man other Internet Marketers credit with perfecting affiliate programs in the industry, should have been the one to so heavily influence Antion's career. Defying conventional wisdom, Antion formed few joint ventures and relied very little on affiliates. He never criticized or dismissed them—he just wasn't particularly interested, preferring to be a bit of a loner, and he tended to attract like-minded clients who shared his opinion that whatever path you follow to success is "awesome," providing it's ethically and morally irreproachable. That, too, ran contrary to the message of most Internet Marketing, which often implies that there is a "right" way to do things and that it can be codified and packaged and sold.

Antion always "cherry picked" advice from those marketers he admired (like Rudl), and has offered especially high praise for some. For example, he says, "John Reese's 'Traffic Secrets' seminar was the best seminar I ever attended in my whole life, whether I was speaking or not.... That guy knows his stuff. He's credible. He's a good guy. He's not a sleazebag.... I visited the "BigSeminar" once, but I attended that whole thing for John Reese," and "Alex Mandossian's, 'Exit Strategies' was one of the most brilliant teleseminars I had ever heard." Many people fail on the Internet because they just try to get visitors, according to Antion, and if someone leaves without buying, the marketer just tries to get another visitor instead of asking how to turn that exit around or otherwise monetize it. "On that particular point, [Mandossian] has been a major factor. I've been making a fortune on that for a long time. I credit him for teaching me that." Although Antion never spent nearly the amount of time schmoozing at Internet Marketing events as the other gurus did, he did manage to learn what he needed to learn from people he encountered—including, in at least on instance, a stripper. No, it's nothing like that. "She showed me how to keep my flyaway hair in place with a little gel. Cool." He is mum about what kind of tip he left.

## Enter Your Code and Press # to Connect

Are teleseminars "Internet Marketing"? Technically, I suppose not. But they are live events, and the ones I'm concerned with are those held by Internet Marketers, so they deserve to be included.

If one person "invented" the teleseminar, his or her name may be lost to posterity unless someone else has some evidence of its beginnings. But I can tell you which Internet Marketers have raised it to an art form. One is Alex Mandossian, who got his start on Madison Avenue in the traditional marketing world. In the 1990s, he was part of the team that brought us some of the best known

Infomercials ever: Suzanne Somers and the Thigh Master; Ron Popeil and the RONCO Food Dehydrator; and Telly Savalas and Players Club International. He made millions for his clients as a consultant for television advertising/ shopping networks, voice/fax broadcasting, catalogs, and direct mail campaigns. But in October 2000, after the birth of his son, Mandossian realized that although he loved what he did, he was working sixteen hours a day, and that at that pace, he would have no time to watch his son grow up. He gave his company three months notice, and just before the end of the year he and his family relocated to San Francisco, leaving behind his $300,000 job and the comfortable life he'd known for more than a decade.

He started with a niche he knew well but that no one else seemed to want, and launched a website: *marketing-withpostcards.com*. While he still worked long hours, he did it from home, so he could take a break and spend time with his wife or play with his son. While he did grow the site into a successful operation, it was in live events that he made the biggest impact on the Internet Marketing world: teleseminars, webinars, Podcasts and virtual book tours. All these "live" events had one thing in common: they were location-independent. Speaking from wherever he happened to be, Mandossian could reach hundreds of people without their having to leave their own homes. This expanded the potential audience exponentially as the speaker could now reach people who might previously have been physically or financially unable to travel—often the very same people most interested in running their own Internet businesses from home.

Mandossian coached thousands of Internet Market- ers, and many more went through his *Teleseminar Secrets* training, making him the undisputed master teleseminar strategist. Even Tom Antion, already a professional speaker, owed a large part of his success to Mandossian.

But one student from the latest wave of Internet Marketers embraced the teleseminar in a big way.

It's amazing the number of Internet Marketing gurus I've spoken with who have attention deficit disorder. I don't know if that's a coincidence or a causal relationship. I do know that Tellman Knudson has called himself "more ADD" than anyone else you'd ever meet, and when I spoke with him, I began to sense that he might be right. But rather than ADD being detrimental to him, it gave him a calling in life—and the temperament to pursue that calling.

Immediately before launching into his online career, Knudson was a hypnotherapist and neuro-linguistic programming practitioner. Before that, he had eight failed businesses—perhaps in part because he admittedly had a hard time finishing things; three-quarters of the way through a project he generally grew bored and was ready to move on. To deal with his ADD, Knudson learned some techniques and principles that helped him achieve more in his personal and professional life, and he soon began passing on these methods to others with the disorder. Studying direct marketing on his own, he figured out a few ways to grow his hypnotherapy/NLP services business to help even more people.

By 2005, he had six offices. Unfortunately, there was only one Tellman Knudson. Since he did not want any employees, the maximum number of people he could help in a week was sixty—and even that meant working like crazy and traveling from one office to another. He realized, too, that living in rural Vermont meant that he wouldn't be able to charge more than $75 an hour for his services, yet he had no interest in moving out of the area. He wanted to help more people, but already he couldn't walk down the street without a client or former client stopping to thank him for his help or to tell him some new tale—he had absolutely no down time at all.

His career was still fairly new, but already he felt himself beginning to burn out.

Knudson wondered if there was a way that he might be able to help more people, to expand his reach. Perhaps, he thought, he could record his sessions and sell them—and maybe even get them online. To begin, he made several CDs and wrote some sales letters without any guidance, then sat back and waited for traffic to flow in. It was a long wait. Several failed websites later, he read Shawn Casey's e-book, *Mining Gold on the Internet*, and things started to turn around, even though by then Casey's book was so outdated that half the links were dead. He subscribed to Casey's newsletter and focused on learning everything he could in as short a time as possible.

Knudson started his online business almost entirely on adrenaline. He had managed to make the hypnosis business successful technically, but it wasn't highly profitable. After paying bills, student loans, apartment rent, office rent, and everything else, he wasn't making much. There wasn't much left over after expenses, and he'd cut up all his maxed-out credit cards. All he had to begin his online business was $50 in cash.

All the newsletters and eBooks told him that list building was key. He'd gotten pretty good at the basics of list building through his offline marketing—for instance, he'd mail out a flier with a special offer, and new clients would turn up. Ready to start his online business, and invest that $50 well, Knudson took stock of what he didn't have: knowledge of copywriting, programming, graphic design, editing audio—and product. Then he looked at his assets: the $50, a business idea, determination....and his list of about 300 people he knew were interested in Neuro-Linguistic Programming.

He sent out an email, telling people he had an idea for a company but that he needed people to help out with copy, programming, and the rest of it. In the end, he and six others formed a company and launched *ListCru-*

*sade.com.* They all worked on a percentage of the earnings. The first step had to be learning a lot more about list building, yet he could not afford to buy any home study courses. Sure, that would have been an investment that paid for itself over time, but he simply didn't have the capital outlay. He had no credit and a business that was barely covering its own bills. He worked sixty hours a week, so he had little extra time, either. Inspiration struck: "What if I interview experts who already have products and pick their brains about list building? In the end we can sell the interviews as product, and sell it through affiliate links. Everyone gets a percentage."

The first person Knudson interviewed was Dr. Robert Anthony, a self-help expert. The plan for the series was to alternate between marketing and self-improvement interviews. Dr. Anthony would help people learn to get the right mindset for making a lot of income. Knudson reasoned that having a great list wasn't going to do any good if people weren't going to be motivated to use the lists. They would also need to know how to bounce back from the negativity if their families were constantly harping at them to stop wasting time on the computer and do something productive with their lives. Without something to raise their energy level, they'd wind-up hunched over and drooling on the keyboard. They would need self-confidence, and Dr. Robert Anthony could provide that.

Knudson needed to hold onto that mindset himself. He lived in a three-bedroom apartment with his partner, Jody, and two other roommates. His computer was so loud he couldn't have it turned on while he was in the room using the phone, so he had to do interviews on a wireless phone from one of the roommates' rooms if he wanted to leave his computer turned on to record everything. Knudson drove his local friends crazy talking about his work. None of them were computer people. They were loggers, cheese makers, artists, potters—people who live in a rural, borderline-arctic community. To keep himself motivated, he had to rely on Jody, the team, and his own inner drive.

He knew he could do it. In one of his earlier projects, after he received about forty "No"s, he changed his sales approach. He would say to the prospective customer: "Hey. I'm not going to try to convince you to say "yes." But could you please tell me what I might have done to make this offer more appealing so that the next person I approach is more likely to say yes?" The advice was painful, but he applied it anyway. The next person said "No" anyway. After many iterations and tweaking, his proposals started to generate favorable responses. He learned his lesson and used that knowledge with ListCrusade.

Not all his earlier projects had failed absolutely. One *had* met with success. The problem was in that case, Knudson didn't control the list or the product. He got checks in the mail, but he had no input. At the heart of it was a product he had done with Kevin Wilke and Matt Gill of Nitro Marketing (a team Knudson calls "awesome") called the *Nitro Marketing Mindset*. Knudson's contribution was the Neuro-Linguistic Programming component called modeling: he could create a series of hypnotic sessions that would help to instill certain skill sets into the customers who bought this product. Wilke and Gill had first met Knudson when he responded to an ad for someone to be the project manager for all of Jack Zufelt's online marketing business. Knudson invested a lot of time and energy in the application process—at the time, the opportunity seemed to have been made for him—and ended up on a three-person shortlist. Then, before Wilke and Gill made any decision, Knudson realized it would not work and told them why: "I'm sorry. This is potentially an awesome opportunity and I'm ideal in most ways, but I'm going to turn it down. If I take this position, I'm not going to serve you well. I'll stick at it for three months, then end up more focused on my own goal. I'm looking to bring my own techniques and principles about attention deficit disorder to the world. That is my goal. I can't meet that goal working for someone else." The Nitro team understood. His honest appraisal impressed them enough that when he came up with the idea of the "Nitro Marketing Mindset," and pitched the idea to them, they readily said "yes." It was a success, and Knudson ended up with a nine- or ten thousand-dollar royalty check that paid off most of his debt. It didn't change his lifestyle except in two indirect ways: first, it let him concentrate on his own projects, and two, it showed him that it was possible to make money online. On the downside, he didn't own the list, so he couldn't reproduce that success. But that's what gave him the idea for ListCrusade.

Knudson's goal for ListCrusade was to build a list of 1 million subscribers within six months. The deal: anyone who did a half-hour interview with Knudson and sent out one promotional email to his or her list would have that interview go out to every person on Knudson's list in every future mailing *ad infinitum*. In other words, if they promoted him once, he'd promote them forever. They never have to do another thing.

It worked. *ListCrusade.com* may not have made its 1 million subscribers (yet), but it did make, as Knudson put it, "millions and millions and millions of dollars anyway." That's pretty impressive: from debt to multimillionaire in two years. Part of his success began when Knudson signed up for *Teleseminar Secrets*—the very first time Alex Mandossian had taught the course. Knudson realized that it was going to be another modular step-by-step system. Ever the creative type, Knudson always hated playing by the rules, being told what to do. (He'd never been fired from a job, surprisingly. That may be because once he takes a job, he always does extremely well and gets numerous raises and promotions until he lands the top position available—then gets bored and quits.) He wasn't happy to find strict rules in Mandossian's manual, but he followed them anyway, every last click. He listened to every single live teleclass. He did every bit of homework assigned and did it in real time.

By class three or four he had his first teleseminar set up, and using his list, the company made $14,000. (Knudson finally gave in to popular demand and launched a list building product, too). When he and his colleagues saw the final tally, Knudson *claims* he said, "Holy monkeys! We just made fourteen grand!"

Knudson had reason to be excited. Up until then, they had been making about $10,000 a month, and that was being split among the seven employees. Each of them got 10 percent, and the remaining 30 percent was invested in growing the business. So everyone was earning $1000 a month, or $250 a week. Adding a teleseminar added a zero to everyone's paycheck. He started doing one every week, and each one earned $20,000 to $25,000. Their best teleseminar to date pulled in $260,000. Alex Mandossian may have cracked the teleseminar code, but Knudson mastered following it.

He set his big 1 million subscriber goal for a practical reason: it attracted the Big Names. The B- and C-level marketers all said it couldn't be done, but the A-level marketers said, "Let's go for it." The next thing he knew, Knudson had Jay Abraham's signed seal of approval on his home page. While some on his wish list are still unscheduled, such as Mark Joyner and Alex Mandossian, Knudson has managed to work his way through a very impressive list in a short time: Harv Eker, Joe Vitale, Mark Victor Hansen, and Jack Canfield. Knudson liked to think big, believing that what holds a lot of people back is that "they just think too damn small."

His big think has made Knudson very, very rich. He still works, but he doesn't do it to make more money. That was never what drove him then and what drives him still is his dream of helping millions of people with attention deficit disorder not only learn how to cope with it but even learn to use it to their advantage. That's what gets him out of bed every day. The name he gave his company says a lot about the man: Overcome Everything.

# Sittin' Pretty

Maybe he was inspired by Alex P. Keaton, the television character who read the *Wall Street Journal* and was preternaturally concerned (for an elementary/junior high student, that is) with money—or maybe not, since the show *Family Ties* might not have aired until after Matt's bedtime since he would have been only around nine years old when the show went off the air in 1989. But "Alex" would have been impressed by Bacak's managing to leverage a regular paper route into a thriving, profitable lawn-care business. Bacak grew up in a middle-class family in Youngstown, Ohio (the "Keatons" lived in Columbus, Ohio). Though extremely diverse culturally, Youngstown was never diverse economically; the once-thriving city still hasn't fully recovered from the 1970s, when changes in the steel industry forced the closure of one plant after another and left thousands of people—including the elder Bacak—in search of new employment. The Bacaks weren't poor, but they were surrounded by a city filled with people in economic shock, and maybe that's why they lived on budgets: if the budget said $20 for shoes, that's what Matt Bacak had to spend. But as Bacak got closer to adolescence, he started to feel self-conscious, as many kids do at that age, and realized that he didn't like being the only one in his class wearing shoes from K-Mart.

His dad was sympathetic but firm. If Bacak wanted more money for shoes, he would have to find a way to earn it. Soon Bacak had picked up several paper routes. It didn't make him rich, but it did teach him to enjoy having a little bit of spending money. He'd been thinking about how to earn even more when he realized that when he went to people's houses once a week to collect payment for the newspapers, people were already standing there with their wallets or their checkbook in hand. Why not add an upsell? Bacak offered to mow their lawns, too, for $20 a yard. The first week he tried it he picked up ten lawn-care clients. Before long he'd gone from a kid in twenty-dollar K-Mart sneaks to a kid with $200 in his pocket every week. Soon enough, delivering papers *and* mowing lawns *and* going to school got to be difficult. He didn't cut back, though, he cut a deal—he knew a kid who wanted to earn money for baseball cards. Bacak offered him $5 a yard to do the mowing. All Bacak had to do was just deliver the papers and collect the money, paying out the $5 and keeping $15 for himself.

Bacak's grandfather saw him earning money and told him that he needed to do something with it besides keep it in a shoebox, and gave his grandson a subscription to the *Wall Street Journal*. Bacak would read the paper and dream about all the wonderful things he could do when he had money, but meanwhile he just scraped his way through school with a 1.7 out of 4.0 average. His teachers despaired of him, but school held no interest for him since it seemed that nothing he learned there would be of much practical use later, and he told them so: "This doesn't matter. When I go out into the real world, this stuff is not going to work. You're not teaching me how to make money—you're teaching me how to become an employee."

Much as he disliked school, Bacak tried to get into college, to no avail. He says he finally had to "beg in front of a board" to convince them that he should be allowed to enter the University of North Alabama (the state his family had moved to when Bacak's father's employer went bankrupt). UNA finally admitted him, but put him on probation for his first semester. Oddly enough, that wasn't necessary, as he ended up an honor student with a GPA of 3.9 out of 4.0 that first semester—all because, as he says, he "focused on making it happen." He majored in marketing. Yet even though he was doing well, every time he went home for a semester break or holiday, he dreaded going back to school. His mother would probably say that he threatened to quit school over a thousand times—but he never did quit. Partly that was due to his father's common sense psychology: knowing that Bacak could never walk away from a challenge, he told his son he didn't believe he could ever make it through college. True to form, Bacak bristled and offered a deal. He was currently funding his own education. His deal was that if he graduated in three years, his father would pick up the bill for half the tuition. Bacak the elder lost the bet (but some would say he won the game).

Bacak the younger never lost his "Alex P. Keaton" mentality. While he was still in college, he started two companies out of his dorm room. One, Environmental Waste Consultants, he ended up selling to his business partner, who turned out to be more into his extracurricular activities than into business. The second, *CSRiver.com*, developed websites, intranets, extranets, and databases targeted at politicians. Bacak had gotten involved in that after he helped a friend campaign for College Republican National Chairman. The friend lost, but Bacak and several others sat at the Watergate Hotel and designed a company. He eventually sold that company, too, partly for lack of time, and partly because he believed what so many people had told him—he was just "too young to run a business." And partly it was because he knew he still wasn't "busting through," as he says. He wasn't doing what he really should be doing.

After receiving his B.S. in marketing in three years, then going back to technical school to tack on an Associates Degree in technical engineering, Bacak hit the interview trail. Employers seemed impressed with him, but the feeling wasn't mutual. He was on his third interview with IBM when the man behind the desk reached over and flipped Bacak's tie over so he could read the label, then sneered, "When you come work for us you'll need to wear better clothes." Bacak stood up and walked out the door. The interviewer chased him down, sputtering that he'd been working there twenty years and no one had ever walked out on an interview before. Bacak shrugged. "Sorry, I won't work for a company that tells me where to buy my clothes." (It seems that the "K-Mart kid" had grown some...confidence.)

Bacak took a job with Cisco. He was hired into its new associate sales representative program, signing a two-year contract that stated that for six months Cisco would send him to the Silicon Valley to train as a sales representative. Since Bacak's graduation date was out of synch due to his graduating early, he had to wait out the semester until the rest of the new hires arrived. While he waited, he didn't have much to do, and at work he was surrounded by MIT grads. Cisco finally shipped him out and told him to find a job for a while. He found a temporary tech job in Atlanta, filling NEC Telephone systems, selling Cisco routers, biding his time. Unfortunately, while he was still waiting for the others to graduate, the dot-coms based on hype and hoopla imploded and the market panicked. Cisco cancelled its training program and told him that they couldn't hire him after all.

Bacak stayed in Atlanta. He bypassed lucrative offers from various big companies and still-solvent dot-com companies in favor of a financially iffy sales position with a small company. Every hour he spent in his car, he listened to the Nightingale-Conant tapes his sales manager let him borrow. The job was okay, but he and one of the owners had a less-than-enjoyable working relationship, and Bacak jumped ship after six months to accept an offer from a pre-IPO company selling telephone lines. The time invested in listening to the tapes apparently had paid off: the company had over six hundred sales reps, yet Bacak was the top performer in his very first month. In his second month, having closed out all his deals so quickly that they all fell in month one, Bacak had to spend time rebuilding his sales funnel and pipe-line, and too few of the new deals closed by the month's end. Bacak went into shock when his boss put him on probation and threatened to fire him unless he brought in more contracts. From number one salesperson to one step away from a pink slip in thirty days? He quit.

Bacak had been reading Robert Kiyosaki's *Rich Dad Poor Dad* and *Cash Flow Quadrant*, and working the phones as a pseudo-telemarketer. His job was to ferret out leads in a brokerage firm "boiler room" (just like the movie of the same name) while he studied to become a commodities broker. Somehow word about Bacak's pre-teen entrepreneurial lawn care empire made its way into the Kiyosaki organization—not to mention the two com-panies he'd started during college—and someone there invited him to California, all expenses paid, for a train-ing to learn how to become a cash flow facilitator for Kiyosaki's Cash Flow 101—a game where participants learn how to invest their money. Bacak had never been to a seminar. He'd never been to California. He liked the idea of both, however, and drove straight to the airport after he had just finished, literally, taking the grueling tests to get his Series 3 certification to start work as a commodities broker. He barely made the plane.

The training was a shock to Bacak's system. He came back to Atlanta feeling like an entirely different person ("Some of my friends said I left a boy, but came back a man. They could see it on my face—the changes because of that event."). During one of the breaks, he looked around at the event hosts and the attendees, and saw a room filled with multimillionaires, and at least one bil-lionaire, and thought, "And here I am getting to meet them and talk to them and listen to them and hang out with them. They just talk to me like I belong." One man he spoke with had helped found Keller Williams (a thriv-ing realty company with the vision statement "God,

Family, then Business," not to be confused with the singer/songwriter with the same name), a small-time millionaire who told him to ignore anyone—including his inner voice—who told him that he was "too young." He told Bacak, "You're *always* going to say you're too young. Then all of a sudden the time will come when you're too old, and you're never going to get anything done." Bacak knew it was true.

He returned in the same manner he'd left—racing between airport and appointment, this time to get back to the "boiler room," but nothing else was the same. He made a few calls, then walked over to his manager and said, "I'm done. I'm leaving and I'm not coming back." His manager was astounded—Bacak's series 3 grade was the highest the firm had ever seen—and demanded to know where he was going. Bacak told him about the business he had planned, and when he left the manager shook his hand, saying "I've had tons of people quit on me, but never one with an exact plan. You *should* go." Bacak walked out, vowing never to go back to corporate America again.

His business, of course, was holding Cash Flow 101 events. He had to hold a given number of events to complete his certification as a facilitator, so he put on his first one within a week of leaving his job. One person showed up, but Bacak recorded it and sent in the paperwork. The next week he held a second one and doubled his audience—two people showed up. He sent in another event record. The next week he had six people, and slowly his numbers kept growing.

Once he decided to seriously promote both through the Kiyosaki organization and to some of the people he had met with, he started averaging fifty people per event. He'd line up a speaker and a hotel room. At first it took him a month to get those fifty people there: he sweated each one, hitting a breakfast meeting with a chapter of the chamber of commerce, then driving across town to a networking meeting or two, maybe having dinner with another business group. Then he'd hold an event, and start up all over again in a week or so.

At one event he met someone from the audience we'll call Mr. X. They became friendly. Bacak considered him to be very competent in real estate, speaking and selling, but lacking, extremely, in follow-up and customer service. Mr. X asked Bacak if he had considered promoting his events on the Internet. Bacak decided to try it, and on a Monday emailed a sales letter to a list of everyone he had met through the events—about 2,000 names. Instead of waiting for faxed forms to arrive as usual, he watched as the orders started popping up on the screen. By Thursday the event was sold out. When he realized he had just done in three days what he had been spending thirty days doing, Bacak decided to look a little closer into Internet Marketing.

One of the people Bacak knew was Mike Litman. In fact, Litman had spent many a night sleeping on Bacak's floor. Litman had held six jobs between 1995 and 2000, and hated them all until he started a radio show in which he interviewed well-known, successful people in the personal/financial self-help field. Although Litman has joked that he never had more than three live listeners ("My parents were two of them"), those interviews were his own key to the luxury suite. Litman transcribed the tapes, intending to turn them into a book, but not a single publisher would touch it. In 2001, Litman self-published *Conversations with Millionaires*, and ninety days later it hit #1 on Amazon.com. Litman knew a bit about marketing and the Internet, and he and Bacak spent copious amounts of time concocting great plans and goals—all of which, it turns out, they have achieved—and he helped Bacak with his event promotions.

Litman invited Bacak to an Internet Marketing seminar hosted by Mark Joyner. Bacak went, and he was hooked. He sat next to Ted Nicholas, met Joe Sugarman, and hung on every word the speakers uttered. Then he went back home and started Millionaire Minutes, a sort of email reportage version of Litman's old radio show. He kept sending it to his attendees list, which grew to 10,101. Ironically, all the time he was interviewing millionaires, he was sleeping on a cot in a tiny one-bedroom apartment and living off his credit cards, eating Ramen noodles and Chef Boyardee.

He ended up filing for bankruptcy.

How could that happen? Somehow along the way he'd forgotten all about his most valuable asset: his list. He had failed to work the people on his list, promote to them again and again. So, he figured out what he could do to make his list work for him. He invited them all to an event where he taught people how he had gotten so many people into his live events. He called it "Butts in Seats." After he finished the main part of the course, it turned out that the only question people really had was, "How did you build your list?" His next event, naturally, focused on list building (in fact it was called something awkward but effective, like "How to Build Your List Quickly"), and it sold out. As always, though, Bacak didn't trust success that came too easily, and went back to writing, to promoting other people's products and seminars, and doing the occasional teleseminar. He made his first million online that way. Once he tired of promoting dozens of other people, he hit on the idea of narrowing the focus, of picking just two people and promoting only those two (at first it was a stock expert and a tax expert, but the stock expert has since been replaced by a real estate expert). It's now 2007, and Bacak has broadened his horizons back out again. Now, he teaches people—large numbers of them—how to promote themselves, and he makes sure that they understand the key point: to never forget to make your list count. It all works. The "K-Mart Kid" is now the "Powerful Promoter," and he has three businesses. Each of of his companies is doing at least $1 million in sales per year; one is at $3 million. Oddly enough, his old sales manager from the phone company, the one he liked and who let him borrow the Nightingale-Conant tapes, now works for Bacak.

# Pioneer 2.0

Terry Dean had a lot to learn. The problem was, there weren't that many teachers out there yet. He crossed into the Internet Marketing frontier just behind the vanguard, but the handful of those who'd gone ahead hadn't left a clear -cut trail to follow. Tired of delivering pizzas and newspapers to make ends meet, Dean decided to try to make his own trail, chart it, and show others the way.

It wasn't as though he'd be risking an affluent life-style. He had dropped out of Bible College and jumped from job to job, rarely staying more than thirty days. The pizza job was just the last in a long line of dead-end jobs. He and his wife, who worked at a factory, were drowning in debt—the number hovered around $50,000 in 1996—and all their credit cards were maxed out except one. That's the one he used to walk out of Best Buy with a Pentium 75. After poking around online to see what Internet Marketing was all about, he decided to buy licenses to sell other people's training videos (Mark Victor Hanson, Robert Allen) on direct mail and self-help topics. He started with a website created for one of the products, but decided that it was "ugly," crammed with moving graphics, jumping text, and interface elements that were difficult to use. He fixed it up to look more professional—and it stopped selling. Reluctantly, he put back the frou-frou, and the sales came flowing back. (Allegedly he "can't remember " the URL of that ugly site, but I suspect he just doesn't want anyone to see it on the "Wayback Machine," a feature of the Internet Archive website, located at archive.org, where you can check out pages from the past.)

As Dean ventured into the great unknowns of Internet Marketing, one of his first discoveries was evidence that a strong list is key to success. During the first year that he ran his site selling others' videos, he tried a lot of different approaches and techniques, testing to see how little changes affected his results. Then he noticed that his earnings seemed to correlate almost one-for-one with the size of his list: one month he had close to 1,000 subscribers and earned roughly $1,000; not long after he had close to 1,200 subscribers and made roughly $1,200. Thereafter he focused not on selling product but on building his list, devising and testing tactics to see what worked. For example, he tested two promotions head-to-head. In one, he offered a free copy of the list to any new subscriber in exchange for contact information. In the other, he offered a free report and a copy of the list. The promotion with the free report out-pulled the list alone 2:1. When the list reached 3,000 and the site pulled in $3,000 Dean finally let himself believe that his days of tossing newspapers onto people's lawns and smelling someone else's dinner in the back of his car were over for good.

Many of the things he tried came from the videos he sold and a few products he bought such as those by Mike Enlow and Jay Abraham, both of whom focused on traditional direct marketing rather than Internet Marketing. After a year or so, Dean was doing well enough that others began asking how he did it, which inspired him to create his first original products. There were two very early on: the *In Sync Cash Flow System*, a series of five self-executing eBooks he sold for $47, and a series of videos like the one he created to show others how-to design websites with FrontPage. In that video, by the way, he actually filmed himself making a page so users could pop the video into the VCR and create something right along with him—an approach that worked largely because of Dean's soft-spoken but straightforward style. It radiates the message, "Hey, if this guy can do it, I can too."

Other people were out there doing the same things as Dean or similar. Corey Rudl, Jonathan Mizel, Tom Antion, Mark Joyner, Willie Crawford, and a good many others were already soundly established online. Dean, however, wasn't fully aware of it at the time. For the most part he just continued to learn from their newsletters, videos and eBooks, to do his methodical testing, and to build his list. People were starting to notice Dean, however, and in 2000, Ron LeGrand invited him to his first seminar ever, the "Internet Marketing Boot Camp"—as a speaker. The largest audience he'd ever spoken in front of previously was the familiar congregation of his church.  The "Boot Camp" would have well over a hundred strangers.

LeGrand put Dean on the stage for four hours. There he explained what was in his product and fielded questions throughout the presentation. Adding to the pressure was the promise LeGrand had put in the sales letter promoting the event: the $10,000 challenge. Dean, he'd said, would make $10,000 online at the show by sending out just one email. Dean put together an offer for a limited number of licenses for a $495 product, one of his lower-priced ones. He spent about thirty minutes of his presentation going over the email, analyzing what it said, then sent the offer out at 9 o'clock on Friday morning right from the stage. It went only to his own list of about 30,000 names—no joint ventures. They checked the orders at lunch, again in the evening, and then throughout the weekend. When the seminar ended at 4 o'clock on Sunday, the offer had sold out. The "$10,000 Challenge" had earned $33,245. This time, instead of one name corresponding to one dollar of profit at the end of the month, it was roughly one dollar of profit at the end of a *weekend*. No wonder Dean was attracting attention. He sold a lot of product at the end of that show ($20,000 worth), too.

People just getting into Internet Marketing often hear this story and react in one of three ways. A third of them get discouraged, thinking that there is no way they could ever make that kind of money, and they give up. Another third of them get over-confident and over-extended and go broke. And the final third take away the message that if they are diligent, patient, realistic, and willing to learn, they can be successful, too. Dean's goal wasn't to earn $30,000 in a weekend. His goal was to be able to give up delivering pizzas for a living.

After that big success, Dean hit the show circuit. He and Ted Ciuba spoke together three or four times a year doing training sessions, not hawking product, although every time they spoke at one of Ron LeGrand's events they did one of Dean's trademark promotions. At one he accidentally misspelled the email address on the product promo, and still managed to get $7,000 in sales by lunch from people so interested in buying that they figured out how to find the real site; when Dean fixed the address, it pulled in another $13,000. For his biggest on-stage promotion, he tried something a little different—Dean swears by testing, of course—and added a teaser to his regular newsletter: "On Friday at 9 o'clock, I'll send you a special. Pay attention, because it will probably sell out by the end of the week." That was all it said. At the show, he followed the regular formula of writing the email, going over it with the audience, and sending it out to just the members on his list. That weekend the total in online sales was $96,000. He sold an additional $60,000 in product at the show.

The secret to Dean's success isn't a secret at all—it's what he teaches. Building a list is key, but not just any list. It must be a responsive list, which requires two things. One, it must be a targeted list—a collection of people who are genuinely interested in your subject. And two, it must be a list of people with whom you have built up a strong, trusting relationship, which means valuing the people on it. For example, you don't send just any offer. You don't sell anything that you wouldn't buy yourself or send a lot of "hype" emails to your list.

You're honest and "real," right down to writing emails as if you were sitting across the table chatting over coffee with each person—listening, sharing, paying attention.

Dean was one of the first Internet Marketers to say right in his newsletter that he wasn't promising anyone easy money. He actually used the word "work" repeatedly in his sales letters, claiming it weeded out the lazy, the impatient, the unrealistic, and the dabblers, *and* sent him exactly the kind of serious clients he wanted. A client of Dean's from the U.K. once told him he'd bought the product because Dean dared to mention the word "work" as opposed to offering him a guarantee that he would make money without effort. Dean's reasoning was this: "Marketing isn't just the principle of getting everybody you possibly can to buy your products. Marketing is also eliminating anybody you *don't* want to buy your products. The 80/20 rule applies to everything, including the likelihood that 80 percent of your problems are going to be caused by 20 percent of your customers.... I would rather eliminate the whole 20 percent before they even get in." His approach worked. He may have left Bible school, but he still has the demeanor of a kindly pastor in a small-town church. People trust him.

That's why when Dean offered to show others the trail he'd followed, so many people listened—not only when he spoke at seminars but when he mentored people individually or *en masse* through his websites like *netbreakthroughs.com*. On that site he showed members an actual ad test. One week he might compare the effectiveness of different headlines or ways of positioning the site or actual ads. He tested everything from banner ads and eZine ads to newsletters and posted the actual results at the end of the week. By 2004, the site's member list read like a Who's Who of successful Internet Marketers. (FYI: the site is still active, but Dean is no longer involved with it.)

That constant pitch-free connection with his member base strengthened the relationship. So did the fact that he ran tests where the things he tried were dismal failures (he once spent $600 on an eZine promotion that pulled in just $50 in sales). He had two lists, really—the opt-in list of interested people who received his free newsletter, and those who had a paid membership on his *netbreakthroughs.com* site. He pulled people onto the site from the free list by augmenting his usual educational materials with excerpts from or descriptions of longer, in-depth articles that ran on the membership site. He also gained quite a following from his speaking and teaching engagements. Business thrived.

Eventually, the crazy pace caught up with Dean. He had other dreams he wanted to pursue. In 2003 and 2004, he sold off most of his businesses to Kurt Kristensen and retired from Internet Marketing. Sort of, anyway. He still kept his hand in, just not full-time. He ran *mymarketing-coach.com*, a business coaching site where people sign up for a one-hour coaching session, with a 100 percent guarantee that Dean can increase their Internet profits or they can have all their money back. Of course, he didn't accept just any client, only a select few for long-term mentoring. The other part of his time he spent offering up the "politically incorrect ramblings of a pizza delivery driver turned business coaching minister." Dean, an ordained minister now for more than a dozen years, more than achieved his goal of giving up the delivery job that earned him just $8 an hour. He replaced that with a $1,000-an-hour fee delivering personally the hard-earned wisdom of one of the most successful and trusted Internet Marketing gurus out there. I forgot to ask him, though, if you get a pizza with that.

## Focus Group

With no money, no insurance, and no one standing up for him, Stephen Pierce lay writhing on a gurney in a Washington, D.C., emergency room. A drug dealer's bullet meant for his head had buried itself deep in his thigh. The doctors didn't bother to hide their lack of enthusiasm for putting the young gang-banger's case ahead of other more "deserving" types. It's still not clear whether they left the bullet in because it was the best thing to do, or just the most expedient. Today Pierce may be the only multimillionaire who carries a bullet in his leg.

It's a hard-luck story that plays out over and over in the poverty-ravaged areas of America's cities, unfortunately. Smart kids duped into believing they can't do any better, find themselves drawn into the violent but occasionally lucrative criminal side of life. Like any kind of gambling it takes strong resolve to know when to quit. When he was discharged with a sheaf of instructions for changing the dressings and a handful of painkillers, Pierce was sent back out on the streets. The person driving him away from the hospital—someone he loved and respected—said, "Stephen, you've got a brilliant mind, but everything you touch turns to dust. At this rate, you probably won't even live to see nineteen."

He was not off to a good start. Pierce had dropped out of high school, hung out with a tough and violent crowd, and caused so much trouble at home that the landlord had evicted his entire family. At the time he was shot, he was penniless, homeless, and directionless.

A bullet can be a wakeup call. A very powerful wakeup call.

Pierce started reading everything from the Bible to Napoleon Hill's *Think and Grow Rich*. He devoured W. Clement Stone's *Greatest Success Secret* and Norman Vincent Peale's *Power of Positive Thinking*. What he realized was that having endured a string of failures didn't mean he was destined to fail forever. After all, didn't fire create as well as destroy? He started to see that life was filled with tests, and you had to pass many of them to get ahead. Most people took failure as a sign that they shouldn't be trying to do whatever it was they were doing, but Pierce saw it differently. If you fail, you try something different until you get it right. Inspired by his reading, Pierce started a dozen businesses. They all failed. But he didn't quit. He told himself that the greatest wisdom comes not from failing but in realizing why you failed, and figuring out what changes and improvements you can make to get a better outcome. Learn from everything, even success: why did this work?

Pierce's driver on that dark day away from the ER was right. Pierce is brilliant. He's also driven, optimistic and as filled with potential energy as a tightly wound spring. Recognizing that he had a great many strengths, he started a few tentative moves online. He might have been poor, but he had a great head for figures and an avid interest in the financial world. He'd initially looked online to find sites that would let him get into futures trading, something he'd become involved with offline in a big way. There were very few beyond a forum here and a newsgroup there. So he thought, why not start something? People were always asking him to help them out anyway, so why not make it a business?

Pierce started an email newsletter in which he discussed possible trades and provided general information about the market. His daily trades, which were outperforming expensive services offline, caught the attention of a subscriber who wanted to pay him five thousand dollars to teach him the trading methodology. Instead, the savvy Pierce started a paid subscription service and charged $350 a month to join. Soon he had hundreds paying subscribers and was earning over $35,000 dollars a month. A financial whiz and market expert, he wrote his first eBook, *Rapid Fire Swing Trading*, and in the first fifty days it brought in $49,000 (in total it's brought in just under $250,000).

As with Terry Dean, much of Pierce's success can be traced to his personal style. Where Dean is methodical and low-key, however, Pierce is given to flashes of informed insight and radiates a seemingly boundless energy and enthusiasm. Yet they both come off as "real." In fact, another of Pierce's products is an eBook called *The Whole Truth*,wherein he tries to dispel some of what he saw as distortions, lies, and hype online. It was wildly popular—and instantly controversial. As he himself pointed out on one of his websites, fewer than twenty pages were what caused the heated back-and-forth discussion between admirers and detractors. In those pages, Pierce talked about a $97 tool Internet Marketers could use to be assured top positions in search engine rankings—Smart Pages. At the time, it was unclear whether or not this tool was banned by the main search engines (especially Google, which people depended on very heavily for their income). Smart Pages were essentially doorway pages, small web pages packed with relevant keywords that redirected users, often without telling them that the page they had landed on was not the page that the search engine had turned up. The result was a very high page ranking. The problem was, a large number of people considered them unethical if not altogether "illegal" by Google standards. The creator of the Smart Page Creator program, Carlos Martinho, maintained that they were perfectly allowable when used correctly as the redirects weren't "sneaky" (Google's modifier). Others were appalled. And still others allowed that they were probably going to be broadly banned by Google soon enough, but in the meantime, many people would continue to take the chance until the ruling was definitive: "Stephen Pierce still has thousands of Smart Pages out there generating between $10,000 and $20,000 a month. I know this for a fact," wrote Jonathan Mizel on one discussion forum back in 2003. "Google deleted the sites he advertised in *The Whole Truth*, but they caught only a small fraction of his SEO.... Argue all you want, but there are people making tens of thousands of dollars a month with Smart Pages, promoting nothing but affiliate programs. If and when the hammer comes down, they will be far *wealthier* than those who banter semantics on discussion boards."

The controversy didn't hurt Pierce's book sales, but the personal attacks bothered him. He says he was "subjected to torrents of abuse and invective because [his] product performed as promised. In fact, rumors surfaced that Google changed the way they ranked pages because Smart Pages were making it too easy to rank highly. In any case, the debate did obscure many of Pierce's other points. Among his messages in this and other books is the exhortation to believe in yourself and use momentum. Optimism counts, but largely because it can help build momentum, keep you committed, and help you be your own best cheerleader; don't count on others for approval. And don't surround yourself with naysayers and pessimists. He likes to quote educator and actor/comedian Bill Cosby: "I don't know a secret to success, but the way to fail is to try to please everybody."

There's no doubt that Pierce became a towering success in Internet Marketing. Gurus Mike Filsaime and Rich Schefren have both cited him among the key influences in their careers, and Willie Crawford named him as one of his three Direct/Internet Marketing heroes (the other two are Dan Kennedy and Jay Abraham). Pierce is a charismatic speaker who has inspired probably thousands of people in the audiences of dozens of seminars around the world. People respond to his warm, bear-hugging style, and say it makes them feel as though they, too, can succeed…that they if they can learn from their failures, visualize success and believe in themselves—and work hard, of course—they can change their lives as he's changed his.

These days, Pierce is far from broke, and has all the insurance he needs, so he could probably have that bullet taken out now if he wanted to. Yet he leaves it in there as a reminder of those days before he learned the secret: don't expect failure.

# Show & Tell

One of the great copywriting gurus (who shall remain nameless) once remarked that "Internet Marketers are a bunch of incestuous cannibals." Well, he's right. Some Internet Marketers do borrow a little too liberally from their fellow Internet Marketers, and they do seem to survive largely by helping to build up the demand for each other's products. He's also wrong. The gurus in this book—him included—may rely on each other but not in a sycophantic way. Their actual relationships vary, but there's a long list of roles they play in each other's businesses: cheerleader, advice columnist, motivator, friendly competitor, partner, critic, sympathizer, friend—and many more. But one of the most important roles they each play is mentor.

Many, if not most, have acted as mentors for up-and-coming Internet Marketers. Some of them offer their expertise in a one-on-one coaching scenario or through one-on-few avenues like live seminars or teleseminars. And nearly all of them have been informal mentors through their eBooks and other products. Take Terry Dean, the pizza-dude-turned-Internet Marketer/minister who was part of that second wave of pioneers—the ones who had only a few signposts from those who had gone before. Dean used them along with his own sense of direction to make his way in the wilds of Internet Marketing, and along the way he discovered that he truly enjoyed and had a talent for teaching. One newbie he took under his wing was the Millionaire Magician himself, Randy Charach. When Charach released his *Niche Magic* product, Dean was the first (and one of the best known) to promote it as an affiliate to his list. He also called and emailed Charach the day of the launch, every hour or so, to help him tweak the offer in real time.

On another occasion, Charach and Dean were at a Ron LeGrande event in Jacksonville, Florida, chatting about a joint venture Charach was doing with Joe Vitale. Dean glanced over at what Charach was working on and said gently, "So, is that your headline?" For the next two hours Dean worked through the basics of a sound sales letter piece by piece, and that became the foundation for much of Charach's current copywriting.

For some Internet Marketers, teaching and mentoring may be a way of giving back—not necessarily to the very people who helped along the way but to others who might still need a little guidance. One Internet Marketer who turned to teaching very early in his online career feels he owes a great debt to many offline marketers he never even met.

Yanik Silver had been in business for himself since before college. He started out working for his father, who brought his family to the U.S. from Moscow when Yanik was only two-and-a-half years old. The father had $156 dollars in his pocket and far fewer English words in his vocabulary. When his son was fourteen, the elder Silver was fired, but refused to be discouraged; he took the entrepreneurial route and began selling medical products and services—and put the younger Silver to work in "marketing." Actually, the young man wasn't *in* marketing—he *was* marketing. His first job was doing telemarketing, pitching latex gloves to dentists, who snapped them up to prevent becoming infected by the mysterious "new" illness that dominated the headlines and medical pages, AIDS, as well as Hepatitis-C and other diseases that might be transmitted. He made a small salary, but the real rewards—although he probably didn't realize it at the time—were the knowledge and experience he gained.

At age sixteen, Silver started making cold calls to doctors and dentists. When he was about seventeen, a doctor client of his gave him a Jay Abraham tape that changed his selling tactics almost immediately. Why do cold calls when he could do marketing first, and then only call on people who showed an interest? It was a huge revelation. Direct marketing became a passion of his, and he started studying the works of anyone with something to say about mail-order advertising, advertising, copywriting and other components of direct mail. Of course at that age he had other...passions...as well. It's just that when his friends weren't around, instead of popping in a CD of the Goo Goo Dolls or Stone Temple Pilots, he popped in a CD of Jay Abraham, Ted Nicholas or—his personal favorite then—Earl Nightingale. Silver credits his sound foundation in direct marketing to Nightingale's advice: "If you want to become an expert, you read about one subject for one hour per day for three years. If you want to become a world expert, you read about that subject one hour a day for five years." Silver went Nightingale one better, "What would happen if I read about one subject for two or three hours a day for that long?"

As he learned more, Silver branched out. Still offline, he got into Information Marketing, selling a large manual to doctors on how to grow their practices. Talk about a niche product: at first his clients were mainly dermatologists. Then he added plastic surgeons and ophthalmologists. The more contacts he made, the more interested he became in in-person training, and he began doing one-on-one consulting. By July of 1999 he was doing so well, earning from ten to twelve thousand a month, that he couldn't keep up with two jobs, and he resigned from his father's business. He kept up with his own business, full time, while he attended one of the top 25 business schools in the country, full time.  His business earned him $50,000 or $60,000 a year while he worked on his B.S. in marketing. Silver has joked that degree was just that—B.S.—and that he learned more from his marketing tapes and CDs and from running his own business than he ever learned at college.

Meanwhile, he still didn't have so much as an email address online. From what little he'd seen, it appeared that the big businesses on the Internet were either get-rich-quick schemes or porn sites, and he had no interest in getting involved in either of those. Then he noticed a few names popping up over and over, like Ken Evoy and Marlon Sanders, who were selling eBooks. Silver was fascinated at the thought that these two were selling information, and it cost them absolutely nothing to deliver it. Still, he was hesitant to buy anything online just yet, so he waited until something turned up in print. The first one he saw was Evoy's *Make Your Site Sell*. That convinced him to keep going, and several months later he bought a handful of eBooks, including one from Sanders. What he learned was that the Internet was the perfect direct response medium because it allowed you to get results so quickly: you could test headlines, test new sites, change your copy, and, without waiting for weeks, see what was effective. He adopted the model of the direct response sales letter, and continued honing the copywriting skills he had first developed as a young teen writing ads and letters for his father's business. Some of the ads he wrote for his father eight or nine years ago are still pulling business into the shop to this day, even though they are marketing very complicated pieces of medical equipment, things that before had never been sold any other way except face to face. Silver readily names his copywriting mentors, most of whom he never met: Ted Nicholas, Dan Kennedy, Gary Halbert, Maxwell Sackheim, David Ogleby, John Caples, and Claude Hopkins.

Silver had determined from his studies that a successful working model would be a direct sales letter tied to an affiliate program that would drive traffic to his site. Of course, he didn't have the site yet. He didn't even have a product yet. Operating on the maxim that the type of questions you ask determines the answers you get, he mulled over how he might create an automatic money-making web site that earned money while he slept, wasn't just another eBook, and provided something really valuable that people would be eager to buy. No ideas were forthcoming.

Then, just after Y2K, Silver sat up in bed. Around three in the morning he nudged his wife. "Hey, Missy! Wake up! *InstantSalesLetters.com*!" Missy denied this ever took place, but according to Silver she was less than enthusiastic, and said "Oh, God, Yanik...please go back to bed!" then rolled over and went back to sleep. Although not usually one to ignore her advice, Silver did the opposite. He got out of bed and registered the domain name right then. First thing in the morning he started putting together sales letter templates for all sorts of businesses from manufacturing to retail to service (he later added information marketing). He started with the letters he had written for his father's business, tailoring them to other industries, as well as other letters he wrote from scratch.

The product launched in February 2000 without the fanfare and hullabaloo that accompanies today's product launches. But it did get one important mention. Before Silver was ready to accept orders, the product got a mention in Joe Vitale's eZine. Almost instantly the orders began arriving in his inbox, three of them even before Silver woke up that first morning. At $19.95 each, the orders were hardly record breaking, but Silver was as excited as if he'd won the lottery. In a way, he had: his first product was a success. The first month brought in $1,800. The second month brought in almost twice that. Other Internet Marketers began asking about his affiliate program, which he had planned but not created until he knew the product was really going to sell. He calculated that the first month after he launched his affiliate program he made a 138 percent return on investment. By the third month, it had grown to $7,800, then $9,200 the next month. From the outside he looked like an overnight success, as though "this Yanik Silver kid" had dropped online from a parallel dimension—almost no one had heard of him—and people clamored to hear how he had gone from no product to a must-have product in such a short time. That's when he started teaching Internet Marketing. He was barely in his twenties.

By the time Ken McCarthy asked him to speak at a Ron LeGrand seminar in 2002, Silver had already proven he wasn't a "one-hit wonder" by releasing two other successful products, *Autoresponder Magic* and *Million Dollar Emails*. He also revealed that he was about to launch a new product, *Instant Internet Profits*, and took in a few thousand dollars in advance orders, telling people he wouldn't charge them until the product actually shipped. In actual fact, the product existed only as an outline in his head, but with that sort of incentive it wasn't long before it hit the market and eventually became one of Silver's hallmark products.

Silver had spoken several times before at very small events, but this was the first time he would be up on a stage in front of more than a hundred people, most of them complete strangers. One of his most vivid memories of that show is standing nervously while someone attached a microphone to him and thinking, "God, I hope I don't throw up out there." But it wasn't long before it became almost second nature, standing in front of a group and just talking naturally about how his products went from concept to reality. It was another form of teaching.

So was his Apprentice program. Silver keeps an "Idea Notebook" in which he jots down ideas about new products or marketing methods. For his Apprentice program (and he's adamant that people know it existed before the Donald Trump television show of the same name), Silver charged $14,500 per person for a twelve-person class. The first person to apply and get accepted into the program got to choose one of the ideas in the notebook first, the second got to choose next, and so on. Then Silver and the "apprentice" would develop the idea together—

and share the revenue, with Silver earning a 12 percent royalty on each product that started with his idea. It was learning by doing, and a sound way for many of his apprentices to earn back their program fee in less time than it might if they just attended a workshop, then went off alone to develop a product.

By the way, not all those people remained strangers. One of the things you notice when you begin hanging around with other Internet Marketers is that we seem to form unusually strong bonds among ourselves. We are part of our own little microniche. People know a bit about marketing, a bit about the Internet, a bit about buying things online, but it would never cross the average person's mind that that there is such as an industry as Internet Marketing or—a subniche even of that—Information Marketing. Many of us have attended multiple shows, as it's an accepted fact that you can gain as much from the networking with other Internet Marketers as you can from the lectures and workshops. And after a while, friendships form. When you go to your first seminar, it's pretty much the same for everyone: you feel a little intimidated by these people making millions of dollars, people with well known names and a comfortable ease among one another, and maybe you hang back or strike up a conversation with another relative unknown. Next thing you know, *you* are the person making millions of dollars, a well known name, and you feel comfortable with everyone there. Silver, for example, has a tightly knit little group of trusted friends, including John Reese, Jeff Walker, Jeff Johnson, Frank Kern, and Jeff Mulligan.

Corey Rudl used to be one of Silver's closest friends. The two of them were both "thrill junkies," given to adventures such as a Baja racing, bungee jumping, running with the bulls in Pamplona, taking a zero-G flight, skydiving. They had been planning a trip to Russia to fly MiG jets when Rudl, as most people know by now, was killed in a racing accident in June 2005. Below,

Corey's father John discusses the accident that claimed his son's life:

> I read a couple of comments on the Internet, something to the effect that he was only an amateur driver on a racetrack, so possibly it was to be expected. Let me assure you he was an outstanding driver who raced against professionals and won. He also won first-place overall in the 2002 Vancouver Molson Indy sports car event.
>
> Unfortunately, he was not driving when this accident occurred, and if he were, I believe this tragedy wouldn't have happened. The newspapers did not tell the whole story. The local sports car club had rented the racetrack for the day for their car owners to run laps, not race. In other words, they would put a few cars on the track at a time and they would practice driving skills by running against the clock.
>
> Corey had taken a drive with a fellow driver to see how the Porsche handled, as his car was malfunctioning. They were coming down the straightaway at high speed when another car that was miscued came out of the pits right in front of them and they had to swerve violently in order to miss that car. That's what caused the loss of control of the Porsche. They skidded across a grass strip and hit a concrete barrier at high speed and Corey was killed instantly as the car hit the concrete barrier on the passenger side.
>
> —*John Rudl on remembercorey.com*

We've all met colleagues and mentors who turned into friends, and although every guru is hardly on a speed-dial basis with every other guru, and we sometimes have our differences over techniques and tools and what's right, there's one thing we do agree on: going to shows is important.

In 2004 Silver held his first seminar called "Yanik's 30th Birthday Bash." It differed from many internet-marketing-only seminars in two ways: one, with attendance at well over 500 it was (unofficially) the "biggest" to date; and two, you couldn't just buy a ticket and show up. Instead, attendees donated $50 to the Make-a-Wish Foundation, a nonprofit organization that grants wishes to children with life-threatening medical conditions. The seminar ended up directing $25,000 into the organization's coffers. (Silver made nothing on that seminar, although he did charge for the optional workshop on the third day.) For the cause, some of Silver's well known (Corey Rudl, Marlon Sanders) and unknown (Bill Glazer, Janice Weitzer) friends agreed to speak. Silver has a reputation for combining fun with learning. At his "birthday party" (the event was held in January for logistical reasons although his birthday actually falls in August), Mickey Mouse came and sang "Happy Birthday." There was cake, and everyone got a "goody bag."

Silver has long valued veterans who are experts in Information Marketing and Direct Marketing but who remain low profile.  These are the experts who prefer to hear  new ideas directly from the new sources than to attend the major seminars where there is a constant rotation of speakers who turn up again and again and whose talks attendees may already have heard. The success of that Birthday Bash inspired the "Underground Online Seminars," with its "spy" theme; it features people who aren't the "usual suspects" but the ones out there making millions online but flying under the radar, so to speak.

The spy themes are incredibly entertaining, although at one seminar I learned something about the importance of learning the rules and following them. Let me tell you a little story:

I was in D.C. for an "Underground Online Seminar," which Yanik had done up with an Austin Powers theme making every attendee a "secret agent" and using props like life-size cutouts of Mike Myers as Doctor Evil and Austin Powers. Show personnel dressed in groovy clothes, and during breaks we were treated to clips from the movie. Yanik even raffled off a Mini Cooper. But the high point was (or, in my case, should have been) the presence of Vern Troyer, who Yanik had hired to reprise his role as Mini Me and sign autographs and have his picture taken with attendees. At some point, Yanik discussed the protocol for the appearance, discussing the when and where of the signings and photos.

Unfortunately I was not in the room at the time.

All went well until just after the photo shoot. Most people had left the area, so I figured it would be a great time to ask Troyer if he would personalize a photo as a gift for someone. He wrote on it, "You da man!" and signed his name.

I said, "No, YOU da man!" So far, so good.

He smiled. "No, I'm just *me*."

I couldn't help myself. Here I was, towering over a cinematic icon, an actor with a cult following to die for. I honestly thought he would find it funny when I said, "No, you're MINI me!"

Dead silence. Troyer leaned back in his chair, dangling the photo just out of my reach. "You want this?"

I said, "Yes, of course." I didn't have a clue what was wrong, but I knew *something* was.

"What's my name?" he asked.

Thank goodness I said Vern.

With a glower, he gave me the photo, along with a warning—telling me what I would have known had I been in the room during the earlier briefing. "Don't EVER call me THAT again!"

I respected his wishes. After all, I've seen the movies and I know what he—I mean, what the character he plays—can do.

# CHAPTER **7**

∙∙∙∙∙∙∙∙∙∙∙∙∙∙∙∙∙∙∙∙∙∙∙∙∙∙∙∙∙∙∙∙∙∙∙∙∙∙∙∙∙∙∙∙∙∙∙∙∙∙∙∙

## Rhyme and Reason:
### *Focus Your Sites*

# Rhyme and Reason:
## FOCUS YOUR SITES

*A powerful global conversation has begun. Through the Internet, people are discovering and inventing new ways to share relevant knowledge with blinding speed. As a direct result, markets are getting smarter—and getting smarter faster than most companies.*

So began the introduction to a seminal work written in 1999 by four long-time Internet users—an engineer, a consultant, an advertising veteran and a high-tech marketer—that delivered a call to action to businesses everywhere. *The Cluetrain Manifesto: The End of Business as Usual* challenged the old paradigm in which "business" and "buyer" were two distinct entities engaged in nothing more than commerce. Markets, the authors maintained, are not transactions between demographic sectors but conversations between human beings, and the Internet represents a sort of high-tech flashback to the days when people met face-to-face not just to exchange money for goods but to exchange "information, opinions, perspectives, dissenting arguments, and humorous asides." The nature of the Internet "subverts hierarchy": hyperlinks allow users to follow their own paths of thought, not the sequential paragraphing of a glossy corporate brochure; small-town general stores can compete with mega-retailers with equal potential for suc-

**209**

cess; "talking down" to prospects is instant commercial suicide; left unrestricted, intranets can allow entry-level employees to be heard right along with vice-presidents and CEOs; people no longer automatically equate publicity with reality; and brand loyalty is only as strong as the human relationship between the trading parties. The company and product are not just what the marketing department claims but what you actually know from talking with Marge in customer service, Ron in accounting, Steve in engineering, and Kathy, your neighbor who works in human resources.

The people who "signed on" to the *Cluetrain Manifesto* came from everywhere: Fortune 500 companies and mom-and-pop shops; major advertising agencies and one- or two-person design studios; publishers, editors, journalists and early bloggers; engineers, webmasters, independent techno-enthusiasts and consultants; and individuals from every field from law enforcement to social work to academia to archaeology. While many people pooh-poohed the concept, preferring to think strictly in terms of the old MBA models and traditions, the idea of the market as conversation had a profound effect on the direction the technology traveled, right down to the fact that it is still not owned by commercial conglomerates (unlike phone services, cable television, print media and many other modes of communication). The trend has been toward what the media like to call "Web 2.0," which is just a catchy name for listening to both sides of the conversation.

What effect has that had on Internet Marketing, and information marketing in particular? Without being aware of it, many Internet Marketers have been succeeding and failing according to how well they grasp the idea of market as conversation: sites that simply promote products lose ground to sites with rich, engaging, ever-changing content—not "generated copy"—which fits well with the *Cluetrain* premise. Here's an excerpt from Chapter Three, "Talk is Cheap," written by then Sun Microsystems engineer Rick Levine:

> In the same way we distinguish personal attention from inattention, we can tell the difference between a commercial pitch and words that come when someone's life animates their message. Try snipping paragraphs of text from press releases and a few pieces of printed person-to-person e-mail. Shuffle the paper slips. Hand the pile to your office-mate, your spouse, or your next-door neighbor. Can they sort them? Of course they can, in short order. People channel from their hearts directly to their words. That's voice. It comes of focus, attention, caring, connection, and honesty of purpose. It is not commercially motivated, isn't talk with a vested interest. Talk is cheap. The value of our voices is beyond mere words. The human voice reaches directly into our beings and touches our spirits.
>
> Voice is how we can tell the difference between people, committees, and bots. An e-mail written by one person bears the tool marks of their thought processes. E-mail might be employee-to-employee, customer-to-customer or employee-to-customer, but in each case it's person-to-person. Voice, or its lack, is how we tell what's worth reading and what's not. Much of what passes for communication from companies to customers is washed and diluted so many times by the successive editing and tuning done by each company gatekeeper that the live-person hints are lost.
>
> Authenticity, honesty, and personal voice underlie much of what's successful on the Web.... Nascent Web publishing efforts have their genesis in a burning need to say something, but their ultimate success comes from people wanting to listen, needing to hear each other's voices, and answering in kind.

The bottom line: if all you do is sell, sell, sell, you might make a quick buck, but you won't make a loyal or even interested client, and you won't be around to make more bucks in the future. On the other hand, if you share a real passion of yours with people, they will listen. And if you have a product, those listeners will consider buying it. Doing something for twenty years and then taking it online certainly qualifies as authenticity. And making millions by sharing what you know with customers means that everyone wins.

## Abracadabra: Making Millions Appear

You can just imagine the Kodak moments from Randy Charach's family album. Here's Randy as a toddler waving a rubber spoon as a wand...now as a grade school kid in a cape trying to make his homework disappear... now at the high school prom in tails, white gloves and a top hat (with or without rabbit inside), his date dressed in sequins and tights. A showman from the beginning, Charach went straight from high school graduation in 1981 to his dream job: professional magician. He was a natural on stage, and before long the Vancouver native became one of the most sought-after entertainers in the country as a comedy magician, mentalist and motivational speaker. Beginning at age twenty, he also did a six-year stint as Ronald McDonald, donning the red shoes and wig and—after rigorous training on Ronald's voice, mannerisms, and effusive style—visiting pediatric wards in area hospitals and attending events related to the Ronald McDonald House (homes-away-from-home for the families of chronically ill children). Not content to be just technically perfect, Charach immersed himself in studies that could help him become an even greater performer, from body language to hypnosis to personality profiling. He loved the spotlight, and the spotlight loved him: he performed with such well known personalities as Hootie and the Blowfish, Henny Youngman, Richard Dean Anderson, Tony Curtis, and John Travolta.

But that's not why he's known today as the "Millionaire Magician." He began adding that dimension to his life in 2001 when he got involved with the Internet after years of not having so much as an email address. The only marketing he knew was gained through experience in promoting himself as an entertainer and marketing the various offline businesses he owned such as an entertainment agency and a toy company. Still, he knew that his solid performance and winning style couldn't be the only reasons he had no trouble finding steady bookings and making money, and he speculated that it had a lot to do with his concerted efforts to get his name out, to collect testimonials and send out letters, and to find different ways of getting people's attention. It occurred to him that small as his niche might be—marketing for magicians could even be called a micro-niche—there were others out there who could benefit from his expertise. So why not write a book?

Charach went online and started searching different ways of publishing books. He had been thinking along the lines of self-publishing when he came across the concept of doing an eBook. That led him to the sites of many of the big-name Internet Marketers at the time, and ended up buying products from Corey Rudl, Marlon Sanders, Terry Dean, and Yanik Silver. Studying the offline teachings of people like Dan Kennedy, he put the pieces together and saw that most of the things the successful people were doing online were very similar to the things he had been doing offline for the past twenty years.

Charach wanted to promote his book online and was undaunted by the fact that he had no experience at all with Internet Marketing. He was worried about the fact that he really couldn't type.

What he could do, and do well, was speak. He remembered something Terry Dean's material had mentioned, and bought voice recognition software. For about a week solid, he "wrote" his book out loud, putting in intense ten- and twelve-hour days. It was a tightly focused book written specifically about marketing for magicians and variety entertainers. No magic tricks, no stage pointers, just marketing for entertainers. *Secrets of a Millionaire Magician* was Charach's first online product—and his first unqualified success. It sold because he wrote about something he knew intimately and cared about passionately, and he spoke directly to others who cared about the same things. The market held a conversation.

Charach still prowled around other Internet Marketers' sites, and on the site of a fellow public speaker, Tom Antion, noticed a Carl Galletti seminar coming up and decided to try to make a reservation. He reached Galletti in person and was about to ask about a buying ticket when Galletti asked for his name. When Charach told him, Galletti said, "Hey, the Millionaire Magician!" Surprised that the man knew of him, Charach asked if Galletti was a magician. "No, but I liked your copy so much I almost bought your product anyway." Before Charach could ask about tickets, Galletti surprised him again. "I have this Internet Marketing seminar coming up in Las Vegas. Think you could come onstage for maybe five or ten minutes and just tell your story?"

It was magical. Charach was in.

At Galletti's seminar, Charach met a lot of people whose names had become familiar to him—Terry Dean, Marlon Sanders, Armand Morin, Joel Christopher, Frank Garon—and discovered that the mere fact that he had accomplished something online opened a lot of doors for him. Although the whole experience was a little intimidating at first, Charach found the others warm and friendly, and began relationships that have lasted until today. That event led to other speaking engagements— Armand Morin's "BigSeminar," Ted Ciuba's "Think and Grow Rich" seminar. He'd definitely pulled a lucrative career out of his hat. Still, it wasn't long before Charach realized that although he'd made a few hundred thousand dollars in his first few months, those other guys were making some serious money.

Galletti suggested that Charach create a new product that used *Millionaire Magician* as a case study. The result was *Niche Magic*. That book explained step by step how people could take something they love and turn it into a successful product by finding others who share that passion. That became Charach's winning strategy: developing niche products and forming relationships with others who share his interests. For example, he enjoyed playing a little poker now and then (and no, he doesn't use magic to make the "right" cards appear. Really), though he was hardly an expert. After he'd been playing for a year and learned to love the game, he could see that the other players still knew things he didn't. Figuring that there were others out there who enjoyed the game but could use a few winning strategies that any average player could pull off, Charach went to the local casino and interviewed the people who were cleaning his clock time after time at the poker table. From those interviews, he produced yet another niche product, *How to Win at Texas Hold 'em*. In this case he didn't know the secrets, but his fascination led him to ask the experts, and that gave the book the authenticity that made it connect with its audience.

Not everybody does magic. But everybody knows something. Charach was just another regular guy with the drive to succeed. But he'd be the first to tell you that there's a lot of work involved, and a lot of pushing your sleeves up and getting into areas where you may not be fully conversant or comfortable, as in this story:

> I have some sound equipment that I use to record interviews on the phone or in person in my office, equipment I got from Mike Stewart, the audio guy who worked with so many Internet Marketers before he started speaking himself. He's a super guy. I told him, "Mike, I'm really dumb when it comes to this kind of stuff. I'm going to be a pain in the ass. I'm not sure if you want to sell this stuff to me." Mike assured me that he was very patient, and would be

there for me any time. He was. I had set the equipment up and it was working, but something just wasn't right. Things just didn't sound as clear as I thought they should, so for about the ninth time that month I called Mike and said, "I'm sorry, man. I've got to go through this with you another time." Mike said, "No problem. Let's start at the beginning. Right now, what's in front of you?" I said, "The microphone." He asked me to describe what I was looking at, so I did: "It's the microphone I got from you. It's sitting on my desk in a little stand. I'm ready to talk into it." But he says, "No, what exactly are you looking at?" I described it, and he made a very helpful suggestion. Turns out I was speaking into the wrong part.

In Chapter Four of *The Cluetrain Manifesto*, Doc Searls and David Weinberger talk about the industrial revolution as "an interruption of the human conversation." Sure, goods became cheaper and more plentiful, but along the way we lost the personal interchanges of markets past. The Internet brings that back. The authors use the example of a woman in the market for a new computer. Thanks to the Internet, she may go straight to a particular manufacturer's site and even to the local computer store, but it's very likely that before she buys she'll have more than one conversation about it, soliciting opinions and advice from other web sites, newsgroups, blogs, and user forums. She'll email her friends, family, colleagues, and maybe people inside the company who makes the computer.

The authors also mention Amazon.com, where not only can you buy books (and a zillion other things), but you can see reviews and comments from people who have read the book. Many others have since come to recognize the value of this "Web 2.0" interactivity and have added it to their sites.

In 1997, the Internet was abuzz with the exciting "new" idea of Push Technology—seller-created content delivered not by request of the user but sent to seller-specified users at a time dictated by the seller. The rationale was that the Web had simply become so overwhelming that we average users needed someone to tell us what to read and where to shop. The advocates of this (and *Wired* magazine devoted an eleven-page cover story to the glories of Push) were convinced that the whole direction of the Internet would—and should—change. *They were wrong.* Push Technology failed because it stopped the conversation. It turned the Internet into a television set. People don't want information pushed at them; they want to pull it out themselves.

By developing his micro-niche sites, Randy Charach let people pull exactly what they wanted from the Internet. Not generic marketing information or success stories of magicians but marketing for magicians. Not cards or even poker but "Texas Hold 'em." The Internet Marketers who succeed are the ones who "get it." That's actually what inspired the title of that seminal book, by the way. *The Cluetrain Manifesto* came from the words of a "veteran of a firm freefalling out of the Fortune 500" who said that the reason for the company's downhill spiral was painfully obvious to everyone, apparently, except the business-as-usual managers: "The clue train stopped there four times a day for ten years, and they never took delivery."

## Think Big

When you're staring at a pile of bills, recognizing debt collectors on the caller I.D., and searching for change in the couch cushions, it's hard to imagine yourself thinking of making an extra $500 or $1,000 a month as a sign of failure. But failure is relative. One guru whose product launches routinely hit six figures inside of a week once said that if he ever had a launch bring in just $10,000 he would probably have to be talked down off the ledge of a tall building.

With the number of websites growing at a dizzying rate, the gurus realized that the difference between success and failure could be the ability to specialize—to find (or create) a niche. And for most Internet Marketers a niche market would be one that focuses in on a subset of a larger market: not all people who love to fish, but fly fishing in the Rocky Mountains; not all information marketers, but information marketers looking for a guide to selling eBooks by accepting online payments; not just motorcycle enthusiasts, but fans of the Vincent Black Shadow. Yet at least one guru chose his specialty almost purely on the basis of profit margins—a strategy that would send most people into the poorhouse, but that catapulted him into the highest tax bracket in just a few short months.

I knew I was about to interview a different sort of financial mind when my interview with Jeff Mills started out like this: "Back in 1977, I understood the concept of leverage for the first time when I was sitting in a tree house about thirty feet up in my front yard." He wasn't talking about the pulley system/dumbwaiter, either. Mills and his neighborhood buddies used to get together in the tree house every weekend and do Mad Libs and other kid-type things, then trek over to Mr. Toy to buy candy. They learned early on that they could buy a lot more candy if they pooled it all together. At age seven, Mills may not have known the word leverage, but he understood the concept.

Amazingly, he didn't start out on Wall Street. Instead, in 1999 he was working as a youth pastor, earning about $32,000 a year with not much hope of ever earning any more. Debt weighed heavily on him from seminary and Bible College tuition, and from making some unwise choices with his credit cards. Mills resigned himself to never again being debt-free unless he won the lottery or "figured out some super-Jedi investment technique." He knew his best option would be to take on a second job, but the ministry took most of his energy and even more of his time. Though he loved the work, the ministry also

**218**

left his home life a little chaotic, too: his wife went to one church, he belonged to another, and they shuttled their three-year-old daughter between the two; he had his meetings, his wife had hers, and sometimes it seemed as though they saw each other only long enough to say good night and fall exhausted into bed.

He'd heard his friends and parishioners talking about the Internet, and people who were making money online, and thought it was at least worth a shot. Not knowing much about it, Mills signed up for the first thing that sounded promising, a program called *AllAdvantage*. The premise was simple: sign up for free, and *AllAdvantage* would put a banner on your website. Every time you clicked on that banner, they paid you ten cents, seven cents, three cents, or a percentage of a penny. The first day Mills sat at the computer for sixteen hours, clicking the banner every chance he could. He made $1.87. Clearly that was not the way to pay off his debts.

Mills grew up with a Commodore 64, and enjoyed being on the computer, so he didn't let himself get discouraged. He just dug deeper. Like many Internet Marketers, he quickly discovered the idea of selling other people's products as an affiliate marketer. And, like many others, he had no list of his own. He began with safe lists, which were very big at the time, and also mailed to the occasional message board or database. He knew it was just "hit or miss" marketing—throw it against the wall and see what sticks—but he didn't know of any better way until 2003 when he went to his first event, the "BigSeminar", held that year in Orlando, Florida. There, Mills learned that his first mistake was in not at least holding onto the names he did manage to get. Each time he had to redo everything, and he was barely breaking even. Not surprisingly, one of the biggest lessons he learned from Jonathan Mizel that very first seminar was this: Build your list! One lesson he didn't learn, though, was the importance of live events as a way to network with other Internet Marketers. Being incredibly shy, Mills spent a lot of time hunkered down in his room, thinking that all the others there knew each other and were practiced pros. He did meet and spend some time talking with Paul Colligan and Jeff Mulligan—two people he partnered up with three years later.

Mills made a few moves that year that figured heavily in his success. At the "BigSeminar," he bought a copywriting course and learned how to write pretty good copy— good enough that he could get the job done. He also signed up for a mentoring program that cost him $500, but he then joined on as a reseller and began earning $400 for every person he signed up. That was when he caught onto the fact that it takes just as much work to sell a ten-dollar product as it does to sell a hundred-dollar product. At first he was skeptical that anyone would buy "high-ticket products," especially from him as an unknown, considering that even he had debated for days about whether or not to do it. But he did buy it, and by the next day he had five people introduced to *Mentors in Motion*; four of them ended up buying, and he made $1,200 in one day. That's almost fourteen times what he made as a pastor in the same amount of time. Over the course of a year, he earned $80,000 just on that product alone. That let him devote more quality time—and less quantity—to his youth ministry. His exact thoughts were "Ok, the Lord is giving me the vehicle I need to get out of ministry now, come home to my family, do this and sell this product."

Mills believed 100 percent in the Val Smyth's *Mentors in Motion* product, which taught him the foundations of marketing. He even added a little spin to create his own system, and did very well with it, especially when he realized that if he could sell a $500 product, he could probably sell a $1,200 product. Then he sold a $2,500 product. Today he sells an $11,000 product—*coastalvacations.com*—on which he earns a $6,500 commission. Mills found his niche: big-ticket products.

One variation on the big-ticket niche is live events. In October 2006, Mills hosted his first seminar, held in Minneapolis. Attending multiple "BigSeminars" and taking Armand Morin's seminar coaching program gave him the background to set up a live event, as did meeting John Childers, who teaches people public speaking and "platinum selling," which is selling through talking and teaching. Part of his reason for hosting an event was that it gave him an opportunity to bring together many of the greatest speakers available; unbelievably, everyone he invited said yes, even though he knew only a few of them personally. The attendance was only a quarter of what Mills expected, but those who did attend apparently found a lot to like: one attendee began generating so much business—over a thousand phone calls per month to his office—that his employees couldn't handle the volume. It was also the first time his mom and dad got to see and really understand what he did for a living. He has since perfected this niche and it has become his "super-jedi investment technique." It also turned out to be something that he had done all along, just in a different form. As a youth pastor, he taught kids to follow the right path. He now teaches the teachers how to speak more effectively at live events and thus sell their products more successfully from the platform. Not a bad investment, indeed.

## Renaissance Man

The term I've run across many times in relation to Rich Schefren is "serial entrepreneur." He's one of the few gurus who has racked up kudos (and big profits) both offline and online, beginning with his first major success at the age of twenty-two. At first glimpse you might think his style runs counter to the typical find-a-niche strategy that most gurus tout, but in fact he does carve a niche, expand it, and finally dominate—and then move on to another niche. It's not shotgun marketing, it's

Gatling AK–47 gun marketing: dependable, easily loaded, with powerful, rapid sequential fire.

Between his junior and senior years at Case Western Reserve University, Schefren went to work for Arthur Anderson. There he was steeped in the Anderson philosophy that the best consultants didn't have to be accounting or business majors, they only had to be extremely intelligent and adept at mastering complex concepts. A brilliant accounting major himself, Schefren spent two months at the company's St. Charles, Illinois, training facility soaking up "the most comprehensive training that this $6 billion-a-year company had to offer," every day, all day. Then he joined the elite consultants in the Strategic Planning Division.

At the end of the year, Schefren returned to Case Western to finish his degree. Then two semesters into his senior year, he got a doleful phone call from his father suggesting that nothing short of a miracle could save the family clothing business from having to close down its door for good. The past year's losses had totaled over a million dollars. Schefren made his father a proposition: if his father gave him 50 percent ownership in the store, Schefren would make it profitable in six months; any losses that the store incurred on his watch after those six months, he would reimburse his father out of his own previous earnings.

Antique Boutique, despite its prime Soho address, was running $1.5 million in the red. Sure, it pulled in $1.5 million in sales, but its break-even point was twice that. Yet three years later, the cash registers rung in more than $6.5 million, with a quarter of that being pure profit. How did a retail newbie manage to do what experienced managers could not? Schefren carved a niche, expanded it, and then dominated it. While his competitors were trying to win market share by constantly shuffling price, brands, selection, customer service, return policies and every other possible variable, Schefren studied the market. What he saw was a throng of young people much like himself, techno-music club goers and twenty-something urban hipsters. He turned Antique Boutique into something more than a place to buy new and second-hand clothes; he made it a must-see, must-have retail destination. The following comes from a *Crain's* article in February 1996 about the revitalized hip clothing Mecca:

> Schefren had another new idea. He modernized the look of the store and narrowed his selection of vintage clothes to the best period pieces available. He then became the largest supplier of vintage Levi's and even developed a private label collection that copied the look of some of the older clothes… Schefren has transformed the store's rags to riches. Last year, this retail neophyte led Antique Boutique to its biggest year; sales more than doubled to $4.5 million. Antique Boutique is now a cutting-edge retailer with new devotees. It draws everyone from young New York club-going tastemakers to high-profile celebrities such as Madonna, Bon Jovi and Eric Clapton.

Not too long after the store had a $7 million year, Schefren gave the business back to his family and returned to Case Western (he graduated summa cum laude). The final chapter of the story in his words: "The store continued on and had a string of record-breaking years—until some genius who took the helm decided to go after a different customer and therefore changed the positioning. Within a year and a half of the change the store was back in the red."

Not surprisingly, the family asked Schefren if he'd return, but by then he was deeply involved with his next niche: hypno-therapy. His success in that business mirrored that of his experience with the clothing store. It started on a whim. With Antique Boutique safely out of the red and skyrocketing in popularity, Schefren found himself getting bored. After seeing an ad in *Time Out New York*, he visited a hypnosis studio to see if it could help him revive his excitement. It did, but not about the clothing business. He left with a new interest—hypnosis—and started Dynamic Changes Hypnosis with an investment of $7,500. Four years later he had multiple locations, hundreds of employees, and $7 million in revenues.

September 11, 2001, changed everything. All the people who used to sign up for sessions to quit smoking or lose weight suddenly decided (at least for a while) that it was a good time to enjoy life in the present and not worry so much about the future. Schefren was fairly certain he wanted to get out of the business anyway, maybe do something online, and while he was casting around for direction, one of the people he'd hired to help him promote his business—Carl Galletti—mentioned that he was holding an Internet seminar and Schefren should think about going. So he flew to Vegas.

Schefren checked into the seminar and listened to the first speaker, Stephen Pierce, truly enjoying what he had to say, and impressed with the facts he used to back up his assertions. At break time Schefren wandered out to the floor and started playing backjack. And playing. And playing. In what seemed like no time at all he had turned $500 into $10,000, and the casino ended up comping his room and drinks and meals. He never went back to the sessions, and although he left with less than the ten grand he'd had for a while, he'd still made considerably more than $500. But to Schefren the real reward was that for the first time in six or eight months, he hadn't been sick with worry about his business. He had a great time, and that "work seminar" turned out to be the best vacation he'd had in years.

Schefren knew then that the challenge and thrill had definitely gone out of the hypnosis business for him and it was time to move on. He decided to take what he knew about the business and develop a program that other hypnosis centers could follow to improve their companies. He then turned his program into an information product. In the first week selling the program online he made $287,000. He had focused on learning from some direct marketing greats—Jay Abraham, Dan Kennedy, Gary Halbert, John Carlton—many of whom he had actually hired to help *him* when he was marketing Dynamic Changes. Over the next two years, through joint ventures and direct marketing, Schefren earned more than $4 million from his online marketing.

Bob Bly encouraged Schefren to get into eBooks, and suggested he read Jim Edwards's book *E-book: Secrets Exposed* as an introduction. Schefren did about five or ten eBooks, some alone and some with partners. Stephen Pierce's talk *had* made an impact, too, and he bought Pierce's book. Not long after, when a well known Internet Marketer steered Schefren into some dead ends, he started looking elsewhere for help, and for a new webmaster. Recalling that Stephen Pierce had a coaching program, Schefren called him one night and joined; he knew that if nothing else, Pierce could recommend a good webmaster. He did: Greg Cesar. The spiritual Pierce and secular Schefren made an unlikely pair of friends, but they did hit it off, and the coaching was a success as well. Stephen had just released *The Whole Truth*, the best selling eBook for a long time, and he was doing the coaching program at the time with big-name Internet Marketer Jonathan Mizel. It was called the *Smart Marketing Coaching Program*, and Schefren signed on for $250 or $300 a month. Schefren and Pierce actually became close friends at the second "BigSeminar." (Schefren had mind-mapped every call during the coaching teleseminar, and showed the notes to Pierce, who responded in his usual brainiac/streetwise style: "Interesting.... What the hell is it?") He also met a number of other Internet Marketers with whom he would later become friends, such as Armand Morin, John Reese, Alex Mandossian and Ryan Deiss. Schefren would walk into a seminar feeling like a stranger and walk out with a list of private email addresses and cell phone numbers; it was heady stuff for someone who had been on the scene just two short years. He soaked up everything he could. At one point he must have seemed a little too earnest, as John Reese drew him aside and cautioned him, saying "Dude, chill out a little bit. You're going to upset everybody if you keep going back to the well too frequently."

Fast forward a few years. Schefren had done multiple successful projects on his own and with other Internet Marketers such as Jay Abraham, Stephen Pierce, John Reese, and Armand Morin. But he found himself working ridiculously long hours just like all of his friends. It puzzled him, since he got into the online world thinking that it would help him automate a lot of what he wanted to do, and would help him maintain personal control over large projects. Yet clearly that was not what was happening. Then he had an epiphany: you can succeed doing everything yourself—for a while—but you can't grow. With the Internet you can leverage technology, but only to maintain. You can't use technology to build another eBook; some human has to get involved at some point. If you don't have employees, there will be problems, since there is only so much you can outsource. Schefren came to the realization that just as he had in the clothing and hypnosis businesses, he needed a staff—he needed to build a company.

That was the genesis of his "YOU slide," a now infamous slide he uses during his presentations. It shows the ugly truth that for most entrepreneurs, the business owns them. The slide itself shows all the different aspects of an Internet Marketing organization and how every post in that organization is filled with "you." He also created a companion piece, a classic mind map showing all the different duties that go into Internet Marketing and how they each siphon off a little bit of your time. It starts with "you" at the root, and branching off are all the things you have to do. It's everything from copywriting and web page design to accounting and list building. Everybody agrees that these are all necessary components, but they look at them individually. When Schefren put them all in one graphic representation, the mind map and the "YOU" slide, it's obvious why some Internet businesses simply can't survive. His message resonated with the people in the room, almost all of whom were successful, established Internet Marketers—Reese, Alex Mandossian, Rob Bell, Mike Filsaime, Jim Edwards—and they knew *exactly* what he was talking about. That launched him on his current successful online career, which is coaching Internet Marketers on how to turbo-charge their businesses—to make them run better, faster, and more efficiently. The main promotional piece was the now-famous (or infamous, depending on your point of view) *Internet Business Manifesto*, and the follow-up *Missing Chapter*, which stated that one of the biggest reasons online businesses fail is that people just jump in thinking they see an opportunity, and don't think things through. They don't pay attention to the words of that other Internet manifesto, which said that "Markets are conversations." If your strategy is to let the market decide what your business should be instead of first listening to what you have and want to say, you will fail. Schefren envisioned a future in which there may be fewer one- and two-person outfits and more organizations with greater numbers of resources and employees—that is, companies. But since the phrase has never applied to him, he certainly wouldn't see it as "business as usual."

## Nitches and Neeshes

Believe it or not, the word niche did not originate from anything related to business or marketing—although these days it is impossible to wander around in either of those two fields without tripping over the word at every turn. It should be pronounced to rhyme with "rich," but if you prefer rhyming it with "quiche," well, go for it. Experts still wrestle over the etymology of the word, but most sources say it comes come the Old French *nicher*, to make a nest, and the Latin *nidus*, nest. It was borrowed to describe a recess or inset in a wall built to hold an object of reverence or beauty. When marketers of every sort discovered the word, they snatched it up and refused to let go, and overuse has turned it into one of those metaphors that's lost its visual anchor. We don't see honored spaces; we see pie charts.

That's a shame, because as Internet usage expands exponentially, so too does the need to differentiate one product, service or organization from another. Most successful Internet Marketers deal in "niche" markets; all successful Information Marketers do. That doesn't mean you have to stay in one pigeonhole forever, only that each product needs to be something that somebody wants. Many gurus, myself included, have made huge leaps from one market to another and done well that way. For example, I fell in love with computers and video games when I was sixteen years old. I combined the two about a decade ago when I co-founded Springer-Span (Hudson the dog was the mascot), which we later renamed *ClassicGames.com* for reasons that should be obvious. It was the Internet's largest selection of java-driven multiplayer games. In the beginning, given the total number of users online, I considered that a fairly narrow focus. But the Internet grew, and the site grew so fast we had to keep subdividing the users (three separate game areas became four, which became six) to keep from frying the servers—between November 17 and December 5 of 1997, the number of registered users jumped from 50,000 to 60,000. Finally it got so big that—oh, darn!—it caught the attention of a bigger company, who bought us out. The site is now Yahoo! Games.

But *ClassicGames.com* was part of a larger business I began in 1995 with my business partner Ken Burge, called InfoMedia, Inc. Our first website was *WorldVillage.com*, a family-friendly portal to software reviews, downloads, chat rooms, forums, online games, contests, newsletters, offers, banner ad exchange programs, email, and a search engine. I am still the (self-appointed) mayor of this cybertown, and my benevolent dictatorship has prohibited the kinds of things wise parents shield their children from, such as violence and pornography. It was and still is a niche product (family-friendly Internet), divided further into even smaller niches. Gamer's Zone, for example, was a kind of WorldVillage version of *ClassicGames.com*. I still operate the site because I still find that there's a market for it, but I certainly haven't restricted myself to that area. I have dozens of sites, including *DealofDay.com*, *SafetySurf.com* and *FamilyFirst. com*, but I am currently best known as an AdSense expert and creator of The Next Internet Millionaire reality show. My best-known niche is people who want to learn to use Google's AdSense to make their websites profitable.

That's the difference between a hobby and an online business: profit. Even if you are truly passionate about something, as I always have been about *WorldVillage. com*, if you plan to devote enormous amounts of time and energy toward your passion you owe it to yourself— and your family and friends—to at least make sure it isn't sabotaging other parts of your life. There are more important rewards than money, but unless you're already sitting on a pile of principal, you need to spend at least a little time earning grocery money. When I first started *WorldVillage.com*, I knew the content would be mostly software reviews and downloads, chat rooms, articles, shopping areas and freebies, and my model was based on free content, with the site financed entirely through advertising. The types of advertising have changed, of course, as new trends come and go, and I've tried everything, I think—that is, everything within the bounds of the law and my conscience. I've used banner ads, affiliate programs, pop-ups, pop-unders, interstitial ads (like commercial breaks before you get to the destination page), floaters, mapped ads, contextual ads, embedded hyperlinks, hover ads, and even—can you believe it?— offline advertising. There's a whole lot of advertising going on out there: the Interactive Advertising Bureau and PriceWaterhouseCoopers LLC reported that Internet advertising in the just the first quarter of 2007 was just under $5 billion. That's right, billion. That's 26 percent higher than the first quarter of the previous year ($4.9 billion, up from $3.8 billion.)

I'm biased, of course, but I really like working with AdSense.

Before you can make money from people visiting your site and from buying your products, you have to get them there in the first place. That's a crucial part of the "marketing" part of Internet Marketing. There is one Internet guru whose presence and product changed the course of the industry. Jeff Walker first started experimenting online in 1990—long before the World Wide Web—using online forums on Genie, CompuServe, Prodigy, and AOL. His passion was trading on the stock market, and he found the Internet to be a valuable source of information and a great way to find other would-be traders and stock-trading communities. In 1994, the first piece of spam he ever received landed in his inbox. Of course, back then it wasn't called spam yet, nor was it even thought of as particularly bothersome. All told, Walker got an email maybe once every two or three weeks, "spam" included. This piece of "unsolicited bulk email" turned out to be the key to Walker's success; like the first dollar any business earns, he could have tacked it up to his wall and pointed at it years later and said, "This is where it all began."

The email featured a promotion of Sheila Danzig's *Turn Your Computer into a Money Machine*, a 3.5-inch floppy that covered the basics of direct marketing and information marketing. It took Walker a week of tense deliberation to decide that he could afford the $99 price tag, but eventually he mailed in his check for the course. It taught him how to sell ads on AOL and CompuServe—how to sell information. The idea appealed to Walker, and it made perfect sense: people have been selling information for eons, after all. The online world made sense to Walker, and despite the fact that he knew almost nothing about how it worked or how it would evolve, he understood that eventually people would be paying a lot of money for all kinds of information online. It would be cheap and easy to produce and would be delivered digitally. An entrepreneur at heart, Walker worked his way through the course, then sat back and smiled, knowing he'd found what he'd been looking for.

Still, while he was a quick study, he was a slow implementer, and it took him two years from when he bought the course in 1994 until he started publishing seriously online. In 1996, he launched an email-based newsletters for day traders, back when hardly anyone knew what day trading even was. He charged $700 a year, a courageous move considering that almost no one was charging *anything* for information online at the time—everyone thought that the Internet and all the information it contained should be free—let alone an amount that high. Randy Cassingham was selling his *thisistrue. com* humor newsletter, though at a substantially lower cost, and another Internet Marketer was selling information about the stock market for $99 a year, but such people were far and few between.

Walker didn't even have a domain registered. His website address was the name of his ISP followed by /~jwalker. With that kind of domain name you could actually get a listing in Yahoo—you didn't need your own dot-com, which around that time would have cost around $200. Walker started his business for $35, the amount he paid for his post office box at Mailboxes, Etc. He already had an ISP connection, a computer, and a free place to park his website, so his five-to-six-page newsletter cost him almost nothing. He built his first list by publishing the newsletter for free before initiating the $700 fee, and by the middle of 1996 he had several web pages with eye-catching charts and graphs, and the traffic starting trickling in. He garnered some media attention, including a mention of the PBS show *Frontline*, that brought in hundreds of new subscribers overnight, and listed his site with all the search engines of the day.

When Walker started charging for his newsletter in 1996, he used an approach that would eventually become part of his most famous offering, *Product Launch Formula*: building anticipation. He began teasing his subscribers, telling them that although he planned to start charging a fee, he was first going to give away some valuable tips and techniques. At the end of the year he sent a six- or seven-page email that served as a sales letter (his first real one ever). His only guide was that $99 floppy and a few materials from other sources on information marketing. He emailed his sales letter, which included instructions on where to send a check or money order for the subscription, and went to bed. Half expecting that nothing would come of the mailing, Walker felt only a little jittery and slept surprisingly well. So the next morning he was shocked when he saw his inbox which held a message from a man in Switzerland who explained that he had mailed his check for $700 to Walker that morning.

The theoretical had become reality. Not only had he made a sale, but he had made a major sale: he had offered quarterly rates for $225, but here was someone—from another country, no less—signing up for the entire year. That first offer netted just $2,000 or $3,000, but it was a subscription, so it did generate renewals. He admits he could have done more for the launch, but there was so much he and his content writer didn't know then about how to do things. The price was right, but Walker hadn't been able to spend anything on advertising. Nevertheless, that first year (and remember, this is only 1996), his cut of the $20,000 or $30,000 in sales was $10,000 or $15,000. Friends and family were astounded since the general consensus until then had been that "Jeff sits around at the computer in the basement all day, wasting his time, probably playing video games...."

Walker followed that launch with another email-based stock market product in 1998, sending it to his growing list. This time he made $35,000 in a week—more than he'd ever made in an entire year before that. The reality took a while to set in. As a consultant working in the stock market, finance, and investing, Walker got to do what he loved and had worked toward all his life, yet he'd never expected success to come from such an unusual venue. He was just doing what he knew best.

And it was an unqualified success: in the summer of 1999 his wife Mary retired, and they bought a house in the mountains. Walker needed to scratch together $70,000 to put a down payment on the new construction, but still hadn't sold his other house. By that time he'd been running his business almost four years and done half a dozen small product launches, and between that experience and his expertise in finance, he knew that the only sensible way to get the cash was to work for it, and he set out to design a new product. This time he planned a serious product launch. It was March 2000, and he needed $70,000 in April to hold onto the new house. He had his list, he had his product, and he had an elaborate rollout plan for his email–based product. In one week he did $106,000—his first six-figure income in seven days. That's when he started to build a reputation for "Six in Seven."

Remember the earlier discussion about how "easy" it was for the pioneers way back when, and how much more difficult it is now to be successful on the Internet? And how the only way the gurus have gotten rich is by selling to each other? Walker is the perfect example of why that is simply not true. First, he didn't do anything with those products he started up in 1996 that couldn't be done now: he wrote a newsletter packed with valuable information, and he sold it to people who wanted that information. Second, he didn't get rich through joint ventures or partnerships but all on his own. And third, he didn't cobble together a "book report" from other Internet marketers and try to palm it off as an in-depth information product aimed at other Internet Marketers; he wrote down what he knew about investing, and he wrote it for the general public. Did he always earn "six in seven?" No. As a matter of fact, he admits that the $106,000 week was his only six-in-seven to date. But he routinely earned $20,000 to $30,000 in a week. That's not chump change.

That doesn't mean that Walker worked all alone in his basement cave making everything up as he went along. A researcher by nature, he sought out others who were doing things online. Many were in his niche, the stock market niche. Others were not. One of the first people he connected with was Paul Myers and the two have been great friends now for more than a decade. Walker also found Ken Evoy and early on bought Evoy's *Make Your Site Sell* product, for which he paid "twenty-seven dollars or fifteen dollars or some insanely low price." He also subscribed to *I-Sales*, a discussion list by John Audet, and bought *Amazing Formula*, a Marlon Sanders product. He went to a few live events, starting with a Jay Abraham seminar that Myers comped him into. All Walker had to do in exchange for his free seminar ticket was write reviews on attendees' websites. These attendees had paid $5,000 to attend, and they expected good content. They weren't disappointed; Walker's reviews impressed people and opened some doors.

Walker reveled in the excitement of live events, going from eight in the morning to midnight, talking into the night with the people he met there. Walker never considered himself an Internet Marketer who sold investment-related products but as an investment consultant who sold products on the Internet. Nevertheless, he'd still tell you that going to live events is the single-most important thing a would-be online entrepreneur can do. They require traveling; they often come with a hefty upfront price tag, and for anyone who's not a natural-born networker they can even be painful. But Walker always viewed live events as another investment. To him, it wasn't just the information he could learn from the speakers, workshops, and panel discussions, and it wasn't even just the contacts and relationships that he'd make that made a live event a worthwhile investment. It was mostly the confidence building he got from being around others who have similar ventures and are enjoying great success. Seeing the dream played out over and over by others helps you dig deep.

When Walker headed off to another event soon after the Abraham seminar, he'd been feeling as though he'd won the lottery, earning almost $300,000 a year. Though still not used to the idea that all his hard work had finally paid off, he was feeling pretty sure of himself. Then he struck up a casual conversation with over lunch with a man who let drop that he was making $100,000 a month. The amount seemed inconceivable. Yet the man was just another attendee, not trying to pitch a product to Walker, and had no reason to lie.

Maybe it was hearing that casual admission of serious profits that put Walker in a different frame of mind, but he always considered that conference as pivotal to his later success. It was 2001, one of Jonathan Mizel's "Boulder Summits." Mizel had been in the business for a year or so before Walker and was already a marketing maven whose success trajectory was steep and still climbing fast. Website technology was exploding. Pop-ups were the popular new technology—"you could rule the world if you put pop-ups on your site"—sequential auto-responders, pay per click, and how to get your site listed at the top of the Yahoo Directory. At that show, Walker met marketer and pay-per-click expert Don Crowther, with whom he became friends, and another Internet Marketer who was doing well but was not yet the superstar he would become: Yanik Silver. Walker met so many others it might be easier to mention who wasn't there, but conversations with or talks by many of them colored his thinking on his upcoming product releases.  He met with or listened to Marlon Sanders, Alex Mandossian, Jim Edwards, Declan Dunn, Corey Rudl, and Ken Giddens.

Just as an aside, I have to say that Ken Giddens was a fascinating guy. Talk about niche markets—Giddens made a fortune selling clothes hangers, embroidered dog leashes, and pepper spray! But he wasn't one of those slick hucksters who sells people things they don't need for prices they can't afford. He was just a humble genius with an unwavering interest in learning—and a love of teaching. Never afraid to admit when he was wrong— and he rarely was, as he tested everything: if he said something worked or didn't work, you could bank on it...literally—Giddens was one of the unsung heroes of the Internet Marketing frontier, a pioneer who started at the very beginning, building websites for Netscape and Hallmark. Over the years he became an expert in half a dozen areas: search-engine optimization, conversions, traffic generation, niche marketing, affiliate marketing, selling domain names and dog training. Dog training? Well, yes. When Giddens died rather suddenly in October 2005, his family requested that donations be made in his name to two of his "pet" projects, Greyhound Rescue and service dogs: *assistancedog.org* or *goldengreyhounds. com*. Memorial pages and comments by friends and total strangers alike marveled at how someone with such an encyclopedic knowledge of Internet Marketing and a riveting speaking style could nevertheless have been such a regular guy who thought nothing of spending an hour or three discussing the business not just with other gurus but with newbies, wannabes and anyone who wanted to learn. He may have been one of the industry's best-kept secrets, but he also kept the industry at its best.

Walker had never met Giddens, though he did hear him speak at that conference. Maybe it's no coincidence then that Walker decided about that time that while the stock market was interesting, Internet Marketing was *fascinating*: he found himself taking notes on everything from what the speakers were saying to how the actual conference room was set up. He noted how the seminar was organized and how people sold product there. In early January 2003, after the seminar, he got an email from Alex Mandossian's list promoting a free teleseminar with Mandossian interviewing Armand Morin. Walker wasn't familiar with either name, and his first thought was that the teleseminar would simply cover all the basics he already knew from having already been in the business seven years. It was free, though, so with nothing to lose Walker signed on. He did learn a few things he'd never thought of. But the biggest gain for him was learning about the "BigSeminar" scheduled for the first weekend in February in Dallas, Texas.

Mandossian invited anyone who signed up for the $1,0000 seminar from the teleseminar link to attend a dinner the night before the conference started, an event featuring several guest experts for a "mastermind" session. Walker called his buddy Paul Myers to see if he knew anything about the speakers. Myers didn't know about the conference, but he did recommend the people involved, so Walker signed up, booked his flights, and flew down there. When he arrived for the dinner, there were forty others in the room. Walker shyly sat down, and the man next to him asked what his online business was. Walker told him he sold information that taught people about the stock market and that people paid him to tell them what he thought was going to happen. The other fellow smiled and said, "Hey, I'm in a business very similar to that." Walker introduced himself, and they discovered another common bond: they were both from Michigan and had gone Michigan State. Walker's new friend, Jeff Johnson, was a stockbroker who had a client who was thinking about buying a web business. Before he felt comfortable giving advice, Johnson had decided to attend a conference to see if anyone was actually making money online. The two Jeffs hung out together throughout the entire conference (Johnson helped Walker name and crystallize the "Six in Seven" story). They chatted with Frank Kern, John Reese, Jeff Mulligan, Armand Morin, Alex Mandossian, and Jason Potash. In the end Johnson was convinced that Internet Marketing was a solid investment. Whether his client took his advice or not, Johnson himself did; he ended up getting into an online business himself.

And Walker got the speaking bug. The second day into the conference, seminar promoter Carl Galletti was walking through the hall and stopped to shake Walker's hand and introduce himself. They talked about what they did online and Walker mentioned that he had recently done a promotion that made six figures in seven days. Galletti drew him aside and asked if he could record the conversation, then spent twenty minutes quizzing Walker about the Six in Seven. In the end he invited Walker to speak at his event in May. Amazing: eight hours after Walker had decided he wanted to try speaking at a conference, he had an assignment lined up. (He enjoyed that first gig so much that he put up his *sixinseven.com* website not to sell product but to attract more speaking engagements.)

One of the Internet Marketers with whom he had become friendly, John Reese, called Walker in late 2003 to discuss an Internet workshop he wanted to hold, asking for advice on how best to promote it. They brainstormed about how to make the announcement, how to sweeten the offer, how to accelerate response, and then devised a rollout plan.

Reese had a list of fewer than 5,000 people, and had never sold to any of them before, but nevertheless he managed to sell 130 seats to an elite group of Internet Marketers. Standing on the stage in Orlando addressing the group, Reese asked how many people in the audience noticed and appreciated the promotion and thought it was unique and effective. Everyone's hands went up. Reese pointed to Walker, seated in the audience, and introduced him as the mastermind. (That "Traffic Secrets" seminar, by the way, became Reese's *Traffic Secrets* course, which sold $1 million in about eighteen hours—his Million-Dollar Day.) A day or two later Reese published a report about his product and seminar and thanked Walker for his assistance. Walker went from being privately prosperous to being publicly pursued, and his phone rang nearly nonstop with offers for him to speak (Yanik Silver asked him to speak at the August 2004 "Underground Information Marketing Seminar"—probably the last time you could consider Walker "underground") and assist others.

Walker decided to make the leap from being a stock consultant who did business online to an Internet Marketer who happened to know about the stock market, and packaged up what he knew about product launches into a teleseminar series. Then he offered to consult with others for $15,000 plus 10 percent of the profits. He chose a deliberately high price knowing that he would have a limited amount of time to allocate. He also couldn't handle a large number of people, but he wasn't sure how many would express interest at that price. He was surprised at the response—there were far more people interested than he could accommodate. Three who signed up were Brian Sacks, who sells to loan officers, Peter Woodhead, and Corey Rudl (who died, tragically, before the project launch was even complete).

After delivering a number of product launch workshops, Walker turned the concept into a series of calls, and then recorded the course on video. In October 2005 he launched his home study course, *Product Launch Formula*. It was very high risk. Clearly if you're launching a product on product launches and it fails...well, let's just say, the product launch has to be spectacularly successful. He still had a relatively small list (about 1,200 people), and he was hardly the biggest name in Internet Marketing. Nevertheless, he pulled in well over $100,000 in the first hour and over $600,000 in the first week. Better still, he added up all the sales that could be traced to people using his *Product Launch Strategy*: $42 million. Now *that's* success.

# CHAPTER **8**

The More Things Change....:
*Milestones and Roadsigns*

# The More Things Change...:
## MILESTONES AND ROADSIGNS

## Work at Home in Your Underwear

Most Internet Marketers start out working online in their spare time. It's something they either play around with or dedicate themselves to after or before working at their "real" jobs. Unless they are independently wealthy, they need to make money to buy groceries, pay the mortgage, and keep the lights on, and except in a very few cases, Internet Marketers don't earn enough from the get-go to buy much more than an occasional dinner out. For those who stick with it and do become successful, there comes a time when they have to make some difficult, often frightening decisions.

Sometime around April 2004, Mike Filsaime went to Atlantic City to hear Jim Ziegler, owner of Ziegler Super Systems, speak at an automotive seminar about his training program for managers on how to motivate salespeople and improve the sale process. Jazzed with some of the ideas he'd heard and his mind buzzing over the day's event, Filsaime was a little distracted when he answered his cell phone. It was his boss, John Chmela, asking "How was the *Internet Marketing* seminar?" Filsaime said it was great, not even really hearing what

Chmela had really said. Chmela told Filsaime to be in his office at nine sharp the next morning.

It was only when he hung up, puzzled, that Filsaime thought to ask himself, "Wait...did he say automotive seminar or Internet Marketing seminar?"

In the morning, Filsaime sat in the office across the desk of his boss, who reminded him a bit of Gordon Gecko from *Wall Street* with his Rolex, gelled hair, and Armani suits. What followed was a scene that gets replayed many times over by Internet Marketers everywhere once their websites start to do well. Chmela flipped his flat-screen monitor to show Filsaime a website: *mikefilsaime.com*. Filsaime smiled. Chmela glared.

"Something funny, Mike?"

"No, John—I apologize. I'm just a little embarrassed. I didn't expect you to put that website up there." Filsaime tried to stop smiling, but so far he wasn't quite catching on to the situation.

In the PG-rated version of the conversation, Chmela spit back, now more Tony Soprano than Gecko, "You think this is f***ing funny? What the hell is this s**t?"

Taken aback, Filsaime could only stammer in surprise that it was just a website, just something he did on the side after hours.

"A website? Mike, I'm looking on here and I'm not seeing one website. I'm seeing you're doing a lot of things on the side." He was a heart attack waiting to happen. "I don't see how the f*** you can effectively run my store and do all this stuff. Mike, you're working sixty to seventy hours a week. When do you find time *after* hours?"

Filsaime waited him out while listening to the mandatory lecture on what a distraction it was from the job, and then said, "Look John. Our old friend Dennis has a laundromat. Bob has a dry cleaner. Frank has a restaurant. The other managers in here have things on the side."

Chmela wasn't swayed. "They don't run those businesses. Their wives and partners do that."

Filsaime pointed out that it wasn't a conflict of interest; it wasn't as though he was selling extended warranties and taking customers away. But he didn't want to discuss his websites in too much detail, thinking that if you were to ask the average person on the street what someone "playing around" with a few websites made in an average month, the answer would probably be somewhere between two and eight hundred a month. Filsaime was pretty sure that his boss had no idea he was making more money online than he was earning at the dealership, especially since he was earning $13,000 a month as a manager. What he did say was, "Of all the stores you have right now, mine has the highest CSI and the highest copy per vehicle. We're humming. I am the least of your problems, and you know it."

"All right. But don't go to f***ing pieces on me, hear? I need you focused."

The truth was, Filsaime was already going to pieces. He had bags under his eyes the size of couch cushions, cranky as all get out and kept nodding off at his desk (and at least once while he was getting a cup of coffee). He was averaging three-and-a-half hours of sleep a night.

One Monday, Filsaime went to the weekly Atlantic Auto-Mall where he met with the usual roomful of general managers named Tony in Armani and Rolexes. There were already half a dozen people there when he showed up. They'd been comparing sales numbers, cracking jokes, waiting for another dozen or so managers to arrive. Chmela sat behind the desk. When Filsaime walked in Chmela slapped the desk and said "Hey, everybody, it's Internet Boy." Nobody knew what he was talking about, and Filsaime didn't enlighten them, saying only that he had been working with the company's Internet department, which he had. But word got around. Soon one of the Tonys would ask him how much he was making online a month—$1,000? $5,000? And then another Tony would say, "Look you gotta show me how to do this." And eventually, the notoriety started to wear on Chmela, and one day he came into Filsaime's store looking for trouble.

Chmela's salespeople routinely averaged more money than anyone working for the competitors, so when anyone started complaining, he gave his standard speech: "You don't like it, don't let the door hit you on the ass on your way out. You guys are making $150,000 to $200,000 a year working for me. It's my way or the highway." Again, *very* Tony Soprano. Glaring around the shop waiting for someone to make a mistake, he started riding Filsaime. "Why didn't anyone say goodbye to that customer?"

"Which customer, John?"

"The one just walked out. You need glasses?"

Filsaime asked one of the salespeople. "Bill, who was that guy? What just happened?" and found out it was someone who had just bought a car and was just picking up his floor mats, a fact that Filsaime explained to his boss.

"Why didn't he have the floor mats on delivery?"

Again Filsaime got the story, and carried it back to Chmela. The answer did not mollify him.

Millennium Hyundai, where Filsaime was the general manager, worked closely with Millennium Toyota. Against Filsaime's advice, the company had hired an outside company to take over the Internet duties, but at least things were finally starting to get up and running smoothly—or so he thought.

Then Chmela stood at the podium and logged into America Online, went to *MillenniumHyundai.com*. Pecking at the keys, he requested a price quote for a Hyundai Elantra and hit " Submit". Seconds later, the computer responded with, "You've got mail." The message said "Dear so and so. We will get back to you on a price quote on a new Toyota. Thank you. Call Millennium Toyota if you have any questions."

Chmela jabbed his finger in Filsaime's face. "Toyota? I want the price on a f***ing Hyundai. Why the f*** do I want to hear from Millennium Toyota?" Filsaime shrugged, and pointed out that the Internet work had all been outsourced, and that he had already called the agency to point out that bug in the program.

Chmela continued to glare at the general manager. "Let me ask you a question about your priorities. If I went to *mikefilsaime.com* right now and typed in my name and email address, would I get something telling me I would hear back shortly from some other f***ing Internet guy?" Filsaime was pretty sure that his boss still had no idea what he was earning. After his boss spoke next he was sure of it. "I need you to make a decision by tomorrow morning whether you work for yourself or you work for me. No—you know what? I need an answer right now."

Filsaime was shaking. "John, what are you saying? Are you asking me to decide between my online businesses and being a general manager in this store? Are you telling me I can't do both?"

"That's right, and I need an answer right now."

Filsaime was holding back tears when he held out his hand and said, "Well, I'm sorry, John. It's been a great five years."

Chmela flinched like he'd been hit. He said nothing for what seemed liked a very long time. Then he collected himself and said, "Give me the keys—every one—the safes, the front door, the demo, everything." While Filsaime pulled them off his keyring one at a time, his bossed picked up his cell phone and jabbed at the keypad. "Tommy? Be in my f***ing office tomorrow, 9 a.m. You're my new general manager at Millennium Hyundai." Then he walked out the door. Filsaime just stood there, shaking. (You'd never have expected that those two guys would ever become great friends, but once Filsaime left the dealership, it happened. Filsaime calls Chmela "brilliant.")

Everyone in the showroom just stared in shock. They loved Filsaime, and he thought the world of them. As he walked toward the door they all swarmed around, peppering him with variations on the same question: "Dude, what just happened?"

Filsaime, choked up, could barely talk. He muttered something like "F*** him—I don't need this s**t" and slipped outside to call his wife. "Come pick me up."

She was shocked. Then the scary questions started hitting her. "What happened? What about insurance? What about the car?"

But suddenly Filsaime felt at peace for the first time in a long while. "You know what? It's okay. This is going to be the best thing that that could have happened to us—trust me." The very next month his online earnings went from $18,000 to $40,000, and he never has had a single moment's regret.

## Change or Die

It was the summer of 1996. The Scots cloned Dolly the Sheep...Eric Robert Rudolph planted three deadly pipe-bombs packed with nails at Centennial Olympic Park...TWA Flight 800 exploded off the coast of Long Island killing all 230 on board and giving birth to several years' worth of conspiracy theories...the legendary 1995/1996-season Chicago Bulls wrapped up a record-breaking 71–10 season by taking home a fourth NBA championship title...and Jonathan Mizel, Marlon Sanders and Declan Dunn wound down their cross-country speaking tour on the newest frontier in business and marketing, the Internet. Animated as the Stooges, courageous as the Musketeers, and different in appearance as the Bear family, the Three Amigos would take to the stage all day Friday and Saturday, and on Saturday night hit the town—whatever town that was—to relax and critique the day's events. Whether they were drinking coffee at a kiosk inside a Seattle parking garage (I kid you not) or scarfing up a Cincinnati specialty, spaghetti topped with Skyline Chili and a mountain of cheddar cheese, the three always talked shop, and about the cutting edge of Internet Marketing. They were all fearless pioneers, but when they weren't out carving new trails for themselves they were helping each other.

Take that night in July when Sanders and Dunn were hanging out, probably discussing the latest Internet new-comer (eBay) or the latest over-hyped next-big-thing (Push technology), when Dunn pulled out a sales letter he'd just written. By then he'd heard Sanders speak on the subject four or five times, and wanted Sanders to critique his efforts. By then, Dunn had also grown accustomed to his friend's instinctively direct manner of speaking. It was clear that Dunn's headline, more philosophical than practical, didn't knock the socks off Sanders.

"Dec—wut the hail does that mean? It's a wreck." Then Sanders told him *why* it was a wreck.

The next weekend, Dunn showed Sanders a revised version.

"Dec, that's a hailuva lot better. Needs some tweaks here 'n' there, though. Lemme show ya…" And he did.

The third weekend, Dunn showed Sanders one more version. "Hot damn, boy, you got it." And he never had to critique another sales letter of Dunn's again. He was *that* good a teacher, and Dunn was *that* quick a study.

Dunn's comfort zone hovers close to the edge. He likes exploring what's hot, what's in the works, and what's out there, and he's got the brains and the energy to do it. (The first time I saw him speak at an Affiliate Summit, he was running up and down the aisles, ponytail flying, as he led an audience sing-a-long of "We Will Rock You," pounding on the tables. To say he's a charismatic speaker would be an understatement.) In fact, his early training and work revolved around education and training—his Master's degree is in Instructional Technology—and he'd been on and around the Internet since 1986. In 1993, he was working in the San Francisco Bay Area creating a series of multimedia presentations for K–12 students and Bay Area and Silicon Valley businesses. He spent two laborious years digitizing graphics and images, and writing Lingo programs to produce (somewhat) interactive CD-ROMs. The work was engaging, but frustrating: by the time he created a product that would be compatible with a dozen different PC and Mac systems, he joked that the CD-ROMs would probably run on only about 200 computers in the country. But he wasn't laughing.

Dunn abandoned the CD-ROM idea and took his multimedia product online. On April 25, 1995, he launched *remember.org*, a research and education "cybrary" dedicated to honoring those who died in the death camps in Germany during WWII. (Millions of hits later, *remember. org* remains active today.) Dunn was doing some webmastering for PBS, ABC and Travelocity when he got a call from an old friend he'd met some years before when he used to jam with other after-hours musicians at a high-tech store. Jonathan Mizel told Dunn that he was holding an Internet Marketing seminar along with another friend: Mizel would be the "marketing guy," Marlon Sanders would be the "copy guy," and Dunn would be the "Web guy." For Jonathan Mizel, never being content with doing things on a small scale, one seminar became several, which became a seminar/event management company that raked in $10–12 million in its first year. That's how it came to be that Mizel, Sanders and Dunn spent a year and a half as Internet Marketing Nomads, teaching others and themselves. They created two how-to products, a video and a book, each of which Mizel leveraged into major affiliate deals. The sales seminars were always packed, and because everything was still so new and unknown, the excitement level was palpable as the gurus talked about how everything was shifting—not just the way people used the Internet, but media in general. The three of them were constantly pumped up, and they kept the audiences hopping. (During one seminar in D.C., the power went out. Other presenters were lost without their PowerPoint slides and gave up. Mizel, on the other hand, said, "I don't need no stinkin' lights. Dec, let's go find some candles!")

The day after Sanders gave him a crash course on copywriting, Dunn started shipping *Director of Sales*. It went to six figures, but although it made him a lot of money, Dunn wasn't interested in teaching people how to sell websites all his life, and he let that part essentially sell itself while he developed something more substantial. In 1997, he released the *Beginner's Guide to Internet Marketing*, followed by *Insider's Guide to Affiliate Programs* in 1998. His next product ("one of the best books I've ever written that no one ever really bought"), a more analytical book called *Net Profits*, was never a big seller on its own but did respectably well.

Dunn's forte was always spotting trends in their earliest stages. He was a natural tracker, seeing the bent twigs and hearing the snap of branches off in the distance that lead him down the right path almost instinctively. As a result, he was usually six months to a year ahead of the pack in terms of new techniques and technologies. His affiliate book was a perfect case in point; it hit just as the concept was gaining serious momentum, and he sold about a thousand units in six weeks at $97 a copy, despite the fact that his "little blue book" (it reminded him of Chairman Mao's little red book) had no images or graphics. At the "Beyond the Banner" conference in 1998, Dunn mingled with the big names in affiliate marketing and joint ventures—Todd Crawford and Lex Sisney of Commission Junction; Heidi and Stephen Messer of LinkShare; Gordon Hoffstein of BeFree—and came away with a joint venture deal that led him to come out with *Winning the Affiliate Game* the following year.

With the profits (and with his growing network), Dunn switched his focus from multimedia design and development (when he ran Inetdesign) to marketing services and business development with his new company, ADNet International, which he built into a multimillion-dollar agency. ADNet survived, even thrived in, the dot-com meltdown since that stock market fiasco filtered out the hucksters who were more interested in what kind of yacht they planned to buy when they became dot-com millionaires than they were in building sound businesses.

Dunn saw early on where the dot-com frenzy would lead. Many of the companies that flamed out were "so screwed up, [he could] talk about them" freely since there was nothing and no one left to take offense. Most people remember *Pets.com*, an online purveyor of pet supplies and accessories. The company launched in August 1998, went from its initial public offering on the NASDAQ to liquidation in less than a year. It's a classic example of someone getting so caught up in the thrill of the roller coaster ride that no one bothers to lay any track to follow. The company had millions of dollars in venture capital and won numerous awards for its site design and its advertising (including a $1.2 million Superbowl ad. The business may be gone, but who doesn't remember "Because pets can't drive"?). Yet the company was a castle built on sand (actually, Emeryville, California is known for its mudflats, but who ever heard of a castle built on a mudflat?). Home base was a part of the city built directly over the bridge from San Francisco in one of the worst traffic nightmares you could find. The problem with this is that shipping was supposed to happen right in the middle of that nightmare. The company should have had its shipping facilities outside the city but con-venient to services. Not only were they handicapped in the shipping department, no one there knew how to run a warehouse, and so in an average day they could only ship about fourteen packages. Even their market-ing was all wrong. They advertised on other sites, yet didn't even bother to make the ads clickable so people could be linked to the store and actually buy something. But perhaps the biggest mistake was failing to base the business on a sound market plan. You may make money

selling little dog outfits and catnip mice and ferret tun-
nels, but the minute you start trying to sell 50-pound
bags of dog food you're going to end up in the dog house
yourself. It costs more to buy it and ship it than you can
charge for it. Drs. Foster & Smith, a pet-supply company
that has been very successful online, succeeded because
it operated according to sound business principles, and
because it offered only those products that it made sense
for people to buy and have shipped across the country,
such as unique bird perches, pet medications, grooming
supplies, and iguana lamps.

That ability to evaluate a business's shortcomings
after the fact is a talent in and of itself, but "20-20 hind-
sight" is far more common than the ability to hatch an
idea from possibility to product according to a sensible
business and marketing plan. Too many Internet Marketers think of themselves as just self-employed individuals
and not as business entities. And planning a business?
What about knowing what your product should be or
the best way to reach your market? That is as much art as
it is science. It helps if, like Dunn, you are somehow able
to recognize the "next big thing"—six months to a year
ahead of anyone else. With his multimedia background,
he was drawn to the technologies and programs like Flash
that integrate audio, video, and animation, the programs
that are quantum leaps ahead of the early applications
like PowerPoint and MacroMedia Director. Dunn leapt
immediately into the world of social media, the "Web 2.0"
concept of integrating user-supplied content. Social media
sites like MySpace, YouTube, Digg, Wikipedia, and others
differ from plain vanilla websites by enabling interaction
and sharing among site owners, visitors, and communities via blogs, message boards, wikis, vlogs and his current
specialty, podcasts. As with the sites found by surfing,
users select the podcasts to listen to, which automatically
qualifies prospects as people who have at least a passing
interest in your product or subject. And unlike websites,

many podcasts feel almost personal, like phone conversations. With newer technology like the Apple iPhone, they feel like webcam conversations. They surpass eBooks in many ways (depending on the subject of course) since the incredibly small, portable technology (including ear-buds) lets you listen and learn hands-free while you're commuting, running a marathon, or doing the laundry.

Podcasts today are still new enough that many people still don't know exactly what they are or how they work. Essentially they are just compressed audio/video files (such as MP3s) distributed online as downloads or streaming content. You can syndicate them, just as you can articles. Users can subscribe to a series or list, get individual podcasts for free or for a fee, tap into feed readers such as RSS. Sometimes podcasts begin as online teleconferences—these could be anything from classes to "talk shows"—that get recorded; they can be sent as streamed audio, too, although listeners aren't actively participating. You can listen online on your computer (preferably with a broadband connection) or on your iPod (or something similar), or watch and listen on your iPhone. Nearly anything that could be presented on a website, teleseminar, or in an eBook can certainly be done as a podcast, such as music demos for your band, political speeches, instructions, tours, interviews, movie trailers—anything that can be recorded—and without huge investments in time and technology, which would make the podcasts prohibitively expensive.

Most top Internet Marketers have blogs now. Considerably fewer have done podcasts. Dunn runs a site with his business and life partner Jody Colvard—*funmoneygood.com*—that combines the two. The name comes from what could be called the site's mission statement, but works equally well for the couple's shared philosophy on life: "Have fun. Make Money. Do Good." The site focuses on women with an entrepreneurial spirit, an idea of a product or service, and the drive to create an online business.

(Although men aren't excluded, Dunn has said that many of them don't seem to "get it".) He and Colvard created the "Fun Money Good Podcast Program," an intensive ten-week course, to guide people through their very first podcasts. Of course it's a sales tool. Of course it's another way to pitch product. But for Dunn and others, like Paul Colligan, it is a way to get closer to people and relate to them as more than impressions, demographics, seats, targets or eyeballs. Podcasts, because they are about audio and video, allow something approaching conversation—and markets, as *Cluetrain* points out, are conversations.

Of course, these days you can't mention the word podcast without talking about Paul Colligan. He came up through the University of Santa Barbara, one of the four schools connected to the early Internet. Around 1994, Colligan started playing around with an email account that belonged to his fiancé and created a newsletter with a political bent to it. Between that and the Usenet groups, he was hooked, and as soon as the World Wide Web hit the scene, he built himself a little website. One of the people on his political email list asked him what his rates were. Colligan had to ask, "rates for what?" The man thought he was a professional website guru, and even though he wasn't, Colligan quoted him a price. It was 1995. Colligan chose FrontPage, the popular new software for web pages—it was still in v1.1, and not even part of Microsoft Office—to do the job.

He quickly realized that popular does not mean perfect, and that although Microsoft was trying to turn web page design into something almost anyone could do, there were holes in the software big enough to pass a PC through. Colligan mastered the program quickly, including its shortcomings, and for a while ran a small web design shop. When he found himself doing more human resources–related work than design work, he closed the shop and went to work for the first business-specific ISP. Working for an ISP on the West Coast was a challenge—the East Coast divisions' servers went down at 6 p.m. EST for maintenance while the West Coast still had active clients. One day while he was working with the web designers, Colligan starting talking with his boss, Mark Chestnut (*not* the country western singer) about Microsoft and FrontPage and its many idiosyncrasies, and Chestnut had an idea.

He asked himself: "What if we started doing Front-Page classes with Microsoft? And have people buy Front-Page from Microsoft, but web hosting from us? It would be a true joint venture." Microsoft loved the idea, and soon they were the only ISP that could handle FrontPage. They got to use Microsoft's mailing lists, and before long the business had exploded with clients.

When Microsoft released FrontPage 2000 (rev. 4.0, 1999), Colligan ghostwrote *The Idiot's Guide to Front-Page 2000* (and reviewed it as himself), then managed to cut into his own royalties: people would see the book in a store and say, "I'm not going to buy the book—I'm going to go to this *frontpageworld.com* and see what it's all about." That was Colligan's site. He had tremendous traffic, and as he started adding more affiliate links, the checks kept getting bigger. The problem was, the stats were not at all specific. He couldn't tell if one person bought $25,000 worth of product or 1,000 people bought $25 worth of product. Ultimately, Colligan said that if he couldn't get better stats he was going to open his own store. No stats were forthcoming, so he followed through on his promise. The launch date turned out to be less than propitious—September 11, 2001—but before Colligan discovered that his online market was opening at the same time that the world's best known symbol of the free market was under attack, he sent a mailing out to 25,000 people, unlocked the password-protected storefront, and waited. It was only then that he saw the news. No one in the country did much business that day, and the last thing Colligan was worrying about was how many orders had come in during the day. Like so many others, he was glued to the news reports. When he finally decided to check his email later that night, he was surprised to find that he had still managed to make some pretty good sales.

Even on that dismal day, people took note of Colligan's product thanks to several wise marketing moves and, most likely, some people's personal circumstances keeping them from hearing anything about the attacks until many hours after the fact. Before the release, Declan Dunn had mentioned Colligan, singling him out as the leader in new generation of affiliate Internet Marketers; one third of Colligan's sales flow in from affiliates. He'd also been asked by Alex Mandossian to speak on affiliate marketing at the "X10" seminar in Australia 2004; Colligan joked that the first 25 people Mandossian called must have had previous engagements since he was hardly well known. Mandossian knew Colligan, though, since they'd done a joint venture, a teleseminar for Front-Page users. Actually, they began with a webinar with six or seven hundred people signed on; when they followed Mandossian's instincts and switched to a teleseminar, the audience doubled to 1200 people—including Microsoft management. The success of the teleseminar led him to convert his FrontPage manual to audio.

That success also made Colligan an extremely busy man, although in at least one instance that worked to his advantage. In 1995 he had registered the domain *getajob. com*, envisioning a *Monster.com*-style site, totally automated, totally email-driven. With one thing or another, though, he was always too busy to finish it, and it never worked properly. In 2000, one of Colligan's buddies congratulated him saying he'd heard Colligan's ad on the punk radio station—several times, in fact. Curious, Colligan checked out his site, thinking that maybe he'd forgotten to renew the domain name. No, it was still there. It still didn't work. He looked up the stats for the site, a site that never worked and he had never promoted, and found that it had five thousand unique visitors, all from type-ins or bookmarks. So he signed up for an affiliate program with someone who was willing to pay him a nickel a click. Soon after the people at that site called him and said, "Who are you again?" Colligan told him, only to find out that *getajob.com* had more than doubled the affiliate's output, even though they had already had 1,999 *other* affiliates. Colligan was as pleased as they were given that it was all "found" money, but he remained curious about what was driving people to his site. He found out that people were typing in "get" instead of "got," and that created all the flurry. What happened was, one of the last of the dot-com gold rush companies had purchased *gotajob.com*, and since their ad agency had apparently told them that online marketing was dead, they'd put all their advertising dollars into radio and other offline media. Had the gotajob.commers called Colligan several years earlier, he would have sold them the domain for $10,000 without a second thought. But as it turned out, the *gotajob.com* people sponsored MTV Spring Break 2000—and there were multiple commercial breaks during that MTV show. The same typos were happening so after *each* commercial, Colligan earned more than $10,000—and that was after paying his partners. Internet life can be funny that way. Serendipitous things happen that lead you to places you might never have gone on your own. Colligan just seems to especially good at capitalizing on them.

He tells another story about how he had been working for an ISP in Portland, Oregon, he'd spent a lot of time driving between there and Seattle and Spokane, Washington. With all that downtime, he decided he may as well educate himself. He discovered *audible.com*, which delivered a variety of different audio, from entertainment and information to news and educational materials, both online and as audiobooks, as well as radio and television show programs. Right about the time he started his eBook *Podcast Secrets Revealed*, Colligan happened to meet the CEO of Audible. He asked the CEO if he could get his material included and was told that of course Audible was open to "the little guy"—he only needed to be doing half a million in sales to qualify. To Colligan, that was not the cutoff for "little guys," and he went away discouraged. Then in 2005 he discovered podcasting. He didn't think, "Ah, the logical progression in the natural evolution of blogs..." nor "the perfect use of the enclosure XML schema." There's nothing highfalutin about Colligan. He thought, "Now I don't *need* audible.com. I can *be* audible." Podcasting didn't require fancy technology or massive servers. He could be up and running overnight—and he was. His FrontPage products paid the bills while he experimented with podcasts, wanting to be cutting edge, but not over the edge. His theory was that if you stay one step ahead, you're a visionary; two steps ahead and you're a martyr. He was somewhere in between, making a few mistakes that he could have let someone else make first.

What people like Dunn, Colligan, and Jeff Mills understood early on about podcasting that many others did not is that they didn't need to have fancy Internet Marketing shows or to set aside major chunks of time in addition to the long hours they were already putting in. As Colligan once said, it's important (not just with podcasting but with other new developments) not to confuse media (content) with channel (delivery mode). Podcasts are channels. It's easy to understand why a lot of incredibly successful podcasts are simply existing materials such as teleseminars, webinars, or videos, repackaged or repurposed. Think: *leverage*. For example, Colligan and Jeff Mills formed a joint venture to create a weekly show, twenty minutes per episode. Such episodes compile nicely on a CD—eight ten-minute episodes, or eighty minutes total. The CD and individual tracks sell on iTunes to be played online or on an iPod-like device. The CDs get bundled into an audio book and turned into an eBook. That's leverage. One message, many delivery channels.

# Beginnings, Middles, and Endings

Many historical records lend themselves to strictly linear, cause-and-effect structures. The history of Internet marketing is not one of them. As with so many social phenomena, its seminal moments and crucial developments aren't as objective as they might seem at first glance, but are largely subjective—after-the-fact "aha" moments, selective memory, tunnel vision, whitewashing...so much affects how we look back on the past and how we read the story.

Still, there are certain events that happened to these people that can be called "defining" in the lives of these Internet Marketers that I'm calling the pioneers. Many of the gurus and mentors I interviewed mentioned launches and tweaks by other Internet Marketers as important milestones in their developments as online businesspeople. Many of them you have just read about, from Jonathan Mizel's *Unlimited Traffic Technique* and *Online Marketing Newsletter* and Sheila Danzig's *Turn Your Computer Into a Money Machine* to Corey Rudl's affiliate programs and his *Car Secrets Revealed* eBook, Mark Joyner's *Search Engine Tactics*, and John Reese's *Million-Dollar Day*. One thing every guru mentioned was the importance of attending live events with other Internet Marketers. For many it was one of Jonathan Mizel's "Boulder Summits" or Ken McCarthy's "System Seminars" or any of a hundred different boot camps, workshops or conferences. For me personally the turning point was Armand Morin's "BigSeminar" in Los Angeles in 2005.

But I couldn't end this story of Internet Marketing history without giving a nod to certain technological advancements that everyone admits played an important role in the history of Internet Marketing. Obviously, without an Internet there would have been no history to tell. And without the World Wide Web things would have played out much differently. Of course, there were some obvious practical technological necessities that make Internet Marketing yield such spectacular results—high-speed connections, image compression formats, low-cost personal computers, ISPs, HTML...the list could go on forever. But it's the milestones and moments that never attracted a lot of attention outside the industry that also need to be mentioned.

Internet Marketing is part of e-commerce, and commerce means buying and selling, which means transferring funds from point a to point b. The early Internet Marketing pioneers had no safe, easy online way to do this. Buyers could go online to learn about a product but they would then have to use the telephone to charge items to a credit card, or use snail mail to send a check or money order. These additional steps made "online shopping" awkward, and discouraged many would-be buyers. Sites that did accept credit cards online in the early days were risky; using them was tantamount to leaving your wallet open on a table in a crowded room and walking away. Without the development of security protocols that made it possible to transfer sensitive data online, Internet businesses could not have thrived the same way. In 1995, a significant number of users were interested in buying online but only a relative few actually had.

Underlying the advancement was the introduction of Secure Sockets Layer (SSL) and its successor, Transport Layer Security (TLS). You can imagine TLS as a virtually impregnable transport tunnel for armored cars underneath the information superhighway. Initial cryptographic specifications and protocols for SSL were developed by Netscape, then refined into TLS by the Internet Society's Internet Engineering Task Force (IETF), a volunteer-based standards organization comprising working groups or "BoFs" ("birds of a feather": somewhat informal or ad-hoc manner teams of people interested in and knowledgeable about a given topic). The working groups or BoFs work only on particular components of the protocol (for example, routing or infrastructure), and then disband. The IETF works hand-in-hand with the World Wide Web Consortium (W3C), the International Organization for Standardization (ISO), and the International Electrotechnical Association (IEC), especially with respect to TCP/IP and Internet protocol suite standards.

If TSL is the protected transport tunnel, shopping cart systems are the armored cars that travel there. The earliest ones were extremely rudimentary, although they did at least fulfill the basic need of enabling online credit card transactions. Today's versions go beyond simple electronic ordering forms, combining additional functions such as customer histories, discount programs, shipping options, search, upsell, and order management. There are dozens of shopping cart solutions for online storefronts and other websites selling products.

Transferring funds, of course, requires that they be accessible online. None of the above would have been possible without the development of online banking and other funds-transfer systems. These allowed users to debit finds directly from their own checking accounts or from third-party "banks" such as PayPal.

Another important step along the path came when Adobe Systems developed an open standard, device-independent page description format that could transfer WYSIWYG documents electronically, complete with fonts, images, graphics and layout information. Adobe developed the Portable Document Format (PDF) in 1993 for desktop publishing, but coincidentally it gave Internet Marketers a way to distribute information effectively, efficiently and in an aesthetically pleasing format.

Internet Marketing relies heavily on the power of search engines, and the elaborate functionality of such giants as Google and Yahoo! changed online business from an interesting sideline of commerce in general to a major if not the dominant business methodology. Retrieving information was just the beginning. The first search tool, Archie (Alan Emtage, McGill University, 1990), let users download directories and search filenames—but not content. Gopher (Mark McCahill, University of Minnesota, 1991) was a document indexing system. The first real full-text "web crawler" search engines that could locate individual words within the content of any web page became available several years later: WebCrawler (Brian Pinkerton, the basis for the major search engines that followed University of Washington, 1994); Lycos and Infoseek (1994); AltaVista and Excite (1995); and Dogpile, Inktomi, and Ask Jeeves (1996).

Google appeared in 1998 and quickly became the number-one search engine due to its PageRank algorithm, which relies not just on the frequency of a term's appearance but also takes into consideration (through methods that can best be summed up as magic) "importance," as determined by real people, not computers. Google searches multiple file types: HTML files, caches, indexes, PDFs, spreadsheets, text documents, Flash/Shockwave files, and other formats. Google also expanded way beyond searches to standalone applications, extensions, and other programs—including, of course, two advertising and analysis programs that Internet Marketers have come to depend on, AdWords and AdSense.

Whatever the advancement or breakthrough, the technology will certainly continue to change and mature as new technology, new programs, new software, new whatever-it-is-that-we-need comes about to make the Internet smarter, faster, safer, and certainly more productive for everyone who wants to partake.

# CHAPTER 9

Social Truth:
*Don't Take My Word For It*

# Social Truth:
## DON'T TAKE MY WORD FOR IT

SO, THERE YOU HAVE IT. THE INTERNET MARKET-
ING PIONEERS didn't succeed because they had it easier
than people today. They made it easier for people today.
They made it possible.

Are these gurus some strange breed, now extinct?
Hardly. They were ordinary people trying to find a way
to make money and for whatever reason they stumbled
onto the Internet. But no matter why they flocked to
this "new fangled" technology. One for one, the guys
and gals talked about in this book each had two important ingredients: passion and persistence. One without
the other may get you started on the Internet, but the
one alone will not bring you the kind of success these
gurus enjoyed. For, while they forged the trail, it still
isn't a codified superhighway, where all you have to do
is punch in some numbers or letters and, poof, out comes
streams of money. It is still "difficult," to start an Internet market venture. In fact, I would dare to say that you
don't know difficult until you, yourself, experience some
of the things that the Internet Marketers who you've
been reading about had to go through to get where they
are today. Because, you see, while the early gurus certainly forged a path so that instead of having to figure
out how something works you can now read a book

and then figure out how it works, and while technology today makes it all a little more "user friendly," it still takes one person making the decision to learn how to do it and then be willing to climb all the mountains that get in their way. Countless moms, grandpas, college students, teenaged boys or thirty-something women have tried or are trying to forge their path on the Internet. And, may I repeat, it is never easy. History is something that is happening right now, and even as you read this, there are Internet marketers who are overcoming insurmountable obstacles and helping us to be inspired. Perhaps one of the most inspirational is this one, which Eric Holmlund has graciously allowed me to reprint from his *ericstips.com* website.

> **Ladan Lashkari: *If This Girl Can Succeed, So Can You***
> I want to tell you about a young woman who has overcome some extreme obstacles on her brief but challenging journey to Internet marketing success. Her name is Ladan Lashkari, and when I say she's a young woman, that's an understatement. At just 20 years old, she has a youthful look that defies the maturity she's developed in such a short time.
>
> I suppose in the online world, youthful success is not entirely unusual (I met a couple of 21-year-old Internet millionaires last month in New York), but this story hasn't even begun yet. The fact that she's a girl making money on the Internet becomes much more significant when you realize where she comes from.
>
> She lives in Iran.
>
> When I came across that tidbit of information on one of her sites I was like, "Are you serious?"
>
> Make no mistake. Like most Americans, I'm ignorant in many ways…but I have heard a few things about Iran and its culture. I know just barely enough to understand that a girl becoming a successful Internet marketer in Iran is about the same as the Denver Nuggets winning the Superbowl — and yeah, I know those are two different sports.

So I had to find out if it was true.

After several email exchanges, and some online investigation on my part, it became apparent that she is indeed the real deal. As I've gotten to know her a little bit over the past week, an incredible story has unraveled that needs to be told. Maybe you'll watch her life story in a movie some day, or see her on the front cover of Time magazine. Either way, just remember that you saw it on Eric's Tips first ;-)

Lashkari was born and raised in Tehran, Iran, and lives there to this day. There are political, economical, and religious obstacles that make it difficult for anyone to be a successful Internet marketer in Iran, and in most cases even more difficult for a woman to do so.

With respect for Lashkari, I'm not going to get into the details of the specific political and religious barriers that many women face in Iran, but just be aware that this story runs even deeper than I'm able to write about.

If Internet marketing was a wrestling match, she's starting the competition with one hand tied behind her back simply because of the place she was born into the world.

Next obstacle: the language barrier. Although you wouldn't know it from her articles and sales letters, Lashkari was not born into an English-speaking family. She started learning the language at eight years of age, and devoured every English book she could get her hands on. Even at such a young age, she began to realize that fluency in English would open up more doors of opportunity throughout her life. Throughout her teen years, this fervor grew as she tackled the language head-on.

A true entrepreneur, she decided that she wanted to become independent and produce her own income. When her family bought a computer, she quickly began experimenting with ways she could turn it into an income stream. She tried all kinds of business; teaching Windows, graphic designing with PhotoShop, website design; she even learned C++ programming.

Even though she was able to make money through those avenues, she knew that there was a bigger opportunity out there. At sixteen years of age, she discovered the world of Internet marketing through the late Corey

Rudl's website. She bought and studied his Internet marketing course, along with other eBooks and resources.

She knew right away that this was the business she wanted to be in.

Her friends and family tried to convince her that becoming a successful Internet marketer in Iran would be impossible, and that she shouldn't continue to waste her money. If you've ever faced the negative energy of friends and family, you'll understand that it's a powerful force that can quench your enthusiasm and ultimately abort the launch of a new business. Fortunately, her father believed in her, and the resistance of others made her more determined than ever to find success.

After about a year of learning and studying the business, she launched her first website — and the rest, as they say, is history. But that history has not been without its fair share of bumps and valleys.

Jumping into business forced her to take her English proficiency to a new level. For a long time it was difficult to read and comprehend the many technically oriented eBooks that she acquired. And if reading comprehension was a challenge, writing was an even bigger issue. It would take her six hours to write and proofread an article, but her determination paid off. Today if you search for her name on a search engine, you'll find a slew of her articles indexed all over the Internet.

And as if writing weren't enough, she wanted to write her own sales copy. Anyone who's ever successfully written a sales letter will concur that being a good writer doesn't make someone a good copywriter. I'm amazed to say that Lashkari is a good copywriter. Being a copywriter myself, I wouldn't say that if it weren't true. She applied the same vigor to learning the craft as she applied to learning the language itself.

She studied articles and courses from the top copywriters, and practiced until she had developed her own style. While there is obviously some innate talent at work here, I'd say that she is also a testament that copywriting can be learned.

## The U.S. Embargo

Starting her business was the beginning of a long uphill battle. Because of the U.S. embargo on Iran, she faces obstacles that most of us wouldn't imagine. As I mentioned, her culture has already tied one hand behind her back. The language barrier effectively tied the other one. And the following problems essentially tied her feet…a situation that would cripple most marketers and paralyze them from moving forward in business.

Most people wouldn't jump into a new business with their hands and feet tied. It's impossible, right? Just don't use the word "impossible" around Lashkari.

**To start with, she couldn't get a credit card.** That makes it pretty tough to buy anything online, wouldn't you say? My business relies on my credit cards for many things. Not a day goes by without several business-related charges to my credit card. As I think about it, many of the products and services that I use come from sites that only accept credit cards.

**She can't open a PayPal account.** Again, this limits her ability to make online purchases. It also rules her out of participating in a large number of affiliate programs that only pay commissions via PayPal. Of course, probably the biggest disadvantage of not having a PayPal account is not being able to accept PayPal payments. She estimates that this one issue is costing her many thousands of dollars in lost sales.

**She can't get a merchant account,** so it becomes very difficult to sell anything online.

**She can't have a bank account in U.S. dollars.** So that rules out another possibility of making or receiving payments.

**To make matters worse, she can't have any bank account that accepts wire transfers.** This cripples her ability to receive payments from affiliate programs to her bank account, or from merchant services for her own products. So even if she can find a way to sell a product online, getting that money into her own hands is a huge obstacle.

**She can't cash any USD checks.** That rules out most of the other affiliate programs.

**She can't travel.** It's almost impossible for her to get a visa to travel outside of Iran. This means that she has not been able to go abroad to attempt to open up accounts, and she cannot attend any Internet marketing seminars.

Those are just <u>some</u> of the barriers created by the embargo. There are many more limitations imposed by the Iranian government.

## Other Barriers

On top of these physical barriers, she also faces another kind of discrimination that continues to this day. In a business built upon online image and perceived trust, she has been severely disadvantaged by the way much of the world views Iranians.

As she puts it, "The reactions are not very pleasant."

She thinks it's mainly due to the way the media has portrayed Iran and Islam. This has made it difficult to be open and build relationships online, as she has found that even her own subscribers, customers, and business associates look at her differently when they discover she is from Iran.

She says, "Some people even act like I am a terrorist." She has received "hate" emails through her websites and also on forums.

"I know who I am and where I stand," says Lashkari, "but what the media shows the world and what my country's government does has nothing to do with me. So I just wish people in the West – especially the United States - would understand this difference."

**We take so much for granted. To show you how much, let me ask you a few questions:**
- *Do you have a credit card?*
- *Do you have a PayPal account?*
- *Can you open a US bank account?*
- *Can you receive US checks?*
- *Do you have the freedom to travel?*
- *Could you go to an internet marketing seminar?*

Maybe you didn't answer "Yes" to ALL of those questions, but for each question you answered "yes" to, you are starting one step ahead of Lashkari.

Let me ask you a couple more questions:
• *Are you fluent in English?*
If you said "Yes", take two more steps ahead.

• *Do people view you as a terrorist?*
No? Take three more steps ahead.

If this girl can do it, so can you. It doesn't matter how old or young you are…it doesn't matter where you live in the world…it doesn't matter what other internal and external factors are trying to hold you down.

You can succeed.
In spite of all her challenges, Lashkari views Internet marketing as an easy opportunity to take advantage of, and she encourages others to do as she has done…
"I think there's nothing hard about it. It's the perfect kind of business for people who want to be independent and work for themselves in a business that there's no limit to your success."
If you're just getting started, she has more advice.
"When you are just getting started, you should know it might take some time to make the amount of money you expect, and you should keep on and don't give up - no matter how people around you try to disappoint you. I think this is the most important and difficult part. It's where most people give up."
In the three short years that she's been in business, she's worked hard and implemented many strategies that she's learned by studying other successful marketers. Out of everything she's tried, she deems list building as the most important component of her business,
"Nothing is more powerful than building a targeted, responsive list and building a relationship with that list."
While her income may not yet be on par with the Internet marketing superstars, she's earning a living online that

**273**

would impress even those of us living in a more generous economy (she recently earned US $6300 in a month).

The thing that must be kept in mind is that she is making more money than about 95 percent of the people in her country, and bringing home more income than her country-men who have 30+ years of experience in their careers.

I'd love to see what she'd be capable of achieving out-side the restraints of her county, and so would she, which is one reason she is considering a move to a locale more conducive to her business — such as Canada or Australia.

She says the biggest key to success is, "Believing in yourself, and promising yourself that you <u>will</u> reach your goals and won't let anything or anyone stop you."

When I asked her what makes her different from those who fail, she said that her success is derived from her persistence in facing and overcoming challenges and obstacles. She points out one of her favorite quotes from Ross Perot: "Most people give up just when they're about to achieve success. They quit on the one-yard line. They give up at the last minute of the game, one foot from a winning touchdown."

When she's not working on her business, she enjoys reading self-improvement books (who would have guessed?), dancing, watching movies, spending time in nature, and going out with friends. In other words, she's just a normal girl with big plans and an indomitable positive attitude.

Today she has more than 20 websites, and she hopes to expand her business by 400 percent while continuing to help others find their own success.

You can learn more about Lashkari and her business at ladanlashkari.com.

As Lashkari says, "If a young girl who got started when she was only 16 years old, with no previous business expe-rience, with English being her second language, with less than $30 to her name, in a country where you can't have a credit card or PayPal account and is under a strict embargo from United States, and so many more limitations…if such a girl can succeed, how is it possible that <u>you</u> can't succeed - while you may not even have one of these limitations?"

– ©2007 Eric Holmlund, reprinted with permission

The Internet is a world wide phenomenon, and it is all the aspiring business men and women—whether it be the "Pajama Mama" here in America who helps people who want to work from home, or a kid from Jakarta, Indonesia who uses a computer at a library or an Internet café to make money with Adsense. He's going to save his money so that he can buy a computer and move back home to be with his family. Both of these two people talk about the challenges involved with making a success out of Internet marketing. But no matter who it is or what they are selling, the Internet is full of possibilities and potential for making those who work at it hundreds, thousands, even millions of dollars. Not bad when you consider that you really can sit at home in your underwear or your 'jammies, and make it happen!

# Crystal Balls

If I could see into the future, I'd be considerably more well known (and well off, I suppose) than I am now. But I can't. I am a firm believer, however, that for the most part, the best predictor of behavior is past behavior, as long as you aren't too literal with the interpretations. With that caveat, let me take a stab at what the next chapter(s) in the history of Internet Marketing might describe.

**Access** – We've already seen a trend toward portability, of having easier and more ways to access the Internet. Even many basic cell phones allow Internet access. The introduction of Apple Computer's iPhone just confirms that there will soon be more ways for people to get online. Heck, maybe we'll go back to having "phone" booths on the corner, except they'd be Internet access portals. As with audio and video, I'm sure the Internet will find its way into the family car, as well. Maybe ISPs will go the way of phone and cable companies, consolidating into fewer but more powerful companies.

**Advertising/Marketing** – It's funny. The Internet Marketer in me wants to say that online marketing is only going to get more exciting and creative, since my specialty relies on it. Yet the Internet user in me wants to see less intrusive, more targeted advertising that doesn't interfere with what I'm doing online. A good balance might be combining some form of "profiling" based on user history with a way for users to pull in ads featuring products or subjects of interest (rather than having them pushed at users). As for style, we've tried a lot of different things from popups to popunders, static banners and blinking boxes, audio, video, advertorials, hard sell, soft sell, sales letter…everything I've touched on in this book. It would be easy to throw up our hands like the apocryphal patent officer and claim that it's all been done before. But history suggests otherwise. There is always something new to try.

**Internet as Multi-Media** – not only do we now have all the "Web 2.0" goodies like Youtube and MySpace, the Internet has long been merging with other traditional forms of entertainment. We can download music, watch movies, listen to the news, and I'm proud to say, even watch a full length, made-for-Internet reality show. As I finish up this manuscript, *The Next Internet Millionaire* has debuted its first two shows, and I'm getting frantic requests for easy ways to download the shows onto iPods. Who knows what other Internet Marketers will create as a way to reach not necessarily a broader audience but definitely more people who are interested in their product. If there is one constant about Internet Marketers, they're almost all mavericks in their own way, meaning they don't like tradition very much and are always looking for that something new to keep them interested.

**Internet Marketers** – The next generation of Internet Marketers will have grown up in a world that always had an Internet and a World Wide Web. They will have become accustomed to establishing relationships with faceless strangers (or avatars thereof), with names like snickerdoodle44 and speedweederdude, through chat, email, forums, MUDs, and blogs. Thus when they get around to selling online, they may find the personal relationship building aspect easier than for those, back when, who felt the Internet was one of those carnival arcade games for toddlers where you tug on a string attached to a bucket and you get to keep whatever comes out (everybody gets something, but not all of it is worth anything).

They will also be incredibly computer savvy—actually, technology savvy in general with their iPods, Xboxes, videocams and TiVos. Will they have it easier than those who came before? In most ways, absolutely. There will probably be Internet Marketing courses in schools and colleges, and for some it will just be a matter of studying and testing. This review of the past tells me one thing, though, that these newbies might want to know. If you want to become successful in Internet Marketing, it doesn't hurt to study business, but what you really need is patience, persistence, a little bit of imagination, a lot of willingness to take risks—and to brush up a wee bit on your history.

# Notes:

Bush, Vannevar. "As We May Think." *Atlantic Monthly* 176 (July 1945):101–8.

Licklider also introduced the idea of timesharing on computers: the mainframe could work on as many as 30 projects at a time by switching from one to another as necessary. The projects were fed in and used by people sitting at dumb terminals (that's not a slam but a real term for a keyboard/workstation that has no "computer" built in—a shocking idea these days) cabled to the mainframe. This was the only kind of "personal" computer in the 1960s and 1970s.

Berners-Lee, Tim. W3.org "Answers for Young People." World Wide Web Consortium. Retrieved 10 February 2007.

Enlow, Michael. "Who is Mike Enlow? The Story Behind One of America's Foremost Private Detectives—Who Can Help You Get Almost Anything on Anyone!" *pisecret. msg*.Z, INTEC Investigative Technology, 1992. Retrieved 13 February 2007 from ftp://coast.cs.purdue.edu/pub/doc/privacy/enlow_pi/.

**The Long Tail**—A term coined by Chris Anderson in his book of the same name, this is a statistical distribution graph that looks like a shelf bracket lying on its long end: a high-amplitude value dropping in a sharp but steady curve that then "tails off" in a slow and gentle decline. The values within the tail section of the graph are The Long tail, and their aggregate can in some instances account for greater volume overall than the high-amplitude values in the spike.

Guerilla Marketing originated in 1983 by Jay Conrad Levinson in his book *Guerrilla Marketing:Secrets for Making Big Profits from your Small Business*. (New York: Houghton Mifflin, 1998 (1983). Designed primarily for entrepreneurs and small businesses on a budget, it is an unconventional way of performing promotional activities on a very low budget. Many Internet Marketers also consider themselves "Guerilla Marketers" because it is a form of marketing that is built on building relationships, not only with your existing clients so that you can build referrals, but even with your competition. Most important, Guerilla Marketing stresses using current technology as a tool to empower marketing, exacly what Internet Marketers do.

Levine, Rick; Locke, Christopher; Searls, Doc, and Weinberger, David. *The Cluetrain Manifesto: The End of Business as Usual.* New York: Perseus Publishing, 2000. (First printed version: the original was presented online, and is still available at cluetrain.com).

# DIRECTORY OF
# INTERNET MARKETERS

The following directory of Internet marketers is a work in progress. To be included in the online version, please visit the directory at http://www.ClickHereToOrder.com/Directory/

| First Name | Last Name | Web Address |
|---|---|---|
| Jay | Abraham | www.abraham.com |
| Jeff | Alderson | www.jeffalderson.com |
| Markus | Allen | www.marketing-ideas.org |
| Gary | Ambrose | www.garyambrose.com |
| Nathan | Anderson | www.seoclub.com |
| Tom | Antion | www.GreatInternetMarketing.com |
| Jon | Atwood | www.jonatwood.com |
| Matt | Bacak | www.powerfulpromoter.com |
| Bart | Baggett | www.bartbaggett.com |
| Tom | Beal | www.tombeal.com |
| Larry | Benet | www.larrybenet.com |
| Anthony | Blake | www.ablake.com |
| Justin | Blake | www.universityofinternetmarketing.com |
| Chris | Bloor | www.chrisbloor.com |
| Alexander K | Brown | www.ezinequeen.com |
| Jimmy D | Brown | www.123webmarketing.com |
| Russell | Brunson | www.dotcomsecrets.com |
| Jeremy | Burns | www.jeremyburns.com |
| Rick | Butts | www.rickbutts.com |
| Brad | Callen | www.bradcallen.com |
| John | Carlton | www.marketingrebelrant.com |
| Shawn | Casey | www.shawncasey.com |
| Jeanette S. | Cates, PhD | www.OnlineSuccessNews.com |
| Greg | Cesar | www.1stadvantagesolutions.com |
| Teri & Doug | Champigny | www.champignyweb.com |
| M. Alisande | Chan | www.thisalicat.com |
| Randy | Charach | www.randycharach.com |

| | | |
|---|---|---|
| William | Charlwood | www.williamcharlwood.com |
| Michael | Cheney | www.michaelcheney.com |
| Ewen | Chia | www.ewnchia.com |
| Paul | Colligan | www.frontpageworld.com |
| Shawn | Collins | www.ShawnCollinsConsulting.com |
| Jody | Colvard | www.funmoneygood.com |
| Christine | Comaford-Lynch | www.mightyventures.com |
| Holly | Cotter | www.HollyCotter.com |
| Simon | Coulson | www.internetbusinessschool.com |
| Willie | Crawford | www.williecrawford.com |
| Don | Crowther | www.greatresults.com |
| Jim | Daniels | www.bizweb2000.com |
| Van | Day | www.ThatOneWebGuy.com |
| Terry | Dean | www.terrydean.org |
| Frank E | Deardurff III | www.frankdeardurff.com |
| Costa | Dedes | www.costadedes.com |
| Ryan | Deiss | www.profitdiary.com |
| Glenn | Dietzel | www.awakentheauthorwithin.com |
| Declan | Dunn | www.dunndirectgroup.com |
| Brian T | Edmondson | www.listprofitacademy.com |
| Jim | Edwards | www.igottatellyou.com |
| Ray | Edwards | www.rayedwards.com |
| T. Harv | Eker | www.peakpotentials.com |
| Michael J | Enos | www.auctiontnt.com |
| Jose | Espana | www.joseespana.com |
| Ken | Evoy | www.sitesell.com |
| Brad | Fallon | www.bradfallon.com |
| Harris | Fellman | www.successincentives.com |
| Mike | Filsaime | www.mikefilsaime.com |
| Reed | Floren | www.reedfloren.com |
| Michel | Fortin | www.successdoctor.com |
| Sylvie | Fortin | www.workaholics4hire.com |
| Andrew | Fox | www.dominatingcb.com |
| Stephanie | Frank | www.stephaniefrank.com |
| Rick | Frishman | www.rickfrishman.com |
| Carl | Galletti | www.carlgalletti.com |
| Rosalind | Gardner | www.netprofitstoday.com |

| Allan | Gardyne | www.associateprograms.com |
| Frank | Garon | www.internetcashplanet.com |
| Matt | Garrett | www.lazygitmarketing.com |
| Derek | Gehl | www.marketingtips.com |
| Randy | Gilbert | www.success-bound.com |
| Adam | Ginsberg | www.adamginsberg.com |
| Jeremy | Gislason | www.surefirewealth.com |
| Matthew | Glanfield | www.affiliatemarketingformula.com |
| Henry | Gold | www.henrygold.com |
| Marc | Goldman | www.goldbar.net |
| Michael | Green | www.howtocorp.com |
| Jermaine | Griggs | www.nittygrittymarketing.com |
| Todd | Gross | www.toddgross.com |
| Gary | Halbert | www.thegaryhalbertletter.com |
| David L | Hancock | www.davidlhancock.com |
| Mark Victor | Hansen | www.markvictorhansen.com |
| Marc | Harty | www.prtraffic.com |
| Jason | Henderson | www.bigmarketingonline.com |
| Mark | Hendricks | www.hunteridge.com |
| Christina | Hills | www.shoppingcartqueen.com |
| Michael J | Holland | www.nichemastery.com |
| Eric | Holmlund | www.ericstips.com |
| Tom | Hua | www.tomhua.com |
| Jason | James | www.membershipriches.com |
| Bob | Jenkins | www.teachersinbusiness.com |
| Jeff | Johnson | www.searchenginevoodoo.com |
| Terry | Johnson | www.freelistexchange.com |
| Mark | Joyner | www.markjoyner.name |
| Daniel | Kennedy | www.dankennedy.com |
| Harlan | Kilstein | www.overnight-copy.com |
| Tim | Knox | www.timknox.com |
| Tellman | Knudson | www.listbuildingblog.com |
| Michael | Koenigs | www.mikekoenigs.com |
| Drew | Kossoff | www.rainmakeradventures.com |
| Tony | Laidig | www.thecoverexpert.com |
| Dave | Lakhani | www.boldapproach.com |
| Ladan | Lashkari | www.ladanlashkari.com |

| | | |
|---|---|---|
| Jonathan | Leger | www.jonathanleger.com |
| Simon | Leung | www.simonleung.com |
| Mark | Ling | www.affilorama.com |
| Mike | Litman | www.mikelitman.com |
| Chris | Lockwood | www.lockwoodletter.com |
| shelley | Lowery | www.web-source.net |
| Jaime | Luchuck | www.jaimeluchuck.com |
| Ben | Mack | www.profitablemagic.com |
| Alex | Mandossian | www.alexmandossian.com |
| Nick | Marks | www.marksenterprise.com |
| Jason | Marshall | www.jasonstanleymarshall.com |
| Perry | Marshall | www.perrymarshall.com |
| James | Martell | www.jamesmartell.com |
| Kenneth A | McArthur | www.infoproductblueprint.com |
| Ken | McCarthy | www.kenscopyclinic.com |
| Stu | McLaren | www.myideaguy.com |
| Michael W | Merz | www.im4newbies.com |
| John-Paul | Micek | www.johnpaulmicek.com |
| Jeff | Mills | www.jeffmills.com |
| Jonathan | Mizel | www.cyberwave.com |
| Michael | Morgan | www.outsourcecopy.com |
| Lorrie | Morgan-Ferrero | www.red-hot-copy.com |
| Armand | Morin | www.armandmorin.com |
| Jeff | Mulligan | www.CBMall.com |
| Paul | Myers | www.talkbiznews.com |
| Alex | Nghiem | www.wealthautopilot.com |
| Michael | Nicholas | www.successtriggers.com |
| Daniel | Nickerson | www.youmetdan.com |
| Dr Kevin | Nuley | www.drnuley.com |
| Eben | Pagan | www.hottopicmedia.com |
| Charlie | Page | www.directoryofezines.com |
| Michael | Penland | www.instantcashmarketing.com |
| Craig | Perrine | www.maverickmarketer.com |
| Rhea | Perry | www.educatingforsuccess.com |
| Lynn | Pierce | www.lynnpierce.com |
| Stephen | Pierce | www.stephenlive.com |
| Michael | Port | www.michaelport.com |

| | | |
|---|---|---|
| Jason | Potash | www.ezineannouncer.com |
| Robert | Puddy | www.robertpuddy.com |
| Rick | Raddatz | www.xiosoft.com |
| John | Reese | www.income.com |
| Frank J | Rumbauskas Jr | www.nevercoldcall.com |
| Paulie | Sabol | www.pauliesabol.com |
| Marlon | Sanders | www.amazingformula.com |
| Christine Carter | Schaap | www.pathpartners.com |
| Rich | Schefren | www.strategicprofits.com |
| Scott | Schilling | www.scottschilling.com |
| Ted | Schneck | www.trafficarb.com |
| Jeremy | Schoemaker | www.shoemoney.com |
| Thor | Schrock | www.thorschrock.com |
| David P | Schwartz | www.thetoolwiz.com |
| Alice | Seba | www.internetmarketingsweetie.com |
| Harvey | Segal | www.supertips.com |
| Neil | Shearing | www.scamfreezone.com |
| Wendy | Shepherd | www.wendyshepherd.com |
| Liz | Sherwood | www.lizsherwood.com |
| Yanik | Silver | www.surefiremarketing.com |
| Anik | Singal | www.affiliateclassroom.com |
| Dr Mani | Sivasubramanian | www.ezinemarketingcenter.com |
| Segovia | Smith | www.segoviasmith.com |
| Paul | Smithson | www.xsitepro.com |
| Socrates | Socratous | www.mydigitaldispatch.com |
| Mike | Stewart | www.internetaudioguy.com |
| Stuart | Tan | www.stuarttan.com |
| Dave | Taylor | www.askdavetaylor.com |
| Lynn | Terry | www.clicknewz.com |
| Antonio D | Thornton | www.moneymouthmarketing.com |
| Len | Thurmond | www.Lenthurmond.com |
| Howard | Tiano | www.imoutsourcerer.com |
| Sterling | Valentine | www.sterlingvalentine.com |
| David | Vallieres | www.infoproductlab.com |
| Wayne | Van Dyck | www.simplemoneymachines.com |
| Joe | Vitale | www.mrfire.com |
| Brian Keith | Voiles | www.briankeithkillercopyclinic.com |

| | | |
|---|---|---|
| Martin | Wales | www.customercatcher.com |
| Jeff | Walker | www.productlaunchformula.com |
| Neil | Waterhouse | www.waterhousereport.com |
| Keith | Wellman | www.keithwellman.com |
| Mark | Widawer | www.landingpagecashmachine.com |
| Phil | Wiley | www.ozemedia.com |
| Kevin | Wilke | www.nitromarketing.com |
| Dr Ralph | Wilson | www.wilsonweb.com |
| Bryan | Winters | www.pushbuttonpublishing.com |
| Michael | Wong | www.mikes-marketing-tools.com |
| Mike | Woo Ming | www.theoutsourcecode.com |
| David | Wood | www.solutionbox.com |

To view the most recent directory or to apply for inclusion, visit our web site at http://www.ClickHereToOrder.com/Directory/

 INDEX

# M

# N

# O

Oracle · 12
    Ellison, Larry · 12

# P

PARC · 7
PayPal · 105, 106, 262, 271, 272, 274
PC · 3, 25, 26, 92, 121, 122, 127, 250, 255
PDF · 25, 262, 263
phishing · *see* scam
Pierce, Stephen · 80, 108, 109, 112, 191–5, 224, 225, 226
    *The Whole Truth* · 108, 194, 225
    *Unleash Your Marketing Genius* · 112
Podcast · 171, 253, 254, 255, 259
point–and–click · 7, 9, 10, 61
pop-ups · 229, 235
Potash, Jason · 70-5, 238
    *eZineAnnouncer.com* · 73, 74, 75
    *ArticleAnnouncer.com* · 75
Project MAC · 7
Push Technology · 216, 217, 249

# Q

Quantum Computer Sevices · *see* AOL

# R

Reese, John · 51-3, 63, 75, 110, 112, 121, 122, 123, 138, 170,
    202, 225, 226, 227, 238, 239, 260
    *InfoBack* · 53
    *Traffic Secrets* · 112, 170, 239, 260
ROI (Return On Investment) · see Joyner
Rudl, Corey · x, 64, 80, 97, 123-5, 127, 165, 168, 169, 170,
    188, 202-3, 204, 213, 236, 239, 260, 270
    *Car Secrets Revealed* · 64, 124, 260
    *Insider Secrets to Marketing your Business on the Internet*
    · 65, 125

# S

TCP/IP · 8, 9, 262
teleseminar · 68, 75, 96, 113, 115, 133, 138, 146, 170, 171, 172, 176, 177, 185, 196, 225, 237, 239, 254, 257, 259
text ad · 33, 62, 63, 110
Thuerk, Gary · 20-2

# U

Unisys · 27
UNIX · 7, 8, 11, 55
    USENET · *see* networks, early

# V

viral marketing · 63, 109, 110, 111, 112, 113, 114, 122
Vitale, Joe · 41, 68, 177, 197, 200

# W

Walker, Jeff · 129, 138, 202, 230-9
    *Product Launch Formula* · 129, 232
    "Six in Seven" · 233, 234,
Warrior Forum · 19, 50
web, definition of · 9
Web 2.0 · 87, 210, 216, 253, 276
WebGenie · 130, 131
webinar · 74, 171, 257, 259
Weinberger, David · 216, 279
Wellman, Keith · 113, 114
"White Hat" business techniques · 36, 81, 84
Williamson, Ramon · 138
Wilson, Dr. Ralph · 48
    *The E-Mail Marketing Handbook* · 48
    *Web Marketing Today* · 49
*Wired Magazine* · 61, 62, 217
    "The (Second Phase of the) Revolution Has Begun" · 61
Wolfe, Tom · 33
    *The Right Stuff* · 33
World Wide Web · xvi, 3, 8, 9, 12, 13, 25, 47, 49, 53, 55, 56, 60, 86, 163, 164, 261, 276, 278
WWII · 5, 250
WYSIWYG · 25, 26, 55, 262

# X

# Y